Children in Care, 1834–1929

Children in Care, 1834–1929

The Lives of Destitute, Orphaned and Deserted Children

Rosemary Steer

PEN & SWORD
HISTORY

First published in Great Britain in 2020 by
Pen & Sword History
An imprint of
Pen & Sword Books Ltd
Yorkshire – Philadelphia

ISBN 978 1 52672 801 2

Typeset by Mac Style
Printed and bound in the UK by
CPI Group (UK) Ltd, Croydon, CR0 4YY

Pen & Sword Books Limited incorporates the imprints of Atlas,
Archaeology, Aviation, Discovery, Family History, Fiction, History,
Maritime, Military, Military Classics, Politics, Select, Transport,
True Crime, Air World, Frontline Publishing, Leo Cooper, Remember
When, Seaforth Publishing, The Praetorian Press, Wharncliffe
Local History, Wharncliffe Transport, Wharncliffe True Crime
and White Owl.

For a complete list of Pen & Sword titles please contact

PEN & SWORD BOOKS LIMITED
47 Church Street, Barnsley, South Yorkshire, S70 2AS, England
E-mail: enquiries@pen–and–sword.co.uk
Website: www.pen–and–sword.co.uk

Or

PEN AND SWORD BOOKS
1950 Lawrence Rd, Havertown, PA 19083, USA
E-mail: Uspen–and–sword@casematepublishers.com
Website: www.penandswordbooks.com

Contents

Acknowledgements

I thank Ian Wakeling and his staff at The Children's Society Records and Archive Centre for not only allowing me access to the society's records but for agreeing that I could use the full names of the children in the book. I am particularly grateful to archivist Gabrielle St John-McAlister for her patience in answering my numerous queries. My thanks also to the staff of the London Metropolitan Archives, Newham Archives and Local Studies Library, Norfolk Record Office, Staffordshire and Stoke-on-Trent Archives Service at Lichfield (although sadly the branch has now closed), and Suffolk Archives (Ipswich and Lowestoft branches) for assistance with my research.

I am grateful to the many local people who have encouraged and helped me with my research into the Dickleburgh charity, including Moira Croskell, headteacher of Dickleburgh Church of England Primary Academy, and her predecessor James Richards, for allowing me access to the school records. Mike Tinsley, Brian Baker and Carl Roe have been most helpful too in making the collections of the Dickleburgh Village Society available to me.

My thanks also to David Waller of Fegans and Irene Fry, John Sayer and Gale Fewings in Canada for information about Louis Fewings. I am also grateful to Jenny Keaveney for directing me towards her article about Louisa Brandreth, née Jackson in the Gaskell Society Newsletter. Peter Higginbotham's excellent websites on workhouses and children's homes as well as his numerous books are a must for anyone researching aspects of the poor law and I am grateful to him for highlighting several sources and examples that I could explore further.

It has been a privilege to meet, either in person or online, descendants or relations of some of the Dickleburgh children or of the foster parents who looked after them, including Jean Freeman-Allen, Nikki Lund, Sue Perry, Gwen Pooley, Maggy Roberts, Pauline Spinlove and Nigel Wells.

I am most grateful to them for sharing memories (and photographs in some cases) of family members who were part of the Dickleburgh story.

I thank Laura Hirst and Aileen Pringle of Pen and Sword who have supported me throughout the production process, and a huge thank you to Kate Bohdanowicz whose wise and experienced editorial guidance has turned my research and writing into a published book. I am most grateful to Brian and Angela Woodley for their most generous hospitality on the many occasions I visited London to research at The Children's Society Archive and to Angela and my brother Dr John Rogers for their helpful comments on the typescript. Last, but certainly not least, I thank my husband, Norman, who has supported and encouraged me throughout my studies and the writing of this book, eagerly reading and commenting on every chapter as I completed it, with a glass of chilled white wine waiting for me. He has endured cries of 'Found him' as I discovered yet another lost child in the census returns or poor law records, and he has done more than his fair share of domestic duties!

Permissions

Permission to reproduce items to illustrate this book was given by The Children's Society, Dickleburgh Church of England Primary Academy, Dickleburgh Churchwardens and Parochial Church Council, Dickleburgh Village Society, Fegans, Peter Higginbotham, Norfolk Record Office, Gwen Pooley and Pauline Spinlove. I also thank those who permitted me to quote from published works including:

Lost Children of the Empire, © Philip Bean and Joy Melville, 1989. Reprinted by permission of HarperCollins Publishers Ltd.

Nation Builders, © Gail H. Corbett, 1997/2002. Reprinted by permission of Dundurn Press Ltd.

13 Penny Stamps, John Stroud, © Church of England Children's Society, 1971. Reprinted by permission of The Children's Society.

The Home Children, © Phyllis Harrison, 1979. Reprinted by permission of J. Gordon Shillingford.

Introduction

My mother, I remember, tried to prepare me for what was inevitable by telling me I was going away to the country, there would be a lovely garden and a lot of other little girls to play with. I couldn't understand why if it was so nice mother kept crying! What I didn't realise was that mother wasn't coming with me![1]

Winifred Price

For centuries, there have been children who have not lived with their birth parents for a range of reasons and have been taken into the care of the state, voluntary societies, other families or employers, temporarily or permanently. Local authorities are now responsible for the care system and for 'looked-after children' as they are usually known. These terms reflect the view that such children and young people are vulnerable and need properly managed arrangements for their care with professional social workers, care staff and key workers to support them. Official and news reports over the past few years show that there are many challenges facing looked-after children in the twenty-first century, emotional and practical, including negotiating the transition into adult life. Sadly, many examples of adults who have abused or otherwise failed children, particularly in institutional care, are now coming to light, and forming the subject of public enquiries and police investigations.

In the nineteenth century, different terms were used for such children; many described their circumstances – orphans, deserted children, paupers, Home Children (British children who emigrated to Canada under the auspices of the state or voluntary societies), workhouse children, ins and outs (children who, often with their families, were in and out of the workhouse, staying only a short time). Other terms were pejorative, especially those used to describe street children, many of whom were never taken into care and lived, and sometimes died, on the streets –

guttersnipes, street urchins, ragamuffins or street arabs. Although 'children in care' is a modern phrase, not in use in the period covered by this study, it has been used in the book to refer to children who were not living with their birth families but were resident in an institution, such as a workhouse or children's home, were boarded out with foster parents or who had emigrated to Canada under the child migration programmes.

The origins of this book lie in a study of the lives of over 300 children who came into the care of a charity in the village of Dickleburgh near Diss in Norfolk, which was started in the 1870s by the rector's wife, Louisa Brandreth, to prevent a family of local children from going into the workhouse. From small beginnings, the charity grew, with two certified cottage homes for girls and a certified boarding-out scheme in the village, accepting workhouse, destitute and orphaned children from both urban and rural areas across the country. The Waifs and Strays Society (now The Children's Society) took over Mrs Brandreth's charity in 1888, although she remained in charge locally until 1899 when she and her husband, the Rev Henry Brandreth, retired to Cambridge. The charity closed in 1912 because the village school had reached capacity, so presumably the village could no longer sustain the additional numbers of children coming through the charity.

This book extends the localised study of the Dickleburgh charity across the country to cover the main period of the Poor Law Amendment Act (the 'New Poor Law') from 1834 to 1929. It starts with a detailed description of the Dickleburgh charity followed by consideration of some of the attitudes and legislation which shaped the poor law system and charitable support over many centuries, focusing on how pauper children were affected. An overview of the social and economic conditions of the time, including consideration of some of the key social investigators and commentators such as Henry Mayhew, Charles Booth, Charles Dickens and Andrew Mearns, places issues about children taken into care in context. The book explores the range of provision for children in care, both by the state and by charitable organisations – workhouses, poor law schools, children's homes, training ships, industrial schools and reformatories, boarding out, adoption and emigration – and looks at how legislation, changes in thinking and new ideas about the care of pauper children affected provision.

Research into the care of pauper children has often been anonymised, but this book includes examples of *named* children, particularly Home Children and those from the Dickleburgh charity. Using a range of sources, such as published personal accounts, the records of the Waifs and Strays Society and other charities, poor law records, census returns, parish and school records, newspapers and passenger lists, it explores the lives of some of these destitute, orphaned or deserted children. It looks at why children came into care within the context of the social and economic conditions of the time, and what became of them after leaving care, usually when they left for employment in their early to mid-teens.

This study also explores other aspects of the care system at this time, such as how far children were treated as individuals, arrangements for the care of siblings, how those with mental health issues or learning disabilities were treated, and whether there was any affection or ongoing relationship between the children and those who cared for them. This approach allows the voices of the children themselves to be heard, chiefly through letters and reminiscences or, in the case of a few of the Dickleburgh children, through the memories of their descendants. It is unlikely that many of these pauper children would feature in any other study, other than individually within the context of family history, so this book also has the benefit of highlighting the lives of some of the least regarded of society.

Chapter 1

Mrs Brandreth's Charity for Workhouse, Destitute and Orphaned Children

None but those who have had the care of such [pauper] children can know what a deadening effect their loveless surroundings have had on them, and how eagerly they respond to love and care.[1]

Mrs Louisa Brandreth, c.1895

Louisa Brandreth started her charity for workhouse, destitute and orphaned children in Dickleburgh about 1875, when she and her husband, the Rev Henry Brandreth, rector of Dickleburgh, took charge of some children 'whose father was dead and their mother gone away' to keep them out of the workhouse.[2] These were probably the Gardner children, Rosa, William and Lucy, whose father died of smallpox in 1872 after the family moved from Dickleburgh to County Durham, and who seem to have been deserted by their mother, Maria, a few years later. In 1875, Maria had an illegitimate daughter, Mary, in Norfolk and later that year married William Eyre Jenner in Brixton, London. William and Maria Jenner had six children between 1877 and 1894, all born in London, and there is no indication that Maria ever returned to Norfolk or saw her other four children again. Mary, the illegitimate child, was brought up in Diss, a few miles from Dickleburgh, by her maternal grandparents, Robert and Maria Todd, probably from birth, but it seems they could not take in their other grandchildren, Rosa, William and Lucy, who were resident in the children's home in Dickleburgh by 1881.

The Brandreths may also have helped the three Ford children from Dickleburgh in similar circumstances a few years earlier, before the formal start of Mrs Brandreth's charity. Their mother died in 1871 and their father James probably deserted the children shortly afterwards. By 1881, the three Ford children were all 'in care' in some way. The eldest, William, aged 15, was a carpenter's apprentice, living with his master in the nearby village of Starston, and Alberta, aged 12, was recorded as the adopted child of Arthur and Charlotte Garland, a childless couple living in Dickleburgh, although she kept her own name. Margaret (or Maggie), aged 10, was boarding in Dickleburgh with Rebecca Turner, a 70-year old widow. Maggie was admitted to the Waifs and Strays Society at the age of 20, presumably as a special case as she was hearing and sight impaired. According to her Waifs and Strays case file, she had been living with Mrs Turner in Dickleburgh 'all her life' and Mrs Brandreth had always helped with clothing for her, suggesting that she had been involved in Maggie's care for many years.[3]

Mrs Brandreth was born Louisa Victoria Jackson in Birmingham in 1838, the youngest child of Henry Augustus Jackson, an officer in the Dragoon Guards, and his wife, Mary. According to Mrs Gaskell, the nineteenth-century writer, whose daughter Meta went to school in Liverpool with Louisa and her sister, Anna Maria:

> [The two girls] lost both father and mother in one fortnight; they were great friends of Meta's who had also received much kindness from Colonel and Mrs Jackson. The latter was dying of cancer, the former was a strong handsome healthy man; But he dropped down dead in the street just a fortnight before his poor wife died after five years' illness.[4]

Louisa was just 17 when her parents died and, although she herself was subsequently well supported by friends and family, it seems likely that this personal tragedy may have influenced her later work with pauper children.

Henry Brandreth was about four years older than his second cousin Louisa Jackson; he was educated at Eton and Trinity College, Cambridge, then taught mathematics at Eton and Rugby. After he was ordained priest, he served several curacies before his appointment to the living of Dickleburgh in 1871.[5] Philip Green, an acquaintance of Louisa, wrote in 1871 to his sister Isabella:

> H Brandreth & Louisa Jackson are to be married on the 8th June....
> He comes from his living in Norfolk in the middle of every week to

see her (in Derbyshire by a night train and back the same way), & she thinks it so bad for him & his parish that they are going to be married directly.[6]

Over the next seven years Henry and Louisa had four children, Rosalind, Ashton, Ernest and Roland, though tragedy struck Louisa again as by the time Roland was born in 1878, his two older brothers had already died.

The Rev Henry Brandreth was a formidable temperance campaigner and took every opportunity to expound his views on the evils of drink in the Dickleburgh parish magazine, often including a form for signing the pledge. A lasting memorial to Henry's mission to tackle the problems of alcohol locally is the temperance reading room that he opened in the village in 1874. He took to verse in the parish magazine, *Home Words*, in February 1876 to explain his vision for it:

> A public-house, without the drink
> For sober recreation
> Where you may smoke, or read, or think
> Or join in conversation.

Unfortunately, the parishioners did not share Henry's vision for the reading room, and he closed it down the following year when he discovered that 'games were being played for money and for beer' there.[7] Henry was persistent though and in 1879, he reopened it, probably on a different site closer to the rectory, writing in the parish magazine:

> The principal event of the past month in Dickleburgh has been the re-opening of our Reading Room and Coffee House. I think it of great importance that there should be a room where a respectable man can sit or read or talk without being expected to drink to his own hurt for the good of the house.

The reading room (possibly in its third incarnation) survives to this day; a corrugated iron building probably dating from the early years of the twentieth century. After major restoration some years ago, it is now the home of the Village Society and houses a community archive and permanent local history exhibition.

Louisa opened the first of the two children's homes in the village, Rose Cottage, in about 1875 to house twenty girls and by 1878 it was certified by the Local Government Board to receive children from poor law unions across the country, enabling the unions to get at least some of their children out of the workhouse and into better surroundings.[8] A second home, Lee Cottage, opened in Dickleburgh in 1883, raising the capacity available in the village to forty-six girls. It closed twelve years later, and the resident children transferred to a newly acquired home in Lowestoft. In 1888, both Dickleburgh homes were taken over by the Waifs and Strays Society (now The Children's Society). In practical terms, this probably made very little difference to the homes in Dickleburgh; Mrs Brandreth continued to run the charity locally, raising funds and begging for items for the homes, finding 'situations' for the girls and liaising with the poor law unions. Significantly for historians, however, the charity's involvement meant that a case file was created for each child admitted to the Dickleburgh homes from July 1888, as well as for the forty-five children already resident in the homes on that date.

No records of Mrs Brandreth's charity or the Dickleburgh Boarding-Out Committee have been located but other records help to fill the gaps, especially where there is no case file for a child. Some children were baptised after they came to Dickleburgh, such as Agnes Hurst who was recorded in the Dickleburgh baptism register as an orphan from Wickhambrook, Suffolk, the daughter of John and Hannah Hurst, living at the children's home in Dickleburgh.[9] Her parents had died within a fortnight of each other; her mother on 18 July 1877 and her father, an agricultural labourer, on 31 July 1877. Some baptism entries record the names of foster parents, such as that for Mary Grace Hammond, daughter of Edward and Emily Hammond, of Stowmarket, who was not yet 3 when she was baptised in Dickleburgh and boarded out with Absalom Feaveryear in the village. Some of the later entries provide fewer details about the children, perhaps because the workhouse staff did not pass them on. Mary and Louis Fewings were baptised on 9 December 1909, boarded out by the West Ham Guardians, 'parents unknown'.

The Waifs and Strays Society case files provide a rich source of information about individual children before, during and sometimes after their time in care, including a few letters written by the children themselves. Many case files also contain letters from Louisa Brandreth, chiefly to Edward Rudolf, the founder and honorary secretary of the Waifs and Strays Society, which reveal much about the workings of the Dickleburgh charity as well as about Mrs Brandreth herself and her attitudes to the children in her care. A note by Mrs Brandreth on Martha Thurlow's application form provides interesting insights not only into the poor law authorities' definition of disability, but also into contemporary attitudes to morality:

> The Guardians can make no payment for Martha, as the father is an 'able-bodied' man though deaf and dumb. Her home when not in the workhouse is a most immoral one, from which we are anxious to rescue her and we have a vacancy at Lee Cottage.

The 'immoral home' probably referred to the fact that Martha's widowed father was cohabiting with a woman by whom he may have had one or more children.

Mrs Brandreth spent much time sourcing clothing, bedding, treats and other items for the Dickleburgh homes. In the December 1890 Waifs and Strays magazine, *Our Waifs and Strays*, she acknowledged donations of fourteen umbrellas and requested toys, dolls or books for the children for Christmas. Seven years later, *Our Waifs and Strays* carried her request for blankets, sheets, serge for fourteen winter frocks and framed sacred pictures for the children's bedrooms. In 1899, she thanked Mr Rudolf for sending hymn books and a parcel of books to the home and asked for clothing to be sent: 'stockings … vests, pinafores, school frocks or materials … large size night gowns'.[10]

Mrs Brandreth mentioned on several occasions the difficulty in training older children sent to Dickleburgh from the workhouses. In 1894, she suggested that if the Burton-upon-Trent Guardians would not fund Fanny Parker for another year, as she was not yet ready to go out to service, then she should be sent back to the workhouse as she was a very naughty girl and deserved punishment. However, Mrs Brandreth was concerned that the Burton workhouse was very badly managed and returning would 'mean ruin to the girl'. She added that she was convinced that it was unwise to take girls as old as 14 from the workhouse, especially Burton, as there was 'so much to unlearn'.[11]

Other society records give information about the Dickleburgh charity and the children, particularly the annual reports and *Our Waifs and Strays*. In the November 1888 issue, there was a detailed account of the charity describing the circumstances of some of the earliest children who came to Dickleburgh, although their real names were not given, so they are not easy to identify, particularly if they had left the homes before the society took them over. Two that could be identified, however, were Esther and Ellen Oakes (a third sister, Emma, had already left the home a few years earlier) from the neighbouring village of Burston: 'Amongst our flock are two children who were exposed so much to cold and want during the severe winter of 1882, that, when received into the Workhouse, the younger child was so terribly frost-bitten that she lost all her toes.' It is possible that Ellen was affected by frostbite before that, as in 1881, parents George and Mary Oakes and four of their children were living in Burston, but Ellen was on her own in the local workhouse, aged 4; perhaps her parents were unable to cope with her disability.

More difficult to identify is 'Lavinia': 'the little gipsy of seven [who] fell from a high gate on Wormwood Scrubs, where her caravan halted', who was taken in by the sisters at St Peter's, Kilburn before being admitted to Dickleburgh. She would tell 'strange, weird stories ... of her nomad life' and died after a long illness a few years later. It is possible the child was Annie Webb (although that was probably not her real name either) who died at Rose Cottage on 30 March 1886, aged 8, of 'Suppressed Scarlatina, Uremia'.[12] She is buried in Dickleburgh churchyard. The information about Annie and her parents recorded in the Dickleburgh baptism register cannot be verified so perhaps she was 'the little gipsy' mentioned in the 1888 report. Some children arrived in Dickleburgh with little or nothing in their possession, like the 'little London waif, rescued from a life of theft and misery.... The only treasures the child brought out of the wealth of the great city, were a chestnut, clasped tightly in her hand, and a penny, given to her by a kind man at the station.'

Being taken into care must have been a frightening experience for a young child, as shown by this memory by an unnamed lady (subsequently identified as Winifred Price) of a train journey in 1908 to Burston, two miles from Dickleburgh, recalled some sixty years later:

I was six when my father died and my mother was left with three children, she also had her grandmother living with her.... I remember going into the office at Kennington Town Hall ... and mother crying and the next thing I was on the big station, Liverpool Street I suppose, and being popped on to the train and we were off! I can remember the bewilderment and misery of that long journey with strange people, occasionally the guard came to see if I was all right and at Ipswich bought me a glass of milk and a bun. We eventually arrived at Burston and I was met by a (to me) grim bespectacled person with a little bonnet on her head, and was lifted up on to a high dog cart between the 'ogre' and the driver, to say I was terrified was putting it mildly.[13]

In the September 1894 edition of *Our Waifs and Strays*, an account of a visit to the Dickleburgh homes by some ladies from the local Girls Friendly Society (GFS) branch showed what life was like for the children:

We found the children at play in their playground, and a very happy group of maidens they looked, all dressed alike in print frocks and clean white pinafores. It was interesting to see how eager the children were for a kind word or look from Mrs Brandreth ... they evidently looked to her as their best earthly friend.... The housework is entirely done by the children as well as the mending of their own clothes. This is splendid training for girls going out to service. But the motto of the Home is not 'all work and no play' as was evident from the number of dolls and toys, and a rocking-horse, which we noticed in the little ones' day-rooms. Upstairs – the little beds so carefully made – were placed some two, three, or four well-lighted and thoroughly ventilated rooms. We heard that strict silence is kept by the children in their rooms.

The policy of keeping siblings in care together was a feature of Mrs Brandreth's charity and continued after the Waifs and Strays Society took over the running of the two girls' homes. It became easier to keep brothers and sisters together once a certified boarding-out scheme was established in the village from about 1890, providing foster placements for boys as well as girls. There were numerous examples of siblings of both sexes in care together including the Mallett and Adams families from Burton-upon-Trent; each family had six children in care in the village, in both cases five girls and one boy. The four Peet sisters from London were resident in Rose Cottage in 1881 and several other families had three children living in Dickleburgh, such as Rose, Mary and Albert Wheal from West Ham and Rose, Beatrice and Edith Newberry from Kirkley near Lowestoft in Suffolk.

Brother and sister pairings were very common; both were usually boarded out, but with different foster parents. Louis Fewings and Herbert Hayes from West Ham were fostered in Dickleburgh by Edward and Ellen Lockett, who had a son, Alfred, of similar age to the two West Ham boys. Edward ran a newsagent's shop in the village. Louis's sister, Mary, was fostered with Miss Anna Catchpole in the neighbouring village of Shimpling, again with another West Ham child, Agnes Clarke; all four children attended Dickleburgh School.

Siblings were not always admitted to care at the same time, as in the case of Emma and Margaret Bruce. The children probably went into the Stowmarket workhouse in Suffolk around 1882 and by the following year, both their parents were dead. The older child, Emma, came to Rose Cottage in 1886, but Margaret seems to have languished in the workhouse for another three years, before she too came to Rose Cottage. Margaret was only 9, and it seems that she had spent seven years of her life in the workhouse. Mrs Brandreth was clearly keen to see the sisters reunited, writing in a letter to Mr Rudolf now on Margaret's case file: 'I hope that this poor little child may be received from Stowmarket Union House. Her sister Emma is a very nice little girl – & it is well the sisters should be together.' A note on Margaret's application form stated: 'It is the only opportunity they can have of knowing each other.'

The children in the homes and those that were boarded out in the village attended Dickleburgh School, a mixed elementary school next door to All Saints' Church. The old school building, dating from about 1812, is now used for church and village events and meetings. The present primary school, located elsewhere in the village, retains the earliest surviving admission register, which commenced in March 1911. However, the headteacher, Mr Solomon Bye, copied details from the old register of the 185 children who were already at the school when he started the new register. Like the baptism register, the school admission register identifies the children in care in the village, providing details of their foster parents or the name of the matron of the home, as well as the name of their previous school where known. Sadly, it seems likely that Mr Bye destroyed the old admission register when he started the new one, so we only have details of the children who were in care in Dickleburgh from about 1900 in the school records.

The earliest surviving school log book, dating from 1900, is also retained by the school. It records activities, events, inspectors' reports, examination successes, details of teachers and pupil teachers and occasional references to individual children, including some who were in care in the village. We learn that Emily Mallett, who was in the infant class, was absent with a 'very bad toe' and that the previous week she had done nothing but cry, perhaps unsurprisingly as she was only about 4. Florence Saward was mentioned on several occasions, including when she was taken ill in the playground and the doctor advised that she needed two to three weeks off school. On another occasion, she was withdrawn from school in the morning because her foster mother, Miss Howard, was unwell. Robert Donley, another child boarded out in the village, managed to fall in the 'sluice', possibly a nearby deep ditch, and was sent home, presumably to dry out.

The children enjoyed outings and treats on occasions during the year, such as the trip to the seaside in June 1893 and a tea party held in August 1902 for the 'home' girls and some of the boarded-out children.[14] The headteacher was probably less happy than the children about the tea party as it took place on a school day, stating in the school log book: 'This and the wet weather during this week has sadly reduced the attendance.' A major event was the annual Christmas tree, which aimed to give the children a feeling of family and home. This article in the February 1889 edition of *Our Waifs and Strays* paints a happy picture:

At twelve o'clock the doors of the playroom were thrown open, and the crowd of eager children admitted. The Christmas-tree – covered with flags, ornaments and crackers – was brilliantly lighted, and placed in the centre of a perfect wall of toys, dolls, work-boxes, and scrap-books. After the singing of some pretty carols, the distribution of presents began.... Great was the excitement and pleasure depicted on all the faces as dolls and toys were distributed ... each child received no less than four gifts. Mr Dowson, our kind Local Secretary, sent fifty most acceptable story books for the orphans.

It was not only the children in the Dickleburgh homes who benefited from the Christmas festivities, as a large party from the local union workhouse was also invited, consisting of:

all the Union school-girls, with their teacher, and brothers of some of our little ones.... It was very touching to turn from the merry children to a corner of the room where some poor little fellows from the Union might be seen in tears, at meeting their older sisters again.

The rector provided a dinner of roast beef and plum pudding and, after tea and buns, the union children returned to the workhouse, 'laden with oranges and bags of sweets'. The report, presumably written by Mrs Brandreth, ends with a neat summing up of the benefits the Dickleburgh children had over their peers who were still in the workhouse: 'It was surely well for our happy children, rescued from the monotony of Workhouse life, to share their pleasure with those less fortunate than themselves.'

About 1894, with the closure of Lee Cottage imminent, Mrs Brandreth wrote to her friend Miss Mayo who had paid the rent for the home since it opened in 1883, giving an account of the work of Lee Cottage over the previous eleven years. She briefly summed up what had happened to the seventy-two children who had passed through the home, perhaps unusually for the time, recognising the children as individuals, rather than lumping them together as orphans or workhouse children, although still acknowledging their place in society in the servant or labouring class:

Some have done better than others, for of course their capacities and dispositions are very different, but all who have left the Home for service are now maintaining themselves respectably. Many have been for several years in their places, and are now valued servants, and the matrons have received many encouraging assurances that the careful training given to the children has been appreciated.[15]

In the same letter, Mrs Brandreth mentioned that only one child could be called 'a failure', although she does not give the girl's name or any details.

A few children over the lifetime of the charity were sent away from Dickleburgh because of some misdemeanour, including Alice Hall. Alice's case file shows that she was admitted to the Waifs and Strays Society after her mother died, as there were fears for her safety if she were left in her stepfather's care as he was 'a great drunkard' who had broken up most of the furniture in the house. Alice was just 8 years old and was initially boarded out in Cromer in Norfolk, but there were concerns about her behaviour there, so the society requested that she be transferred to Dickleburgh. Having read of her 'delinquences', the Brandreths were initially unwilling to place Alice 'amongst 20 such nice refined little girls as ours at Rose Cottage'. They were also concerned about her attending the local mixed school and the possibility of her 'bringing discredit to the Homes.'

The Brandreths eventually bowed to pressure and accepted Alice on trial, but in less than a year, matters had come to a head, and Alice was again moved on. In a letter to Mr Rudolf in July 1892, Mrs Brandreth wrote that Alice 'had seen & heard very much which is wrong' and Mr Brandreth thought that 'the effect of [her] terribly immoral childhood' meant that she was unfit to attend the mixed parish school. Although Alice had improved greatly and was trying to be obedient and honest, she had written 'most improperly' on her slate to one of the boys in school time; consequently the Brandreths felt they could no longer keep her and the society sent her to its Cold Ash Home in Berkshire.

There are many examples of how Louisa Brandreth provided care and affection to the Dickleburgh children both during and after their time with her, even after she left the village in 1899. Sam Adams was boarded out in the village with Jabez and Charlotte Vyse, a local farming family, while his five sisters were resident in Rose Cottage. When Sam was about 13 and ready to leave school, there was some debate between the Brandreths and Mr Rudolf of the Waifs and Strays Society as to his future, which was recorded in his case file. According to Mrs Brandreth, he was 'a sharp and willing boy [but] he [had] a bad hesitation in speech when flurried.' She suggested that, as he had learned a little farm work while with his foster parents, he could be sent to one of the society's farm schools to learn farming. Arrangements were in hand for this, but Henry Brandreth intervened with further concerns about Sam: 'The difficulty is that the boy who is not very big or strong has a most distressing stammer and if started as a new boy among a party of 30 big & rougher boys it will really be most trying and difficult for him. More than he ought to bear.' It was eventually agreed that Sam would remain with the Vyse family at a reduced cost and they would teach him farm work. Three years later, Sam was still living with his foster parents, described as a worker and 'Boy on farm', so presumably he had bed and board and earned a small wage.

Several children had ongoing health problems while in care in the village, so arrangements were made for hospital visits or periods of convalescence. Lizzie Adams suffered from glandular swellings in her neck (probably tubercular in origin) which recurred every spring and in 1899 she was sent to a Margate hospital for two months for treatment and convalescence.[16] The problem persisted, however, and she returned to Margate the following year and again in 1902, just before she went out to service. Frances Field received treatment for St Vitus' dance (Sydenham's chorea) and Maisey Clark attended the eye hospital; in both cases the medical expenses were reclaimed from the West Ham union.[17]

The 'old girls' of the Dickleburgh homes were remembered at Christmas time, with a present for each on the Christmas tree, packed and ready for posting; in 1897, eighty presents were sent out.[18] Former residents were also welcomed back to the homes for holidays or rest. In February 1889, Rosa Garnham, who was in care in Dickleburgh for about six years during the 1880s, wrote in *Our Waifs and Strays* magazine:

When we go out to service we are not discarded, but come back for our holidays. O, what happy times we have spent in the dear old Home! for which I feel very grateful to my kind friend Mrs B___, and all ladies who have taken an interest in our Homes; and I shall always try to do my best, because it is my duty, and also to please my kind friend.

In the March 1900 edition, it was reported that twenty-five 'old girls' had spent some time at Rose Cottage the previous summer.

Mrs Brandreth retained a keen interest in the welfare of the former Dickleburgh children after she and Henry retired to Cambridge in 1899 and even when she moved to Wanstead in Essex, following Henry's death in 1904. She helped with employment issues and the supply of medical equipment and tried to help any child in trouble. In November 1912, according to her case file, 16-year-old Harriet Pratt, a former Dickleburgh child, was taken to the Waifs and Strays' Clapham Park home by Louisa or her daughter Rosalind after she had turned up at the Brandreths' home in Wanstead dressed only in her apron and cotton dress, having run away following an altercation with her mistress.

Mrs Brandreth also arranged annual gatherings in London for the girls living or in service there. In 1899 she invited Edward Rudolf to a meeting she had arranged at Madam Tussauds, adding she had invited sixty girls though was not expecting all would come.[19] One former resident of Rose Cottage, Mrs May of Shepherds Bush, invited former Dickleburgh girls in service in London to her home; sometimes there might be ten to twelve girls there on a Sunday afternoon, presumably their free afternoon.[20] It was at the gathering at Madam Tussauds in 1899 that Mrs Brandreth noticed that Mrs May was unwell, so she arranged for her to go to the GFS Home of Rest at Brighton and took her there herself. She also took Mrs May's three small children temporarily into care in Rose Cottage.[21]

Perhaps the most remarkable example of the love, care and support given to a Dickleburgh child by the Brandreths and the Waifs and Strays Society is that of Isola Emms who was admitted to the society and into care in Dickleburgh at the age of 16. She was described as a dwarf, suffering from curvature of the spine and learning disabilities. Over a period of forty-five years, Louisa and Rosalind, assisted by the society, ensured that Isola always had a secure home, either in a residential home or hospital or in what we would now call a 'supported placement', with kind people, where she was able to carry out some domestic duties, sometimes for a small wage. At times, the Brandreths took her into their own home when there was no suitable alternative. They ensured that her medical needs were met and managed her funds (mostly from an annual donation from the Mann family of Thelveton) paying all her expenses, including occasional holidays for her, and then banking the surplus for her. As Rosalind noted on Isola's case file:

> She is also very sensitive and it would be a terrible thing for her if she ever had to go into any big Institution where she would be one of a crowd.... It has, however, always been most difficult to find suitable places for Isola. She has never been able to learn to read, or write, or tell the time, and is quite incapable of protecting herself in any way from unkind treatment, and would unreservedly trust anyone who was kind to her. She would therefore be at anyone's mercy and should she be dismissed she would be absolutely powerless to make any arrangement for herself.

Mrs Brandreth's charity closed in 1912 because there was insufficient accommodation at the Dickleburgh school.[22] The children from Rose Cottage and those boarded out were mostly transferred to other residential homes or foster parents elsewhere in the country. Solomon Bye, the headteacher of Dickleburgh School, recorded the dramatic reduction in his school roll in the school log book on 5 December 1911: 'Two girls, Kate Saunders and Kathleen Whiteland are leaving today as Rose Cottage Home is being given up by the Waifs and Strays Society. At Christmas 19 children boarded out by West Ham Guardians are leaving the Parish. Altogether 33 children will be leaving the school.' On 7 December, the rector, the Rev John Forbes, informed Mr Bye that the Stowmarket Guardians were also withdrawing their boarded-out children, so by the end of the year forty-two children had left because of the closure of the charity. This may have been a blessing to Mr Bye, however, as owing to a teaching vacancy, he and one other teacher were teaching 108 children (of about 186 on the school roll) across five standards.

Louisa Brandreth not only established Rose and Lee Cottages as children's homes, but also, over the next twenty-five years, managed both homes and set up a boarding-out scheme in the village. She liaised with the poor law unions and the Society of Waifs and Strays, sought donations and gifts to support the work at Dickleburgh, supervised children in foster care and arranged training and employment placements for the children. She maintained an active interest in the homes and in the children who had left care, offering practical support and friendship to the many former Dickleburgh girls in service in London after her move to Wanstead. The society case files and articles in the supporters' magazines indicate that not only was Louisa Brandreth an efficient administrator and case worker, but she treated the children under her care as individuals, with compassion, even affection. She was not only a philanthropist, and in effect Dickleburgh's own children's social worker for a quarter of a century, but even in retirement she was dedicated to the welfare of those formerly in care. A letter to Mrs Brandreth from Edith Stiff (held on her case file), who had emigrated to Canada a few years earlier, shows the affection in which Mrs Brandreth was held by children formerly in her care. It starts 'My Dear Godmother' and continues:

> I have your Lightness in my bedroom it is so nice to think I have got a friend in the world, would you please to give me Mrs Mann's [the former Matron of Rose Cottage] Address I should like to have it.... I often think it was my best home I had.

Chapter 2

Attitudes and Legislation Relating to the Poor

The working poor are by far the most numerous class of people, and when kept in due subordination, they compose the riches of the nation. But there is a degree of ignorance necessary to keep them so, and to make themselves either useful to others or happy in themselves.[1]

George Hadley, 1788

For over 600 years, there have been systems in place in England and Wales to support, and control, the 'poor' – those who were unable or unwilling to support themselves and their families by legitimate employment. There were three main vehicles for delivering poor relief over this period: self-help and community support, charities and philanthropists, and the state, with the balance between them fluctuating over the centuries.

In medieval times, poor relief was principally provided by private philanthropists and the Church, particularly the abbeys which provided alms and hospitality for the poor. However, with the dissolution of the monasteries in the 1530s, the main form of relief disappeared and the authorities realised a new approach was needed. Legislation from the latter half of the sixteenth century marked the beginning of state intervention. Overseers of the poor were elected annually in each parish to administer all matters relating to the care of the poor within their community, funded by a poor rate levied on the more substantial householders. Support to those in need was either given as in-relief by admission to the parish poorhouse or as out-relief with payments made to those living at home in money or in kind, such as blankets, coal, clothing or bread.

A poorhouse, also known as the parish or town house, was built in Starston, a small parish in Norfolk, in the late seventeenth century; it was demolished after the new poorhouse was built in 1828. The parish was responsible for maintaining the town house, as shown by entries in the churchwardens' accounts relating to sweeping the chimneys and thatching the roof.[2] Unusually, there is a surviving 1801 census for Starston, and this records seven families living in the parish house, a total of thirty-six people.[3]

The overseers of the poor accounts for Starston also show the range of out-relief dispensed by the parish in the eighteenth century, such as a shilling for Widow Brown 'at need', 2s 6d for making five jackets and petticoats for Cattermole's children, 6s 6d for Widow Hubbard in her 'dying illness', three shillings for six weeks' lodging for Sneling and a shilling for a pair of pattens for the girl Norman. The parish also paid for the cost of burying their paupers; the Starston overseers paid around seventeen shillings to cover the cost of Moulin's funeral including a coffin, payment to Widow Strutt for laying him out and to Charles Tuthill for digging his grave, as well as beer for the bearers and the women![4]

In the nineteenth century, there was a huge growth in charitable organisations to help those in need, fuelled by the evangelical revival which linked charity with spreading the Gospel and, in the case of the children's charities, provided a practical response to the number of destitute children on the streets of London and other major cities and towns. Some children's charities, such as Mrs Brandreth's in Dickleburgh, aimed to bypass the workhouse by providing pauper children with better conditions and more family-oriented care.

Much of the legislation brought in over the last six centuries, especially laws that aimed to control the movement of the poor, was informed by prevailing attitudes towards the labouring classes.[5] The phrase 'deserving and undeserving poor' was first mentioned in the 1563 Poor Law Act, together with the 'deserving unemployed', although the concept goes back 200 years or so before that. Over many centuries, the authorities have tried to make the distinction between the workshy able-bodied who supported themselves by begging, crime or deception and those who were unable to work through disability, ill health, age or lack of work, punishing the former and providing help for the latter.

In medieval times, the focus was on preventing, and punishing, vagrancy and begging; in 1349, the Ordinance of Labourers forbade the giving of alms to 'valiant beggars'. The 1388 Statute of Cambridge, sometimes seen as the first English poor law, prevented workers from moving around the country without proper reason and required the 'impotent poor' to remain where they were or be sent back to their birthplace. This was the earliest attempt to control the labouring classes by curtailing their freedom of movement. The laws of settlement and removal, first enacted in 1662 but not fully repealed until well into the twentieth century, reinforced the principle of the restriction on the movement of the poor. Each person had a parish of 'settlement' and only that parish would provide the person with poor relief, so if they fell on hard times beyond its boundaries, they would be removed back to their parish of settlement. There were various criteria for settlement such as birthplace, working in the parish for a year or more, apprenticeship or renting a property worth £10 or more per year.

One of the harshest consequences of the settlement laws was that unmarried pregnant women were moved on from parish to parish as, until 1834, the ruling was that although a legitimate child took the settlement of its father, an illegitimate child took its own birthplace as its settlement. No parish wanted to be lumbered with an illegitimate child to pay for if it could avoid it. Even legitimate children were sometimes innocent victims of the laws, being forced to move to a different parish if their parents were removed or died.

Louis and Mary Fewings, who came to Dickleburgh in the latter part of 1906, were caught by the settlement laws following their parents' deaths. Their aunt, Clara Fewings, took the children and their two younger sisters, Harriet and Elizabeth, into the children's receiving home for the Stepney union, in east London, just six days after the death of their widowed father.[6] Clara and her husband Richard, who was a dockside labourer, were probably unable to support them as they already had four children of their own. However, the Stepney Guardians quickly issued a removal order for the children, to the West Ham Poor Law Union, the children's place of settlement, and all four children were removed to the West Ham workhouse at Leyton in May 1906.[7] By the autumn of that year, Louis and Mary Ann were boarded out in the Dickleburgh area, Harriet was probably boarded out within the West Ham union and Elizabeth had died, aged 2, of measles and broncho-pneumonia, still resident in the workhouse at Leyton.

The Poor Relief Act of 1723, also known as the Workhouse Test Act or Knatchbull's Act, empowered parishes to build workhouses and to force the able-bodied to work there in return for receiving relief. Out-relief was limited mainly to widows, the elderly, sick and infirm. This was intended to deter the able-bodied (the 'undeserving poor') from seeking relief, with the belief that they would rather find employment than submit to the workhouse regime to obtain poor relief. In some areas, notably Norfolk and Suffolk, a number of incorporations were set up in the mid-eighteenth century, each with a house of industry serving several parishes, managed by a joint board.[8] Gilbert's Act in 1782 introduced the concept of unions of parishes run by guardians, but effectively reversed Knatchbull's Act (which had proved very expensive) by limiting admission to the workhouse to the sick, elderly and young. The able-bodied might be employed outside with their wages supplemented from the poor rate, a system that continued until 1834, and in some cases, beyond.

From the 1790s, many contemporary economists, political thinkers and writers believed the whole poor law system was in radical need of reform or should be abolished altogether. There was strong criticism of the existing system, citing the cost of providing poor relief as well as corruption and inefficiency. There were also concerns that the system encouraged a dependency culture and that some paupers were living in relative luxury, better off than independent working labourers, so a royal commission was established in 1832 to report on the state of poor law administration.

The royal commission heavily criticised the out-relief system, saying it encouraged high rents, low wages, idleness, large families, and malingerers. It also concluded that the system of putting the able-bodied poor to work was not effective. The resulting Poor Law Amendment Act of 1834 – the 'New Poor Law' – was perhaps the harshest manifestation of the poor laws for centuries. It introduced a central body – the Poor Law Commission – to oversee administration and to bring a level of control and consistency to the system, and it required parishes to join together to form poor law unions, run by elected guardians of the poor drawn from each parish. Each union had to provide a workhouse; some used existing parish workhouses, although these were often unsuitable to house large numbers of paupers, and others erected new buildings. The 1834 Act reversed Gilbert's Act (in theory, though not necessarily in practice) by stopping out-relief for the able-bodied; they had to enter a workhouse to receive relief, and workhouse conditions were made harsher to act as a deterrent. Paupers were divided into classes within the workhouse and a rigorous policy of segregation meant that married couples lived apart, only babies and infants were allowed to stay with their mothers, and even siblings of different ages or sexes were separated in the workhouse.

Charlie Chaplin, the actor, director and musician, entered the Lambeth workhouse in 1896, when he was about 6 years old, with his mother, Hannah, and older half-brother, Sydney. He described their arrival at the workhouse gate where 'the forlorn bewilderment of it struck me; for there we were made to separate, Mother going in one direction to the women's ward and we in another to the children's.'[9]

Children whose mothers were also in the workhouse were usually allowed to meet up with them once a week. Charles Shaw, whose life story was later immortalised in the character of Darius Clayhanger in Arnold Bennett's novel *Clayhanger*, was in Chell workhouse near Stoke-on-Trent as a child around 1840. Some sixty years later, he wrote about Sunday afternoons bringing 'an hour of unspeakable joy' when the children were able to spend time with their mothers: 'This was the one sweet merciful relief in the harsh discipline of the workhouse.... The Sunday afternoon shone through all the week.'[10]

Mothers and children could be separated on a permanent basis within the workhouse system if the children were sent to specialised institutions, such as district schools or grouped homes, away from the workhouse site. Charlie Chaplin and his brother Sydney were transferred from Lambeth workhouse to the Central London District School in Hanwell, about twelve miles out of London, which was upsetting for young Charlie, as not only was he parted from his mother but also from his brother. Sydney joined the older boys at Hanwell while Charlie was with the infants, so they rarely saw each other. He later wrote, 'I was a little over six years old and alone, which made me feel quite abject.'[11]

However, Hannah Chaplin, Charlie and Sydney's mother, was determined to see her boys again, so two months later she discharged herself from the workhouse and arranged for the two boys to be discharged from Hanwell. They met at the workhouse gate, having swapped their workhouse uniforms for their own clothes, and spent a happy day together, playing in the park. They shared half a pound of black cherries, then spent the remainder of the ninepence Sydney had with him in a coffee shop on a twopenny teacake, a penny bloater and two halfpenny cups of tea. In the afternoon, they all returned to the workhouse, 'just in time for tea' said Hannah Chaplin. This meant the boys had to spend another few weeks in the workhouse before returning to Hanwell, giving them further opportunities to see their mother.[12]

In 1835, the Poor Law Commission issued orders and regulations for the management of workhouses under the 1834 Act, which introduced schooling in workhouses and other poor law establishments for the first time; a schoolmaster or mistress was to be appointed and children in the workhouse had to receive at least three hours schooling a day. They were to be taught 'reading, writing, arithmetic and the principles of Christian religion, and ... other instruction to train them to habits of usefulness, industry and virtue.'[13] In the smaller unions, there would be a schoolroom in the workhouse but the larger, urban unions might have a separate school block on the workhouse site.

The new poor law made little, if any, progress in curtailing begging and vagrancy, a major issue for the authorities over the previous five centuries. The casual wards in urban workhouses, known colloquially as 'spikes', were full to overflowing, not with 'valiant beggars', able-bodied men who were too idle to work, but with the homeless, tramps, and 'down and outs', men (mostly) who were unfit to work or unable to get work so had no money for food or lodging. In 1902, Jack London, the American writer, spent two months living undercover amongst the people of the East End of London, writing about his experiences in a book published the following year. London described the workhouse casual ward as 'a building where the homeless, bedless, penniless man, if he be lucky, may *casually* rest his weary bones, and then work like a navvy next day to pay for it.'[14]

London made several unsuccessful attempts to gain entry to a workhouse casual ward and after he was turned away from the Whitechapel workhouse as it was full, he joined a carter and a carpenter who were walking to the Poplar workhouse, three miles away, to try to get a bed for the night: 'The chief difficulty with these men was that they were old, and that their children, instead of growing up to take care of them, had died.'[15] The men explained that it was virtually impossible to sleep on the streets or in the parks at night in London, as the police constantly moved the homeless on, and the carpenter explained how the workhouse system forced him and others into a spiral of unemployment, poverty and hopelessness:

> I go to the casual ward for a bed. Must be there by two or three in the afternoon or I won't get in... . What chance does that give me to look for work? S'pose I do get into the casual ward? Keep me in all day to-morrow, let me out mornin' o' next day. What then? The law sez I can't get in another casual ward that night less'n ten miles distant. Have to hurry an' walk to be there in time that day. What chance does that give me to look for a job? S'pose I don't walk. S'pose I look for a job? In no time there's night come, an' no bed. No sleep night, nothin' to eat, what shape am I in the mornin' to look for work?... . An' there I am! Old, down, an' no chance to get up.[16]

Despite the efforts of the central Poor Law Commission to provide national standards, there was much variation between the poor law unions. Workhouse conditions and diets, the provision of appropriate facilities for children and the amount of out-relief dispensed were often dependent on decisions made locally by the guardians, who tried to keep costs down. The out-relief register of the Aylsham union in Norfolk gives details of cases in 1836, including that of Deborah Bardwell, who was in her thirties with three children and had been deserted by her husband.[17] She was working as a seamstress, not a well-paid job, so the guardians granted her three shillings a week but only until her father appeared before the magistrates; presumably the union felt he should be supporting his grandchildren. Two of the union's existing parish workhouses were being enlarged and adapted to meet the needs of the 1834 Act, so Martha Bird, who was in her late fifties but unable to work because she was lame, was granted relief (of a shilling a week) only until the workhouse was ready to receive paupers. William Greenwood was an unemployed weaver in his early twenties with a wife and four children to support (two others were already in the workhouse); the guardians granted him five shillings a week working on the roads and an additional 1s 6d a week. Some elderly people received relief, such as the widow Mary Smith who was in her eighties and unable to work on account of her age – she received two shillings a week.

There was a strong belief amongst the gentry and middle classes that the structure of society – with the labouring classes at the bottom of the heap – was part of the natural order of things ordained by God. This was expressed by the following verse, which unsurprisingly is never sung these days, from Cecil Frances Alexander's hymn *All Things Bright and Beautiful,* published in 1848, although the sentiments expressed go back much further than that:

> The rich man in his castle,
> The poor man at his gate,
> God made them, high or lowly,
> And ordered their estate.

This overarching belief in a subordinate labouring class, which knew its place and was not expected to rise above its preordained station in life, impacted on the approach to education and to poor relief. From the eighteenth century onwards, there was debate about the type and level of education appropriate for the children of the labouring classes. Many thought education should be limited to providing moral and Christian training, together with reading to enable the poor to read the Bible, though some such as George Hadley thought it was inadvisable even to teach reading: 'What ploughman who could read the renowned history of Tom Hickathrift, Jack the Giant-Killer or the Seven Wise Men, would be content to whistle up one furrow and down another, from dawn in the morning, to the setting of the sun?'[18] In 1856, MP Charles Adderley raised the old spectre of class and the poor's place in society when he urged an increase in educational provision for children of the labouring classes, but added that there should be a restriction in the aims of the education provided:

The object of the present system seemed to be, not to make ploughboys or mechanics, but to make scholars ... if they were to pass a law to compel poor parents to send their children to a school to be made scholars of, they might just as well pass another law to compel the noble Lord to send his children to a school where they would be educated for becoming ploughboys or artisans.[19]

Some were fearful that too much education for the poor might lead to rebellion and threaten the structure and stability of society, like this writer in the *Gentleman's Magazine* in 1797:

A little learning makes a man ambitious to rise, if he can't by fair means then he uses foul... . A man of no literature will seldom attempt to form insurrections, or form idle schemes for the reformation of the state.[20]

In 1807, the MP Davies Giddy spoke in the Commons against providing schooling at public expense for children of the labouring classes:

Instead of making them good servants in agriculture and other laborious employments to which their rank in society had destined them; instead of teaching them subordination it would render them factious and refractory ... it would enable them to read seditious pamphlets, vicious books and publications against Christianity; it would render them insolent to their superiors.[21]

James Kay (later Kay-Shuttleworth), the assistant poor law commissioner and educationalist, had a different view, believing education was key to reducing crime and dependence on poor relief, although he acknowledged the poor's place in society. In 1838 he wrote:

The consequence of the neglect of the pauper class evidently was prolonged dependence and subsequent chargeability as criminals in the prisons and penal colonies... . The duty of rearing these children in religion and industry and of imparting to them such an amount of secular knowledge as may fit them to discharge the duties of their station, cannot be denied.[22]

Many Victorians considered that poverty was not a consequence of social and economic conditions but was the fault of the poor themselves – they were idle, irresponsible and immoral, even criminal. Churchmen could be particularly robust and sanctimonious in their views. In his defence of the new poor law, the Rev Thomas Spencer cited Bishop (Joseph) Butler's view that each person had the power to determine their own enjoyment and suffering, 'for pleasure and pain are the consequence of our own actions'.[23] In his pamphlet, Spencer, who was perpetual curate of Hinton Charterhouse and a guardian in the Bath union, vigorously condemned the old pre-1834 out-relief system, calling it an 'encouragement to improvidence', stating:

> The besetting sin of human nature is INDOLENCE: this indolence, whether mental or corporeal, requires a stimulus to action; and this stimulus is NECESSITY... . Tell the millions of young and middle aged that when they are in need, or old age, their wants shall be supplied, and you remove the stimulus; you rebuke the careful man who, by denying himself, lays up in store for future contingencies.

Spencer considered that there should be pity for farmers and landowners who had had to sell their farms and estates through having to pay the poor rate, and so had been driven into poverty themselves, rather than for 'those who, as "paupers in their own right," ask without shame for that which their own present toil or previous forethought might have provided.'

In her study of 400 case files of the Waifs and Strays Society, Harriet Ward explored the relationships between the poor and those providing charitable assistance. She states, 'the prevailing ideology tended to regard destitution and depravity as manifestations of the same shortcomings: both were seen as culpable conditions that required correction, rather than sympathy.'[24] Joy Parr, who researched juvenile emigration by Barnardo's, said that the 'sturdiest underpinnings [of the emigration policy] ... equated poverty with negligence, intermittent unemployment with idleness, common-law union with viciousness.'[25] In 1910, Lily and Nellie Mellish were admitted to the Waifs and Strays Society, despite concerns by the society that their widowed father and the young woman he was living with were not married. Edward Rudolf feared the society might be accused of 'encouraging immorality, as it is doubtful if relieved, the man would give up the woman with whom he is cohabiting.'

The consequence of these beliefs was that many philanthropic organisations adopted a policy of 'rescue from the environment, rather than rehabilitation within it', which taken to its ultimate became a policy of severance, with the child in care deliberately being denied access to family or friends.[26] Providing financial support for a family to enable them to remain together at home was not acceptable practice at this time. The charities justified the severance policy by claiming it was the only means of breaking the poverty cycle and giving deprived children a chance to grow up to become useful and independent adults and, according to the evangelicals, of achieving salvation.[27]

The poor law remained on the statute book for over a century, causing M.A. Crowther to comment, 'Few pieces of legislation can have had such a lingering death, in spite of its unpopularity and the thinning ranks of its defenders.'[28] There were, though, some changes in policy and practice as time progressed and by 1948, when the last remnants of the poor law system were abolished, it was much diluted. By the late nineteenth century, out-relief for the able-bodied was more common, at least in some areas, as it was cheaper than housing people in workhouses. Old-age pensions were introduced in 1908 and some unemployment benefit in 1911, providing alternatives to the workhouse for some. There was also steady, if slow, progress in providing care away from the workhouse for children.

The 1908 Children Act not only addressed issues relating to wilful cruelty of children, but also negligence, fostering, care in uncertified homes and juvenile offenders. The Act was, according to Heywood, 'a great and fundamental step in child protection', because it drew together many earlier pieces of legislation and amendments into one statute 'which publicly emphasised the social rights of children.'[29] The 1905 Royal Commission on the Poor Law and the Unemployed which reported in 1909, was unable to agree, so produced a majority and a minority report.[30] The majority report suggested improving the current poor law system, but the minority report proposed that the poor law should be broken up, and that all matters relating to children of school age, including destitute children, but excluding the sick or mentally ill, should be dealt with by the local authorities. Although no immediate legislation followed, many of the proposals of the minority report were introduced piecemeal over the following years. The 1929 Local Government Act abolished the poor law unions and transferred responsibility for poor relief, renamed 'public assistance', to the county councils and county boroughs, which also took over infirmaries and fever hospitals. Workhouses were renamed public assistance institutions, although the stigma and shame of the workhouse remained for decades amongst those over whom it had cast its dark shadow for so long.

Chapter 3

The World of the Deprived Child

There, on a door-step, crouches some shoeless child, whose day's begging has not brought it enough to purchase even the penny night's lodging that his young companions in beggary have gone to... . Then, as the streets grow blue with the coming light ... the little slattern girl, with her basket slung before her, screams, *'Water-creases!'* through the sleeping streets.[1]

Henry Mayhew and John Binney, 1862

The nineteenth century was a time of major social and economic change in Britain; industrialisation, particularly the development of the factory system, a significant growth in population, and urbanisation brought prosperity for some but drove others into extreme poverty. Mechanisation of manufacturing processes, especially in the textile industry, meant the decline of small cottage industries such as spinning and silk weaving. With the resultant move from homeworking to factory jobs, family life was changed, childcare became more difficult and older children were less able to contribute informally to the family business. The factory system involved long working hours, dangerous and unhealthy working conditions and harsh discipline, and was highly dependent on child labour.

Immigration, larger families and a reduction in infant mortality all contributed to the rapid growth in population and, combined with urbanisation, resulted in housing shortages and overcrowding. The problem was exacerbated by the demolition of slums, sometimes for humanitarian reasons, but often to make way for new roads or railways. Regardless of the reason for demolition, the slums were rarely replaced with homes that the poor could afford to rent, putting further pressure on housing. Conditions could be as bad, although often more hidden, in rural areas. Economic downturns, particularly in agriculture, the drive for profitability and swings in trade also had a major impact on the labouring poor, with casual and seasonal employment, low wages and unemployment forcing them below the poverty line. Poor housing conditions and sanitation, inadequate diet, and shared and contaminated water supplies led to disease and death, in both rural and urban areas, affecting all ages.

Charles Dickens was one of several social commentators in the nineteenth century who drew attention to the appalling conditions in which many of the poor lived, particularly children. In a letter to *The Daily News* on 4 February 1846, Dickens referred to the pauper children of London as a 'wretched throng ... a vast hopeless nursery of ignorance, misery and vice: a breeding place for the hulks and gaols'. Some four years later, he wrote about the children attending the Norwood district school as 'little personifications of genuine poverty – compounds ... of ignorance, gin, and sprats' adding:

> Generally born in dark alleys and back courts, their playground has been the streets, where the wits of many have been prematurely sharpened at the expense of any morals they might have. With minds and bodies destitute of proper nutriment, they are caught, as it were, by the parish officers, half-wild creatures, roaming poverty-stricken amidst the wealth of our greatest city; and half-starved in a land where the law says no one shall be destitute of food and shelter.[2]

Several major studies of poverty were undertaken in the nineteenth and early twentieth centuries, such as those of Henry Mayhew and Charles Booth in London, and Benjamin Seebohm Rowntree in York. Dickens, Andrew Mearns and James Greenwood were amongst those who published pamphlets, novels or articles in newspapers and journals to highlight the plight of the poor in Victorian Britain, particularly in London. Mayhew was a writer and journalist and published a series of substantial letters in *The Morning Chronicle* in 1849 and 1850, mainly concerned with the London manufacturing trades, as part of its investigation into 'Labour and the Poor'. Over the following two years, Mayhew published his *London Labour and the London Poor* in weekly parts, examining the state of the street trades and labour in the capital including interviews with hundreds of traders and workers, adults and children, as well as those staying in a common lodging house and an asylum for the homeless poor. He addressed issues of the casual labour market and explored living conditions, wages and the domestic lives of those he and his assistants interviewed, as well as asking detailed questions about their trades and occupations, and visiting homes and lodgings as part of his enquiry. *London Labour and the London Poor* incorporated some of the material from the letters in *The Morning Chronicle* and was published in book form in 1851, although the edition published in 1861/2, with additional material, is usually the one used by historians today.[3] The work is richly illustrated with woodcuts, mostly engraved from daguerreotypes (now lost) taken by Richard Beard, a contemporary London photographer.[4]

Many adults and children interviewed by Mayhew and his assistants came from a class that was largely below the radar of contemporary society, so births, even deaths, may not have been registered and few marriages were recorded as many couples simply cohabited. Many were not even known by their real names, but, as Mayhew explained, by some peculiar nickname known to everyone, derived chiefly from some personal characteristic, such as Lanky Bill, One-eyed George or Short-armed Jack. It is likely that many do not appear in the mid-nineteenth century census returns either, so unless they were in receipt of out-relief, apprenticed by the parish or guardians, entered the workhouse or passed through the criminal justice system, there may be little trace of their lives other than perhaps an entry in a burial register. Some of Mayhew's interviewees showed a fear of entering the workhouse, such as the elderly, female pure-finder (a collector of dog faeces for use in the tanning industry) who, having been out all the previous day collecting and only managing to make sixpence, was laid up when the interviewer came:

> No, I have earned no money today. I have had a piece of dried bread that I steeped in water to eat. I haven't eaten anything else today; but pray sir, don't tell anybody of it. I could never bear the thought of going into the 'great house' [workhouse]; I'm so used to the air, that I'd sooner die in the street, as many I know have done … I'd sooner die like them than be deprived of my liberty, and be prevented from going about where I liked.

Many of the children interviewed for Mayhew's study, even those who had been orphaned or deserted, survived with little state or charity intervention. They eked out a living as street traders, mud larks or crossing sweepers, or by begging, thieving or prostitution. Those that still lived at home brought their earnings to their parents to supplement the meagre family income. Deserted or orphaned children and older children striking out on their own might live in groups in cheap lodgings, though when they fell on hard times they would resort to common lodging houses, the casual wards of the workhouse, a refuge or sleeping on the streets. Inevitably some would spend time in prison, or even be transported to the colonies.

Child street sellers were a common sight in London, selling a range of produce and goods, such as flowers, fruit, watercress and matches. They were often sent out to work at a young age by their parents, bringing anything they earned home. Mayhew described an 8-year-old watercress seller:

> Her little face, pale and thin with privation, was wrinkled where the dimples ought to have been, and she would sigh frequently.... . The poor child, although the weather was severe was dressed in a thin cotton gown, with a threadbare shawl wrapped round her shoulders. She wore no covering to her head, and the long rusty hair stood out in all directions. When she walked she shuffled along, for fear that the large carpet slippers that served her for shoes should slip off her feet.

The girl had to be at Farringdon Market between four and five in the morning to buy her stock, otherwise all the watercress would be gone. The trade was subject to the weather; when it was cold, people would not buy it and if there was snow on the ground, there was none available. She went on to say: 'I bears the cold – you must; so I puts my hands under my shawl, though it hurts 'em to take hold of the creases, especially when we takes 'em to the pump to wash 'em. No; I never see any children crying – it's no use.'

The crossing sweeper boys formed into groups or gangs with an appointed captain, often staying together, such as the group of about five boys who lodged in a single room with a woman, her daughter and her 10-year-old grandson, also a crossing sweeper, in a narrow street off Drury Lane:

> 'I've a nice flock-bid for the boys,' [the landlady] said ... 'where three of them can slape aisy and comfortable.'
>
>   'It's a large bed, sir,' said one of the boys, 'and a warm covering over us, and you see it's better than a regular lodging-house; for, if you want a knife or a cup, you don't have to leave something on it till it's returned.'

According to the landlady, the boys were an honest lot for 'they pays me rig'lar every night, which is threepence' though she did take issue with Goose, the captain of the group, who was often out late returning with no money. Johnny, the landlady's orphaned grandson, gave his grandmother and aunt all his earnings and gave further insights into the lives of the boy crossing sweepers saying:

> I don't like the sweeping, and I don't think there's e'er one of us wot like it. In the winter we has to be out in the cold, and then in summer we have to sleep out all night, or go asleep on the church-steps, reg'lar tired out.... . The most of the boys has got no homes. Perhaps they've got the price of a lodging, but they're hungry, and they eats the money, and then they must lay out.

The juvenile mud larks, mostly living in alleyways and courts near the river, spent much of their days wading in the mud along the shoreline in search of items to sell or exchange for food, such as coal, iron, copper nails, rope, bones and, if they were very lucky, discarded tools such as hammers. Mayhew spoke to a group of young mud larks by the steps close to the river: 'There was not one of them over twelve years of age, and many of them were but six. It would be almost impossible to describe the wretched group, so motley was their appearance, so extraordinary their dress, and so stolid and inexpressive their countenances.' A 9-year-old who had been mud larking for three years explained that his father died when he was an infant and his mother now earned up to a shilling a day when she could get work, washing or charing (cleaning). He had no shoes and his mother had no suitable clothes in which to attend church or chapel. 'All the money he gave to his mother, and she bought bread with it, and when they had no money they lived the best way they could,' wrote Mayhew. The boys often injured their bare feet on sharp objects or broken glass; one explained that after going home to dress his injuries, he would immediately return to the shoreline, 'for should the tide come up without my having found something, why I must starve till next low tide.'

Some children resorted to less legitimate means of making a living. In volume four of Mayhew's work, John Binny described young thieves, aged between 6 and 10 as 'Arabs of the city [who] in the evening, when the lamps are lit ... steal forth from their haunts, with keen roguish eye, looking out for booty.' The young thieves usually worked together in small groups raiding the street stalls: 'One will push an old woman off her seat ... while the others will steal her fruit or the few coppers lying on her stall.' Groups of boys also raided shops, stealing items on display or money from tills while the shopkeeper was distracted, or smashing the shop windows and grabbing items from the display, such as sweets or cigars and pipes, running away swiftly before they were caught.

Binny described how pickpockets started young and were drawn from 'the dregs of society ... the little ragged boys living by a felon's hearth, or herding with other young criminals in a low lodging-house, or dwelling in the cold and comfortless home of drunken and improvident parents.' These children were taught how to steal by their companions, even their parents or older brothers, or by trainers, usually experienced and convicted thieves who would then sell on the stolen items, giving the child a proportion of the money. Pickpockets would start by stealing handkerchiefs and gentlemen's pocket books, as well as begging and perhaps opportunistic thieving. Like the young boys, pickpockets usually worked in groups.

Some children started begging in the streets at a very young age, encouraged by their parents, such as this elderly man interviewed for Mayhew's book:

I have been a beggar ever since I was that high – ever since I could walk ... I was turned out to beg by my mother. My father, I've heard, was a soldier; he went to Egypt, or some foreign part, and never came back. I never was learnt any trade but begging, and I couldn't turn my hand to nothing else.

In 1902, Jack London, the American writer, described the young lad appearing in the dock of a police court:

His head was barely visible above the railing. He was being proved guilty of stealing two shillings from a woman, which he had spent, not for candy and cakes and a good time, but for food.

'Why didn't you ask the woman for food?' the magistrate demanded, in a hurt sort of tone. 'She would surely have given you something to eat.'

'If I 'ad arsked 'er, I'd got locked up for beggin', was the boy's reply.[5]

Sometimes begging was more a case of deception – feigning an injury or disability, or a child street seller deliberately jostling a passing gentleman, resulting in the matches or white peppermint lozenges or whatever they were selling, falling into the mud. A few howls of despair would usually shame the gentleman or onlookers into giving the child some cash to compensate for their loss.

Charles Booth was the next generation of social investigator. He was dubious of the accuracy of figures about poverty in London, believing them to be exaggerated, so he undertook his own investigation, using official records such as those of the school board visitors and poor law authorities and working with a team of researchers, including his wife's cousin Beatrice Potter, later Beatrice Webb. He explained:

My first attempt was to enumerate the mass of people in London in classes according to degrees of poverty or comfort and to indicate the conditions of life in each class. In connection with this attempt I mapped out the streets in colours and endeavoured to show by sample descriptions the kind of persons dwelling therein, their habits and the manner of their lives.[6]

Booth's enquiries and the colour-coded maps form a remarkable legacy, equal to Mayhew's work some forty years earlier. Booth popularised the notion of a 'poverty line', defined by a weekly income of eighteen to twenty-one shillings as the minimum for a family of four to five to exist on. He used eight colours, ranging from black to yellow, to denote the street classifications. Booth designated the first two classes – A and B – as 'very poor', below the poverty line, and the next two as 'poor' – on or around twenty-one shillings a week. Individuals and families could rise or sink into different classifications, temporarily or permanently, depending upon changes to their circumstances. These included the earning power of adult children, hard work and good character, a growth in trade or conversely, the growth of the family, drink, death, illness, injury or a trade depression. Booth's work was published in various editions, and an increasing number of volumes, between 1889 and 1903, with the title *Life and Labour of the People in London*. He concluded that the level of distress was worse than the previous estimates, with thirty-one per cent living in poverty across London, rising to thirty-five per cent in east London.

Black (class A) was described as 'the lowest class, which consists of some occasional labourers, street sellers, loafers, criminals and semi-criminals... . Their food is of the coarsest description, and their only luxury is drink.'[7] The children of this class were described as 'street arabs', many of whom were 'separated from the parents in pauper or industrial schools, and in such homes as Dr Barnardo's.' Class B was denoted in dark blue, described as 'casual earnings – very poor ... a deposit of those who from mental, moral and physical reasons are incapable of better work.' Booth concluded that many of them were poor 'from shiftlessness, helplessness, idleness, or drink'. He estimated that there were about 38,000 children under the age of 15 in this class.

The next class, defined in light blue, was described as poor with 'intermittent earnings'. This included many whose work was seasonal or subject to trade variations, such as those in the building trade or dock labourers and stevedores (who docked and unloaded ships). Some earned high wages when they were working, but often spent much of it on food or drink, taking little home. Booth explained that having lots of young children put a strain on the family, stating that it was 'in the years when the elder children have not yet left school, while the younger ones are still a care to the mother at home, that the pressure of family life is most felt.' Class D comprised mostly those with regular, low wages, up to twenty-one shillings a week, plus some at the 'better end' of casual dock and waterside labour, those men who would regularly be selected out of the throng clamouring for work each day. Generally, 'these men have a hard struggle to make ends meet, but they are, as a body, decent steady men, paying their way and bringing up their children respectably.'

Like Mayhew before him, Booth provided details about specific families, streets and houses. Bridget and John Murdock, a bricklayer's labourer, who had four sons, were classified in the lowest class according to Booth: 'Murdock deserted his wife several times, and has been sent to prison for it. She in turn left him in 1877, and has been living with another man since. After this he was in Bromley [Work] House with the children. The two eldest were emigrated to Canada in 1880.' The houses in Shelton Street, one of the 'black streets' in the St Giles area of London, near Covent Garden, were apparently demolished shortly after Booth's team visited. The street comprised about forty three-storey houses, with about eight rooms in each, mostly let singly to families. Many residents were Irish Catholics, often transient, mainly working as costermongers and market porters. Booth described the conditions:

> Drunkenness and dirt and bad language prevailed, and violence was common, reaching at times even to murder. Fifteen rooms out of twenty were filthy to the last degree…. Not a room would be free from vermin, and in many life at night was unbearable…. The little yard at the back was only sufficient for dustbin and closet and water-tap, serving for six or seven families. The water would be drawn from cisterns which were receptacles for refuse, and perhaps occasionally a dead cat. At one time the street was fever-stricken; the mortality was high, and the authorities interfered with good effect so that the sanitary condition of the street just before it was destroyed was better than it had been formerly.

Booth goes on to describe the residents of each household in the street, such as this family, 'a very sad case' who, six months before the property was pulled down, were living on the second floor of No 4 Shelton Street: 'A woman with four small children whose husband had gone to America.

The children were without boots or food, and their mother had to lock them in the room while she went to sell oranges in the streets.'

A few years before Booth, the Rev Andrew Mearns, in his short pamphlet, *The Bitter Cry of Outcast London*, also focused on the housing and living conditions of the poor.[8] Its sensational style, aimed at the middle classes and the churches, attracted much attention in the press, even though other writers and government reports had highlighted these issues before.[9] Here he describes the living conditions of families living in single rooms in tenements in south London:

> Every room in these rotten and reeking tenements houses a family, often two. In one cellar a sanitary inspector reports finding a father, mother, three children, and four pigs.... Here is a mother who turns her children into the street in the early evening because she lets her room for immoral purposes until long after midnight, when the poor little wretches creep back again if they have not found some miserable shelter elsewhere. Where there are beds they are simply heaps of dirty rags, shavings or straw, but for the most part these miserable beings find rest only upon the filthy boards.

Mearns also wrote about the degradation of the common lodging houses, 'often the resorts of thieves and vagabonds of the lowest type'. And for those who could not find the twopence for a night in a common lodging house, 'there is a lower depth still ... they huddle together upon stairs and landings, where there is no uncommon thing to find six or eight in the early morning.'

Benjamin Seebohm Rowntree was influenced by Booth's work and published his own detailed study of the poor of York in 1901. His investigations followed a similar form to Mayhew and Booth, although he named neither the people interviewed nor the streets in which they lived. Rowntree gave examples of households from the different classes; class A contained the poorest such as:

> Odd jobs. Married. Four rooms. Three children. Man drinks. Formerly in good work. Cannot keep a situation. Poverty-stricken. Children not properly nourished. Had parish relief once. Rent 4s.

Widow. Two rooms; Eleven children; the eldest was fifteen when the father died. Four are now working. Sober and very industrious, clean and fairly comfortable. Never in debt; children fairly well clothed and fed. Rooms well kept and of a good size. Parish relief. Rent 2s. 6d.

Labourer. Married. Two rooms. Four children. Chronic illness. Not worked for two years. Wife chars. Parish relief. This house shares one closet and one water tap with eight other houses. Rent 1s. 7d.[10]

Rowntree concluded that the 'poverty line' for a family of five, parents and three children, was 21s 8d per week. He believed that on this, the family could exist on 'mere physical efficiency'. He also introduced the idea of the 'cycle of poverty' for the labourer, with three periods when poverty was most likely and most oppressive – childhood; childrearing; and old age. Rowntree estimated that in York, ten per cent were living in 'primary poverty', whose earnings were insufficient to maintain 'mere physical efficiency', and seventeen per cent were living in 'secondary poverty' where their earnings would have been sufficient for basic survival, had not some portion been spent elsewhere, 'either usefully or wastefully', such as on drink.[11] Rowntree's conclusion that about twenty-eight per cent of the population of York was living in poverty was very similar to Booth's conclusions about London.

In 1912, Dorothy Jewson and her brother, Harry, with a team of nearly sixty people consisting of ministers and clergy, members of the Liberal Christian League and other volunteers, carried out an investigation into the out-relief system operating in Norwich, publishing a report the following year.[12] Dorothy was a suffragist, pacifist, trade unionist, member of the Independent Labour Party, MP for Norwich 1923–1924 and a Norwich City councillor. The Norwich Guardians provided out-relief only to those unable to work – the sick, disabled and the elderly, and their dependents – and to widows with dependent children. The able-bodied poor received in-relief in the workhouse or in some cases through a labour test, whereby the guardians would set men to work on wood chopping, paying them a weekly allowance, part in money, part in food or fuel.

The Norwich Committee of Investigators concluded that in many cases the out-relief provided was insufficient, leading to privation, and recommended raising weekly relief to five shillings for each adult where there was no other income, as well as for widows, with a sliding scale of relief for dependent children starting at four shillings for the first child. The report concluded that of the 812 cases investigated, 471 (fifty-eight per cent) were living in miserable circumstances and of these, 159 (twenty per cent of the total cases) were particularly bad where the amount of relief was insufficient to buy food. The committee also investigated fifteen cases (comprising eighty-six individuals) where the father was on the outdoor labour test, where relief was provided half in fuel or food and half in money, and found that in some cases, relief was 'terribly inadequate'.

Like Mayhew, Booth and Rowntree, the Norwich committee reinforced its arguments with specific examples, such as the widow with ten children under the age of 13, one of which was supported by a charity. She received two shillings weekly out-relief for each of the other nine children, but nothing for herself. The investigators concluded that after paying for rent, heating and lighting, only twelve shillings would remain for food, clothing and other household sundries – just over twopence per person per day. The woman had recently 'completely broke[n] down in health through undernourishment.' One family, comprising parents and three children where the father was on the out-relief test, received goods and money to the value of 6s 9d a week and another, with six children, received 9s 1d.

Poor and inadequate diets, leading to malnutrition and even death, were the inevitable consequence of such poverty. Mayhew was told that poor Irish children would scour the streets and bins early in the morning for discarded cigar ends and scraps of bread and sell the former to buy a small quantity of oatmeal. After washing and soaking the bread, they would boil it up with oatmeal and this would constitute the meal for the whole family for the day. In his introduction to the Norwich report, Seebohm Rowntree stated:

It must not be thought that the absence of frequent deaths directly due to starvation, and of any general complaint of hunger on the part of the poor, proves that they are sufficiently fed... . But [the] effects [of underfeeding] are no less certain and no less deadly. An ample diet of bread, cheap jam, potatoes and tea, does not prevent the slow exhaustion of the body from lack of suitable nutriment. The results of this insufficient diet must be looked for in the high death-rates in those quarters where the poor congregate, especially the deaths from consumption – which is so largely a disease of poverty – and the high infantile mortality.

Girls had fewer opportunities to earn a legitimate living than boys in urban areas; many were unable to gain regular, respectable employment such as domestic service, so might turn to prostitution to supplement their irregular earnings from seamstress work or selling flowers. However, some girls chose prostitution, at least for a time, as they could earn good money and found it an easier life than selling goods on the streets. Andrew Mearns wrote:

The low parts of London are the sink into which the filthy and abominable from all parts of the country seem to flow. Entire courts are filled with thieves, prostitutes and liberated convicts. In one street are 35 houses, 32 of which are known to be brothels. In another district are 43 of these houses, and 428 fallen women and girls, many of them not more than 12 years of age.

Henry Mayhew stated that some flower girls were of 'an immoral character', some being sent out by their parents to make a living by prostitution. The parents of one such girl had sent her out on to the streets to sell flowers at the age of 9, taking her day's earnings on her return home. She was about 18 when interviewed:

She used to be out frequently till past midnight, and seldom or never got home before nine. She associated only with flower-girls of loose character. The result may be imagined. She could not state positively that her parents were aware of the manner in which she got the money she took home to them. She supposes they must have imagined what her practices were.

Another girl turned out by her father some three years earlier said:

> I work at the bootbinding but can't get a living at it.... . If I get bread, sir, by my work, I can't get clothes. For the sake of clothes or food I'm obliged to go into the streets, and I'm out regularly now, and I've no other dependence at all but the streets. If I could only get an honest living, I would gladly leave the streets.[13]

Despite unpleasant and dangerous working conditions and long hours, children employed in factories were in some cases better off than their counterparts who scratched a living on the streets. An Act of 1844 gave some protection to children working in textile factories, prohibiting the employment of children under 8 years old and requiring those aged 8 to 13 to attend an approved elementary school for three hours a day. The Act limited working hours for children in a textile factory to a maximum of six and a half a day which meant that these 'half-timers' could be in work and school for over nine hours a day.

A royal commission was set up in 1862 to enquire into the employment of children in trades and manufactures not already regulated by law. Its evidence revealed much about child employment in a range of industries as well as the extent of education amongst working children. The resulting Workshop Regulation Act of 1867 introduced further regulation, although as with earlier legislation, it was often ignored. Mr J. E. White, one of the commissioners, visited two lucifer match factories in Norwich owned by John Lincoln. Lincoln said that he thought children should not start work until they were 10 and should attend school before that. The commission report added:

> The children that he can get for the match work are quite the poorest of the poor and the lowest of the low. Does not know where they come from. He thinks more is done for children now than there used to be in finding them schools and amusement. The parents will not do anything themselves if they could. They will not give up their drink or anything for themselves for the good of their children or their education.[14]

Mr White considered the conditions in the Lincoln's Bull Close factory reasonable; it was well-ventilated, the benches and racks were of iron rather than wood and the boys who worked with the phosphorus composition wore leather aprons. However, he noted one boy, Walter Thacker, aged 12, was:

> sitting on the hot iron top of the stove stirring a pot of the phosphorus composition with his face bent over it, and he was still doing the same ... about half an hour afterwards. This it appears he does four or five times in the day for as much as two hours altogether. His health by his account has not suffered, but his face is very flushed.[15]

Edward Jolly, aged 14, had worked at Lincoln's Synagogue Street factory for five years. He worked from 6 am in the summer, 7 am in the winter, finishing at 7 pm throughout the year. His job was to fill the frames, cut and box the matches. Edward had attended school for four or five years before he started work, but by then was only attending a Sunday School saying that:

> His matches often catch a light, and smell a good deal then, and make him cough; that hurts him. Has had a cough for 3 or 4 years, at night most. It hurts him down low in his throat like a pin, and in his 'lines' (loins). Can always eat well. Washes in the dipping shop in the same hot water as the dipper does, and so do the rest of them. There is a towel.

Edward said his father was in the workhouse with a broken arm and his mother was going to join him there, although some twelve years earlier, in 1851, his mother, the delightfully named Happy Jolly, was claiming to be a widow. No record of the death of her husband, John Jolly, has been located and it seems likely that John deserted the family before 1848, as Edward was born that year in Norwich workhouse, with no father named. His mother, Happy Jolly, may have entered the workhouse to have the child as she would have had some medical attention there. Nothing further is known of Happy Jolly after 1871, when her occupation is given as wash woman. Her son, Edward, died in the workhouse in 1888, aged

39, from phthisis, a form of tuberculosis, perhaps exacerbated by the long period he spent working in the match factory.

Some children were trained for work, from as young as 4 in some cases, either in general industries, such as knitting, spinning or bootmaking, or in more specialised cottage crafts such as lacemaking or straw-plaiting for the bonnet industry. Mrs Sanders from Princes Risborough had kept a lace school for forty-five years and explained to the commissioner in 1862 that the youngest of the five girls currently in the school was 6 and the two eldest about 12 or 13. She said that she:

> Has had three learners at once only 5 years old, but that is almost too young. She could not teach them as she should; 6 is the best age, you can beat it into them better then. If they come later after they have begun to run in the streets they have the streets in their minds all the while.[16]

Poverty was not confined to urban areas, although most of the inquiries and significant press coverage focused on conditions in London and other cities and large towns. Low wages, casual and seasonal employment, eviction, overcrowding, disease and poor living conditions were present in rural areas too. Rural families were less able than their urban counterparts to turn to neighbours and friends in the community for practical help and so were perhaps more likely to end up in the workhouse. This was particularly true of orphaned and deserted children, who did not have the anonymity of the urban street children, and who had little chance of earning any money or finding suitable accommodation without the intervention of the state or charity.

Local newspapers often highlighted issues of rural poverty and deprivation, reporting on public inquiries, court proceedings and the work of poor law unions and sanitary inspectors, such as an inquiry under the Public Health Act following a cholera outbreak in the village of Mileham, near King's Lynn in Norfolk in January 1849.[17] Mr Lee, the inspector, raised two issues: the state of the labourers' cottages affected by cholera which he had found 'in a deplorable state ... extremely filthy, and without proper conveniences' and a common in the village, which he described as a 'morass or bog, considerably injurious to health'. He also raised the issue of overcrowding in the labourers' cottages stating that at the time of the cholera outbreak, 'a large number of people were generally crammed together into small rooms; in some instances there were from 5 to 11 persons in one bed room.' A local surgeon, C. Wallis, Esq., who had attended some patients with cholera in Mileham, gave evidence to the enquiry:

> I ... am well acquainted with the Sanitary condition of the parish, and consider the outbreak of cholera was occasioned by the ill-ventilation and overcrowding of many of the cottages, by dirt heaps and accumulations of filth close to the doors, by want of proper and sufficient food, by the bad management of many of the labourers' wives, by the high price of corn in 1847, and the failure of the potato crop. I do not think the effluvia arising from the Common to have been so much the cause as those I have stated.

Wallis's evidence provided a concise description of the living conditions of labourers in one Norfolk village and was in accord with a wider view that overcrowding, poor sanitation and filth were the cause of much of the disease prevalent in the nineteenth century, especially amongst the poor. However, the prevailing view in the first half of the century was that cholera was principally caused by inhaling contaminated air or 'miasma', the smell of rotting vegetation and food, animal carcases, human waste, even human flesh. It took an enlightened physician, John Snow, to work out that contaminated drinking water was the cause, although this view was not immediately accepted.

In 1854, Snow investigated a cholera outbreak in Broad Street, Soho in London, discovering that sixty-one people who regularly or occasionally drank from a street water pump in the area had died. It was later discovered that the well supplying water to the pump had been dug only three feet from an old cesspit that had begun to leak faecal bacteria, contaminating the water supply. Snow published his findings the following year. Joseph Bazalgette commenced the installation of a new sewer system in London shortly afterwards, resulting in the confirmation and acceptance of Snow's assertion that cholera was caused by contaminated water, not by airborne smells.

A report to the Burnham District Sanitary Committee regarding overcrowding in Burnham Thorpe, near King's Lynn in Norfolk, featured in the *Norfolk News* on 8 December 1866. A. V. Dennis, Esq, member of the Royal College of Surgeons, visited every cottage in the village and gave details of a dozen of the worst cases of overcrowding he came across, including:

> Mary Futter. One lower and one upper room. In the former she sleeps with two children and a sick son aged 22. In the upper room are five children, the eldest a boy of 16.
>
> David King. He has but one upper room. He, his wife and infant sleep below. Seven children, including a boy of 16 and a girl of 15, in the bedroom.
>
> William Greeves. One bedroom. Ten persons sleep in it – himself, his wife and eight children. The woman told me that her husband was obliged to open the window frequently during the night. One child has had low fever.

Mr Dennis observed that 'there can be no doubt that ... sufficient air cannot be contained in the rooms for so many beings.... . In almost all the cases the children are blanched and unhealthy-looking.' He noted that the most common and fatal diseases in the village were those 'depending upon strumous and scrofulous constitutions [tuberculosis]; ... these, if not really produced, are intensely aggravated by the want of good air.' Although in Mr Dennis's view, the low-lying and undrained nature of the village, and intermarriage contributed to the incidence of these diseases, he felt the dirtiness and overcrowding of the cottages in the village was the main cause.

In rural areas, children helped out in the fields as soon as they were able and even though many attended school regularly, especially by the latter half of the century, they were often absent at key periods in the farming year, collecting acorns, bird scaring, gleaning and helping with the harvest. Some children worked full time on farms at a very early age or were employed in the fields in gangs comprising both adults and children, though the 1867 Gangs Act placed an age restriction on children working in gangs. Evidence from the Royal Commission on

Employment of Children, Young Persons and Women in Agriculture, set up the same year, provides interesting insights into the conditions of employment of children working on the land and the attitudes of parents towards education and child employment.

Mary Cole of Ingoldisthorpe, near King's Lynn in Norfolk, was married to a shepherd and had brought up fourteen children, never taking a penny from the parish.[18] Her boys had gone out to work as young as 6, and mostly had little education, but she had paid for the girls to go to school and they could all read and write. She never let her girls work in the fields, but placed them in service after they left school:

> She was often blamed by her neighbours for not sending her girls into the fields, but her heart was high and she wouldn't... . 'It's the ruination of the country, girls going into the fields; they will make neither good wives nor good mothers; and what do they know of needlework? They get bold and wild and independent of their parents.

Charles Edge of Starston in Norfolk, aged 12, left school when he was about 10, but was still attending Sunday school and had gone to night school with three other boys for three months the previous winter. He could read fairly and write his own name. He explained to the commissioner that he earned two shillings a week, keeping rooks off wheat, potatoes and barley, working from 6 am to 6 pm, and went home for his dinner between noon and 2 pm.[19] Albert Merritt, aged 10, from Almondsbury near Bristol, had a considerably harder working day:

> [He] earned 3s. a week; drove plough; like school better; found himself tired with his day's working; got so much walking. Would leave home at 5 or 5.30 am; go to farm, help to clean out his stable and get the horses ready. Then got his breakfast, which he had brought with him... . Went with the horses on the land, at work till noon; then got a quarter of hour for dinner... . Kept on ploughing till three, then took the horses home, that would perhaps occupy half an hour. When they got home to farm, the ploughman went in to get his dinner in the house while he looked after the horses,

fed them, helped to cut the chaff … home [at] 7 o'clock; had his supper… . Goes to bed at 8 o'clock.[20]

From the early nineteenth century, ragged schools provided some of the most destitute children in urban areas with free schooling and sometimes food and shelter. Dickens described ragged schools as an effort 'to introduce among the most miserable and neglected outcasts in London, some knowledge of the commonest principles of morality and religion; to commence their recognition as immortal human creatures, before the Gaol Chaplain becomes their only schoolmaster.'[21] Thomas Cranfield in London, John Pounds in Portsmouth, and Sheriff Watson and the Rev Thomas Guthrie in Scotland were some of the first to set up schools for those whom Dickens described as 'too ragged, wretched, filthy, and forlorn, to enter any other place', such as charity or Sunday schools. Initially, ragged schools might be set up in stables, barns, lofts or under railway arches. Purpose-built schools came later. The ragged schools' movement grew rapidly, and the London Ragged Schools Union was founded in 1844 under the presidency of Lord Shaftsbury. There was also a steady growth in the provision of other elementary schools for the children of the labouring classes, culminating in free and compulsory education for all by the end of the century.

The nineteenth century saw many improvements, particularly in housing, sanitation, public health, and in the regulation of working conditions, especially for children. There was also a wider range of education available for poorer children, although only the ragged, Sunday and charity schools provided free schooling, so many poorer children slipped through the education net until the last decades of the century. Despite these improvements, however, little changed for many families, even into the twentieth century. They continued to live on or below the poverty line, in overcrowded and dilapidated homes, eking out a living as best they could, with disease and death never far away, for young and old alike.

Chapter 4

Tipping Points – Reasons Children Came into Care

Sidney G, aged 2, mother dead: nine children under 16 at home; father very respectable, has been gamekeeper, but his employer has given up shooting, and he cannot get regular work, so that the family was discovered to be almost starving.

Waifs and Strays Society, Annual Report, 1890,
Case File No. 02376

Poverty was a given for nearly all children taken into care in the period under review, but for most, especially unaccompanied children, there were usually one or more additional triggers that forced them to seek or accept charitable help or state intervention. Research indicates that the most common reason for children being taken into care on a permanent or semi-permanent basis was the death or illness of one or both parents. Desertion, illegitimacy, vagrancy, overcrowding, parental unemployment or low wages, abuse and neglect, the criminal behaviour of parents and concerns about the behaviour or moral welfare of the child were other key reasons why children came into the care of the state or charitable organisations. Any combination of circumstances, such as the death of one parent and the desertion, criminal behaviour or intermittent employment of the other, put children in an even more vulnerable position.

The impact of the death of a parent on a family already living in, or close to, poverty could be severe in the days before the welfare state and widows' pensions. The main consequences were the loss of income if the main breadwinner (usually the father) died, and difficulties with childcare if the mother died and there were dependent children still at home. Often the only solution was for the surviving spouse to remarry (sometimes in haste) or to make other arrangements for childcare so the sole parent could go out to work. Children who lost both parents, and illegitimate children whose mothers died, were particularly vulnerable, as they lost not only their carers but also their homes. Other family members might care for orphaned children, but these arrangements could be short-lived, particularly if elderly grandparents took the children in.

Isabella Timperley's parents, George and Jane, died within three weeks of each other, less than two years after their marriage. George died of pneumonia aged 23 and Jane of 'typhoid fever, haemorrhage and colapse midwifery', aged 21. Isabella, their only child, was just 17 months old at the time of their deaths. It is not known what happened to Isabella in the period between her parents' deaths in January 1887 and her admission to Withington workhouse (Chorlton Poor Law Union) at the age of 5 in February 1892. However, she was resident in the workhouse schools for nearly two years before being taken into care by the Waifs and Strays Society and admitted to Lee Cottage, Dickleburgh in January 1894.

Charles Mellish of Vauxhall in London was in difficulties on two counts in the early twentieth century. As a casually employed house painter, his earnings were low and intermittent, and in 1907 his wife died of consumption after three years' illness, leaving him with seven children aged between 2 and 16. Charles adopted various strategies to keep the children out of care, including sending three of them to live in Brixton with their aunt. Within a year or so of his wife's death, Charles was cohabiting with a young woman who looked after his younger children.

By 1910, Charles was in severe financial difficulties; he had been out of work for some months so was behind with his rent, in debt and had resorted to pawning items, resulting in the Waifs and Strays Society taking two of his children into care, Lily aged 13 and Nellie aged 11. A local mission worker reported that Lily and Nellie were very small for their ages, looking thin and white, probably because they had been very short of food, but she thought they would 'grow with good food and fresh air'. The girls' father remarried, but after his second wife died suddenly the following year, he was left to care for not only his own two youngest children, but also his wife's grandson. Charles could not afford to pay anyone to look after his children, saying, 'I must have a woman to look after the home. My daughter is the proper person now my second wife is dead.' Lily left her job to keep house for her father, despite the concerns of the society about the family's living conditions, calling it a 'dire slum'.

Three brothers, John, James and Peter Miller, were sent to an industrial school by the Waifs and Strays Society after their father, John Miller senior, killed his wife, Mary Jane in 1891.[1] The *Liverpool Mercury's* report on 18 November 1891 of the coroner's inquest was harrowing, not just because of the violence of Mary Jane's death, whose head was split open with a hatchet, but also because it was her younger children, sleeping in the same room as their mother, who found her. The couple's son, John, aged 12, testified at the coroner's court that on his return from school, he saw his mother lying on some straw in the bedroom with a sack over her, but it was too dark to see her face. There was no bed or other furniture in the room. During the evening, John and his two younger brothers, James and Peter, were sent out several times by their father to buy him beer. Their father told John and James to chop some sticks to sell on the streets in order to buy more beer, but they could not find the hatchet they normally used, which later proved to be the weapon used to kill their mother. The family went to bed about 9 pm, all sleeping in the room where their mother lay:

> On waking up they found that the father was gone. They saw their mother lying there with her face covered with blood, and her lips were closed. Witness [John Miller, junior] took the children down the stairs, and told the neighbours, 'Mother's dead, and my father has killed her.'… . The father used to quarrel with the mother when he got drunk, and frequently beat her. Witness had not seen him beat her on this occasion.

The couple's 16-year-old daughter, Sarah, who was not living at home at the time of her mother's death, also gave evidence at the inquest. When her father told her that he had killed her mother, Sarah responded, 'If you have done it you have left us all without father and mother.'

On 11 December 1891, the *Birmingham Daily Mail* reported on Miller's appearance at the Liverpool Assizes where he was charged with murdering his wife. Both his son John and his daughter Sarah were visibly affected as they gave evidence at the trial and Sarah wept when her father became hysterical. The defence gave evidence that Miller was a 'man of low mental organisation, who, when in drink, would not be capable of fully appreciating the nature of the crime.' The judge told the jury to dismiss the question of insanity but to consider the state of drunkenness the man was in at the time. The jury returned a verdict of manslaughter and John Miller was sentenced to twenty-five years penal servitude. In 1901, he was in Parkhurst Prison on the Isle of Wight, described as a lunatic.

It was difficult for widows with dependent children to combine employment with childcare. Some were able to work at home, either on their own account as seamstresses or laundresses or by doing piece work, but women's wages were very low in comparison with those of men, so it was hard to make ends meet. Some widows might earn additional income by taking in lodgers or subletting rooms. Any hint of immoral behaviour by parents or children, ranging from cohabiting to the mother taking to prostitution, or worse, sending her daughters out on the streets, would provoke alarm amongst children's charities, who would often remove the child from the home as soon as possible.

Mary Handley was already a widow with a young son when she married Thomas Varah and she was left with four dependent children after he died in 1901. She also faced a drastic reduction in income as Thomas had been earning twenty-five shillings a week as a railway checker and she brought in a maximum of 5s 6d as a hairbrush drawer (probably piece work at home). Despite a grant of £10 from her late husband's employers, Great Eastern Railway, subletting one room in the house and perhaps a contribution from her eldest son's wages, together with whatever she herself earned, Mary was unable to manage and her daughter, also called Mary, was taken into the care of the society in 1902.

Desertion was another common reason for children to be taken into the workhouse. Emma Calver remarried after the death of her husband, but later abandoned her two children – Kate from her first marriage and William from her second – to the workhouse from where Kate was admitted to Lee Cottage. It is not known what happened to Emma's second husband; perhaps he had walked out on the family some time earlier. A few years later, Emma turned up in Dickleburgh wanting to take Kate out of the home and place her with her married uncle in London, but it seems the girl remained in the home until she went out to service in the usual way.

The Rev Edward Barnes, a minister in Burton-upon-Trent in Staffordshire, referred the Adams children to the Waifs and Strays Society in 1890, asking for help for six 'destitute but very interesting' children in the union workhouse whom he wished to 'rescue from Pauperdom'. Their father had absconded and was believed to be a hotel porter somewhere in America. Mr Barnes was told that their mother had died of 'self-imposed privation – that she might have food to give her children', adding: 'It is a very sad case.' The children spent a few months in the Burton workhouse before they were admitted to the Waifs and Strays Society and sent to Dickleburgh. The father remained a shadowy figure; there were a couple of references to him in the children's case files, one indicating he might contribute to the children's upkeep and the other mentioning a stepmother, suggesting that he had remarried.

Some children, especially girls, were stigmatised within the poor law system because their parents had deserted them. Rachel and Margaret Aldridge's parents had abandoned their four children by 1885, when the youngest was only about 4, and nothing more is known of them. Rachel and Margaret were admitted to the Depwade workhouse at Pulham Market in Norfolk, probably with their two older brothers, but by 1891 the two sisters were still languishing there, recorded as 'deserted children'. By the time the girls were admitted to Rose Cottage in Dickleburgh two years later, aged 13 and 12 respectively, they had spent about eight years in the workhouse. Mrs Brandreth commented that it was much easier to teach the girls good ways if they had them young, complaining that the guardians had refused to send the deserted sisters to the home some years earlier because of concerns that other parents might be encouraged to abandon their children if they knew they would be sent to a home and trained for service.

Unlike some other charities, the Waifs and Strays Society accepted illegitimate children into care, although might require the mother, if she were known, to contribute towards the child's keep at a much higher rate than would be charged to the parents of legitimate children.[2] Victoria Tooke was living with her grandmother when she was admitted to the society in 1899, aged 2. Her mother, Alice, who was only about 14 when she gave birth to her illegitimate daughter, was expected to contribute one shilling a week 'as a recognition of her responsibility', although it seems doubtful that Alice ever paid anything as she was only earning 2s 3½d a week. When she was about 18, Alice had another illegitimate child, a boy called Henry who, according to an undated news cutting on Victoria's case file, she put out to nurse, first with a Mrs Puttock and then a Mrs Utting, presumably so she could continue to work. However, Alice was unable to pay the four shillings a week for childcare, so one evening in December 1901, she took the child out of Mrs Utting's care and abandoned him in a field off the Aylsham Road in Norwich, leaving a slip of paper with him with the words of a children's hymn, starting 'There is a friend for little children.' Alice was convicted of abandoning her child and was sentenced to six months with hard labour. The registration of the death of an Arthur Henry Tooke, aged 1, suggests that the abandoned child died shortly afterwards.

Other family members might take care of illegitimate children if their mothers died or were unable to care for them, but this was often only a temporary respite from the workhouse if these arrangements broke down for any reason, such as the death of the family carer. Esther Jane Burrell was the illegitimate daughter of Rachel Burrell and, by the time she was 2, was living in Aldeburgh on the Suffolk coast with her mother, her grandmother Jane, who had been widowed the previous year, and her 10-year-old brother or half-brother, William. Rachel died aged 34 in 1885 and within two years, Esther's grandmother Jane had also died. By 1887, Esther was resident in the Plomesgate workhouse in Wickham Market, near Woodbridge, and was admitted to Lee Cottage in Dickleburgh in November that year.

Some illegitimate children fared even less well, with no family willing, or able, to take them in even temporarily. In 1901, Wilfred Coleby, aged 2, was an inmate in the Stow union workhouse with his unmarried mother Lucy; he may even have been born there. By 1911, he was boarding with Mrs Saunders in Dickleburgh and his mother was in domestic service in London. Although Lucy's parents lived nearby, there is no evidence they ever provided her or Wilfred with any support or a home.

Overcrowding was another issue for those living in poverty; placing one or more children from a large family into care could be a way of relieving the problem. Walter Copeman's wife died from consumption in early 1890, leaving ten children, seven of whom were still dependent, aged 4 weeks to 14 years. Local reports on the family to the Waifs and Strays Society stated that Walter spent most of his money on drink (he earned an average of thirteen shillings a week) and that the children were in a 'most neglected and wretched state'. The oldest daughter, Jane, who should have been helping her father with the children, was of such 'immoral character' that she had been placed in a home in Norwich. To add to Walter's difficulties, the sanitary inspector had declared the house overcrowded, so Walter had either to move to a bigger house or send some of the children away. It seems Walter did both, as by the end of the year he was living in a three-roomed house in a nearby village with five of his children, including Jane the eldest, while two had been taken into care – Alice to Dickleburgh and her sister Annie or Angelina to another certified home in a nearby village.

Some children were neglected or abused by their parents or step-parents and were 'rescued' by one of the charities, including the National Society for the Prevention of Cruelty to Children (NSPCC) in severe cases. The 1889 annual report of the Waifs and Strays Society provides brief details of 13-year-old Sarah: 'Mother has been in an Asylum eleven years; father died last July; Sarah ran away from a woman of bad character with whom her father had lived, and by whom she was beaten and otherwise ill-treated.' The society's 1890 annual report records the case of 12-year-old George who was orphaned, the deaths of both parents 'hastened by drink'. He had been 'terribly neglected, and amongst bad associates, has been beaten and turned out into the streets to beg.'

Girls could be taken into care because of concerns about their moral welfare and boys might be admitted because they were running wild or associating with criminals. Martha was 11 when she was admitted to a Waifs and Strays Society home in 1889; according to the annual report, it was recommended that 'she be removed from her present evil influences, as she is out in the streets till a very late hour, is left alone all day, and is not attending school.' There were concerns too about the moral welfare of 7-year-old Isabel; it was said that her mother would 'let her go any time anywhere' and the conduct of the child 'with the young boys around her [was] too awful!'[3] She was admitted to a home described as being for children who had lived in the 'midst of vice, even though they [had] not actually fallen' as well as for those who had been led into actual sin. The 1889 annual report also detailed the case of an 11-year-old boy whose father was dead and mother 'immoral and a drunkard ... Charles "is out all hours of the night" and under no control.' Richard, aged 10, rarely attended school, having managed to evade the school board officer, 'getting into dishonest ways and running wild'. According to the Waifs and Strays Society annual report, he was admitted to a home in 1891.

Sometimes neglect was combined with the criminal behaviour of the parents. James Portsmouth and Annie James (or Portsmouth as she was sometimes known, though they were not married), the parents of Rachel and Elizabeth James, were travelling hawkers and pedlars, in and out of prison, and often of no fixed address. In 1903, the parents were convicted with five others at Oxfordshire Quarter Sessions of assault upon PC Obadiah Smith who, with four other men, approached the gang who were sleeping in a cowhouse, together with four unnamed children. A struggle followed, with James Portsmouth hitting the constable on the head with a hatchet and Annie attacking one of the other men with a hoe handle. James pleaded guilty and received nine months' imprisonment with hard labour; Annie was given fourteen days. The parents, described as 'a kind of gypsy tramp' by the Witney union, had previously been jailed for 'neglecting and exposing their children' and they were in prison when the sisters were admitted to the Waifs and Strays Society in 1909. The report from the union stated that the two girls were not deficient in intellect but 'dreadfully backward' in schoolwork due to 'the vagabond life they have led'.

The criminal behaviour of Joseph Henry Humphrey resulted in his three children, from two different marriages, entering care and left his two 'wives' in difficult circumstances. Humphrey left his wife Mary and their two children in Cardiff while he went to Essex, promising to send for the family as soon as he found work. The Cardiff Guardians eventually caught up with him in Ipswich and brought him back to Cardiff to answer a charge of neglecting to maintain his wife and children who had been admitted to the Cardiff workhouse 'quite destitute'. Humphrey was sentenced to one month's hard labour for the offence, but, three months later, he appeared at Essex Assizes and was sentenced to four years' penal servitude for bigamy. The full story of his double life came out in court where it was revealed that while living in Colchester, Humphrey, calling himself Joseph Henry Henry, had married Hannah Sophia Burdett, claiming not only to be a widower, but some fourteen years younger than his actual age of around 60![4] Hannah gave birth to a son, Lancelot Stanley Burdett, the following July in Sprowston, near Norwich, the area from which she came, but within a month of his birth, Lancelot had been taken into care by the Waifs and Strays Society so his mother could return to work. On 11 February 1899, the *Essex County Standard* reported the facts of the trial but could not resist a dig at Humphrey:

> Without offering any excuse for his conduct, he expressed an earnest desire 'to return to his wife and family.' ... the plea of this law-breaker recalls that of another culprit, who admitted murdering his father and mother, but begged for mercy on the ground that he was an orphan. Mr Justice Wills viewed the matter in this light, and his Lordship's sentence of four years' celibacy and servitude is, under all the circumstances, more appropriate as a sequel to this man's offence than the finale which he himself proposed.

Sometimes the behaviour of the child, rather than the parents, was the direct cause of the youngster's admission into care or custody. Children convicted of criminal behaviour were sent to prison, or from the 1850s, to a reformatory, although often serving a short time in an adult prison first. In 1874, William Palmer, aged 12, from Bungay in Suffolk was convicted of stealing a pair of boots. He served twenty-one days with hard labour in Ipswich County Gaol and House of Correction, before being sent to the Suffolk Reformatory at Thorndon near Eye for three years.[5] In extreme cases in the early years of the new poor law, convicted children might even be transported, perhaps first serving time on one of the hulks – old naval vessels moored in the Thames Estuary and off naval ports such as Chatham and Portsmouth – before they left the country. In 1840, John Gould, aged 13, was sentenced at the Suffolk Assizes to seven years' transportation for stealing a silver watch belonging to Samuel Borley, but it was nearly two years before he was admitted to the hulk *Justitia*, moored off Woolwich.[6] The report from the unnamed penitentiary where the lad had presumably been held since his conviction stated that he was 'exceedingly mischievous'.[7] Gould sailed for Van Diemen's Land (Tasmania) on 10 October 1842, one of 270 convicts on board the *Duchess of Northumberland* which arrived in the penal colony on 18 January 1843.

Girls too could be transported; Mary Ann Clarke (alias Amy Gedge), aged 13, and Maria Goldsmith (alias Elinor Vincent), aged 14, 'notorious prostitutes', were convicted of stealing three-and-a-half yards of ribbon and three yards of blonde (this probably referred to blonde lace, a bobbin lace from France) from Rebecca Gaywood of Sproughton, near Ipswich in Suffolk.[8] Both were sentenced to ten years' transportation and committed to Ipswich gaol in 1842 before boarding the *Garland Grove* convict ship that sailed for Van Diemen's Land on 7 September 1842 with 191 female convicts on board, arriving on 20 January 1843.

Children found wandering the streets by the authorities were regarded as vagrants and might be sentenced by the courts to a period in an industrial school. Thomas Royle, aged 11, from Manchester, was admitted to the Waifs and Strays Society in 1891 and sent to one of their homes under the Industrial Schools Act, 1866. Thomas was said to be of 'vagrant habits through being neglected and unhappy home circumstances' and had been sleeping out for over a week when he was picked up, according to the society's annual report. It is not clear exactly what the 'unhappy home circumstances' were, but Thomas's mother, Alice, had died some years earlier and on 4 October 1887, his father Thomas married Edith Lees, a woman around fourteen years his junior. The 1891 census shows the family, comprising Thomas and Edith, and five children aged between 1 and 13, living in two rooms in Ardwick near Manchester. As well as Thomas and his older brother John, there were three younger children, Robina, Edith and Henry. Thomas and Edith subsequently had four more children and it is possible that with the arrival of the younger children, Thomas was neglected and rejected by his father and stepmother.

William Sharp aged 9 from Highgate in London was also admitted to a Waifs and Strays industrial school, although the reasons his parents were unable to keep him at home seem to have had more to do with the boy's wanderlust than an unhappy home life. He was continually disappearing, being absent from home for a week or so at a time, and his parents had received sixteen telegrams from the police from various parts of London during the year, presumably reporting that they had found their son. When questioned, William said he kept wandering off because he wanted to go to sea and be a pirate.[9]

For some families, economic or marital problems were the main factor for the children's admission into care, although this may be difficult to prove if the child was not in the care of a recognised charity that retained detailed records. The Bishop family was together as a family unit in 1891 in Willesden but in 1901, the family was located in four different places. The father Elisha was in lodgings in St Marylebone, London, the mother Fanny was in domestic service in Greenwich (although she described herself as unmarried) and the oldest boy Elisha, aged 13, and the youngest William, aged 4, were boarding out together in Walthamstow, in West Ham. The other two boys, Albert and Lawrence, were boarded out in Dickleburgh in 1901, but by 1911, the whole family, except the oldest son, was living together again, in Kilburn, north-west London, so presumably the crisis, whether marital or economic, had passed.

Although poverty was the underlying reason for children being admitted to a poor law institution or taken into care by one of the voluntary societies, it was rarely the full story. Usually an additional trigger tipped families below the poverty line or placed the children in an untenable position, leaving them vulnerable and without adult care. The most common triggers were the death or desertion of one or both parents, the behaviour of the parents or the child, neglect or abuse, or a reduction in parental income through unemployment, casual work or low wages. In some cases, the tipping point was reached through a combination of factors, though the circumstances of the Miller children's admission to care, involving the father killing the mother, drunkenness, unemployment and mental health issues was an extreme combination.

Chapter 5

Workhouses and Other State Provision

It would seem impossible to discover a place less suited than a workhouse for bringing up children to whom a healthy development of mind and body is of paramount importance. Yet for many years ... the dominant idea adopted by the State for dealing with these poor little creatures was to immure them therein.[1]

Florence Davenport-Hill, 1889

Before the 1834 Poor Law Amendment Act, destitute, deserted and orphaned children with no family to support them were the responsibility of the parish in which they had settlement. The overseers of the poor might apprentice these children within the parish or further afield, or board them out with another local family at the parish's expense. Some children were placed in an institution, perhaps a parish poorhouse or one of the large private schools that took in children from London. Children of able-bodied paupers would usually be supported through out-relief given to their parents. However, the 1834 Act abolished out-relief for the able-bodied poor (in theory, if not always in practice) and placed the emphasis on providing relief through the workhouse. In the decades following the 1834 Act, workhouses rapidly filled up with children, not just the permanent residents, usually those who had been orphaned or abandoned by their parents, but also the 'ins and outs'. These temporary child inmates came into the workhouse, usually with their families, for a brief respite from the grinding poverty outside, sometimes being admitted and discharged several times over a matter of months.

During the latter half of the nineteenth century, there was a growing awareness that the workhouse was no place for a child and the authorities tried various schemes to provide children with care and training more suited to their needs. Urban unions were more likely to experiment with separate and district schools off the workhouse site, and from the 1870s, some larger unions set up 'grouped homes' to house pauper children. These villages of cottage homes were located away from the main workhouse, sometimes even beyond the union's boundaries.

Boarding out or fostering schemes became more common in both urban and rural unions from the 1880s, but it was not until the end of the nineteenth century that the state directly provided individual, or scattered, children's homes similar to the cottage homes that had been the mainstay of some charities – such as the Waifs and Strays Society – for decades. The unions that made separate arrangements for children, such as Stepney, which covered a substantial part of the East End of London, might establish children's receiving homes too, so the young inmates spent perhaps only a few hours in the workhouse before being sent to an institution specifically for children and then onwards to a permanent placement. In the 1850s, two new types of residential care for children were established: reformatories for juvenile offenders who had been convicted in the courts, and industrial schools, mostly aimed at homeless children and those at risk of offending.

Legislation from the 1860s enabled poor law unions to use Local Government Board (LGB) certified homes and boarding-out schemes outside their home union, which were run by charities and voluntary societies, such as Mrs Brandreth's homes in Dickleburgh. Despite these developments in childcare in the nineteenth century, many pauper children continued to spend much of their time in care in the workhouse itself, even into the twentieth century. Smaller, rural unions often could not justify the expenditure on institutions specifically for children, particularly if they had a high proportion of 'ins and outs' who turned to the workhouse during the winter months when there was little work available on the land for their parents.

Apart from physical issues, such as disease and malnutrition, many of the children who came into the care of the poor law authorities had little or no education or sense of right or wrong, with parents or other adults exerting little discipline or control over them. Managing and reforming such children within the poor law system could be extremely challenging. This observation by a schoolmaster from the Tonbridge union in Kent was included in a report by Edward Carleton Tufnell, an assistant poor law commissioner, published in 1841:

The moral state of the children on entering the workhouse, with some exceptions, is very indifferent, being much given to swearing and low conduct, and their amount of education very small, many being nearly destitute of any.[2]

The LGB's 1874 annual report includes an account by 'W. H. R' of his time in a London workhouse during the 1850s. Peter Higginbotham's research has revealed that W. H. R was William Hew Ross, born in 1842, who became a schoolmaster in the West Ham union after leaving Greenwich workhouse and was appointed master of Stamford workhouse in 1871.[3] Ross looked back on his life before he entered the workhouse at the age of about 7:

Need any one be surprised to hear that at the time I am speaking of I could swear like a trooper? I could and did, was never corrected for it, and must say that I never to my knowledge heard God's name mentioned except with an oath... . I was a ragged little urchin without shoes and cap, but generally liked by the neighbours because I was good at running errands, was always considered sharp, knew the names of all the public-houses round about and delighted in playing about the marshes or streets.

Later in the century, there were still significant concerns about the character and morality of children committed to poor law institutions. About 1870, William Imeson, headmaster of the Hanwell district school, which served several London unions, stated that the children in his care were:

the dregs of the population. They arrive here in various stages of squalor and disease; all of them are more or less debased; their intellectual capabilities are of the lowest order; their moral sense is stifled or inactive through suspicion and obstinacy. Many of them inherit the hoarse indistinct utterance of the London costermonger... . Their natural bias is to run the course of their fathers in ignorance, and it may be in crime. With a strangely marked precocity, they are ignorant to a degree that can scarcely be overrated.[4]

One of the major concerns of the poor law authorities was that children brought up in the workhouse would return to the poor law system as adults. Although the 1834 Poor Law Amendment Act established the principle of 'less eligibility', where conditions in the workhouse were intended to be less favourable than those endured by the independent poor who did not seek state relief, in practice this was impossible if the authorities were to provide inmates with the basic necessities of life – food, shelter and clothing. Basic medical attention was provided too, and children were supposed to have three hours of education a day, an advantage few children had outside the poor law system before the second half of the nineteenth century. Writing in 1889, Florence Davenport-Hill described the impact of life in the workhouse on children:

> Condemned to live within the cheerless workhouse walls, children almost cease to be recognised as such. They are classified as 'ins and outs' and 'permanents', and known as juvenile paupers – a name of dire significance, implying that legally, they possess, and can possess, nothing of their own. They are, in short, living in a most debased form of communism, living among hundreds of people who are actually penniless, and yet have all things needful; being fed, clothed, and sheltered without the stimulus of remunerative effort.[5]

This system encouraged, rather than discouraged, a dependency culture amongst not only workhouse children but also pauper adults who were unconcerned by the stigma of entering the workhouse. Some pauper children, especially those who had no other home, returned repeatedly to the workhouse as adults, assured of food and shelter and, as adults, having the freedom to discharge themselves whenever they wished. The Tenterden union in Kent had issues trying to find placements for some of their orphaned 'great boys' who were too old for the school 'and when removed to the able-bodied men's ward, evince no particular desire to leave.'[6] Even William Hew Ross, who turned his life around after leaving the poor law system as a 14 year old, had no ambition for independence when a boy in the workhouse:

> Often … I have looked over to the young men's side, and have envied them exceedingly. No thrashing for them, far more to eat than I had,

as was evidenced by the fact of their always having food for sale to us boys, and they to me always seemed happy; besides they could go in and out as they liked. All this I knew, and longed for the time to come when I could do likewise. Such a thing as getting my own living and being for ever independent of the workhouse never struck me.[7]

For girls as they reached adulthood, the situation was probably even worse, according to Florence Davenport-Hill:

Rejected on all sides, troublesome and uninteresting, and too often vicious, the regular workhouse girl returns finally to the workhouse, which is the only home she has ever known. Brought up in its seclusion, she has no friends, probably few relations, and those of a doubtful kind, outside its precincts, and her only aspiration is to escape for a time from its grim routine for a 'spree', claiming its shelter again when absolutely obliged.[8]

The authorities had concerns, not unfounded, that workhouse girls might turn to prostitution or have illegitimate children when they left. Despite the design of the workhouse to ensure the different classes of pauper were kept separate, with their own wards and exercise yards, it was impossible to keep children apart completely from the adult paupers and their possible corrupting influence. In his report of 1839 on the education of pauper children, Edward Carleton Tufnell wrote:

There is ... considerable danger of moral contamination to the children from their residence in the same house with adult paupers ... a very large proportion of adult workhouse inmates are persons of the worst characters, the very refuse of the population.... . The atmosphere of a workhouse that contains adult paupers is tainted with vice.[9]

Adult female paupers were sometimes used as servants to assist with child inmates and similarly some of the older girls might be used as nursemaids for the infants on the female wards, where they would inevitably come into contact with mothers of illegitimate children. There were casual encounters too as explained by Tufnell: 'Conversation, sometimes of the obscenest description, is carried on over walls and through windows. In going to dinner or chapel there are ready means of communication; doors are accidentally left open; and the adults are employed in carrying or removing furniture or other articles from one part to another.'

Although the 1834 Poor Law Amendment Act made provision for schooling in poor law institutions, there was some variation between unions in the range and quality of education provided, with some guardians feeling that it was unnecessary to educate workhouse children, as it potentially breached the principle of 'less eligibility'. In 1846, there was a clash between the local guardians and the Poor Law Commission over the provision of education in the Martley workhouse in rural Worcestershire.[10] Although the guardians had appointed a schoolmistress from 1839, there had been a high turnover of staff and no one had been in post for nearly a year when matters came to a head. The guardians decided to stop teaching the children writing, justifying the decision to the Poor Law Commission:

Pauper child inmates of the workhouse received as good an education as that generally given in the country and they do not feel themselves justified in going to any expense whereby they [pauper inmate children] might receive advantages that are not attainable by the children of those who support their families without parochial relief.[11]

Although the guardians bowed to pressure by appointing a new schoolmistress who started to teach writing again, the central poor law authority was still critical of the quality of education in the workhouse and continued to insist that the guardians should also appoint a schoolmaster. The guardians replaced the schoolmistress with another in 1847 but ordered her not to teach writing or arithmetic. The matter rumbled on, with the guardians blaming the schoolmistress until they eventually relented in the summer of 1848 and ordered the schoolmistress to teach writing and arithmetic as well as reading.

Although there was considerable uniformity in the design of workhouses built after 1834, often built in a cruciform or H shape to ensure segregation, inevitably some unions tried to convert and adapt existing parish workhouses to meet the new requirements, usually with unsatisfactory results. There were differences in size, especially between urban and rural workhouses, and the amount of money the guardians were prepared to spend on the workhouses was often reflected in the state and design of the buildings and the conditions the paupers were kept in. In 1867, as part of an investigation into conditions in workhouse infirmaries, *The Lancet* published a report about the West Ham workhouse in Leyton. Although the report focused on the provision for sick and mentally ill inmates, it also commented on the 'pitiable condition of the pauper boys' in the main workhouse:

> They are twenty-one in number and of an age fitted to go to school and work; yet here they remain shut up in the ward originally built for imbeciles, tended only by an old pauper eighty years of age, who 'reads them' twice a day. Dressed in the usual workhouse suits of corderoy [sic], with dirty untied boots, and unkempt hair, they looked the very picture of workhouse wretchedness. They are said to be kept here because the district schools are full; but surely some effort should be made to break the chain of poverty and idleness which will undoubtedly gather round them in their present state. It is fair to add that their health seemed excellent.[12]

The problems at Smallburgh workhouse, a large rural institution in Norfolk, related particularly to underuse and lack of plumbing, as reported in 1895 by the *British Medical Journal*:

> It has accommodation for 800 inmates, but only 45 were on the books at the time of our visit, and the master said that 70 would be the largest number, even in the winter. A large part of the house is therefore shut up.[13]

There was no running water in the workhouse, so no baths or laundry facilities; commodes and outdoor privies were the only means of sanitation available for inmates. In 1911, there were seventy inmates in Smallburgh workhouse, fourteen of whom were children.

Some larger unions, such as West Ham in Essex, Chorlton near Manchester and Burton-upon-Trent in Staffordshire, built separate residential school buildings on or near the workhouse site, which helped to keep the children away from the adults. These schools could be very large, housing several hundred children. By 1881, the West Ham union had established schools on its Leyton workhouse site and in 1891, 200 children were living there. However, ten years later there were 325 children resident and on 22 February 1904, according to *Hansard,* Sir Ernest Flower, MP for Bradford West, raised in Parliament the issue of overcrowding in the West Ham workhouse schools. He stated that there were currently 200 more children in the schools than its certificate allowed, with the consequence that:

> The boys are entirely without day-room accommodation; that 144 girls have day-room accommodation of 23 feet 6 inches by 18 feet 2 inches only; that eighty-six infants have a day-room in which they also take their meals of 27 feet 2 inches by 18 feet 2 inches only ... this overcrowding makes it impossible to isolate infectious diseases ... skin and eye complaints are present in the same dormitory.

About 1880, the Chorlton Guardians moved the children into newly built premises opposite the main site to relieve overcrowding in the workhouse, freeing up space for 200 adult paupers. The new buildings comprised six 'homes' each housing fifty children, with living and sleeping accommodation, separate schools for boys and girls, an administration block and accommodation for both a schoolmaster and a schoolmistress.[14] The 'children's pavilions' at Burton-upon-Trent were similar, with accommodation and a school erected about 1886 on the new workhouse site to the north west of the town off Belvedere Road.[15]

Other unions, perhaps the more enlightened ones, took the principle of segregation a step further by opening a separate school away from the workhouse site. In the East End of London, the Stepney Guardians were concerned about the influence of adult paupers on the children in the workhouse, as Davenport-Hill explained:

> The boys lived with the adult male paupers: lying, cheating, and stealing were declared to be their chief characteristics; while the girls,

although they had sometime previously been separated from the women, displayed, equally with the lads, selfishness, stubbornness, and great coarseness of language and behaviour, together with the lack of any spirit of self-dependence.[16]

The guardians' solution was to convert an existing parish workhouse in Limehouse into a residential school for pauper children, both boys and girls. The school was sited near the docks and wharves of the River Thames, about a mile from the main workhouse. It opened as a school about 1840 and closed thirty years later. It was a big establishment with an average of 430 children resident at any one time, with a governor, schoolmaster and schoolmistress as well as other officers, although, significantly, no pauper staff were employed. The boys were taught shoemaking, tailoring, carpentry and spinning, and the girls learned laundry skills, housework, sewing and knitting, as well as the usual schoolwork. Rather than paying a premium for boys to be apprenticed to fishing boat owners, who often mistreated them, the union erected the mast and rigging of a full-sized ship on the school site at Limehouse, and employed a seaman to drill and train the boys to handle a boat, as well as to swim.

There were a few such schools in rural areas too. The Hartismere union in Suffolk utilised a former parish workhouse in the village of Wortham near Diss for its residential school, opening about 1847, housing up to eighty-five children. By the late 1870s, the school was accepting children from the two other neighbouring unions, so it was technically a district school. However, it had probably changed little from its days as a separate school when H. G. Bowyer, who had been inspecting it for thirty years, included an account of the school in his report on pauper schools in the 1879/80 LGB annual report:

There has never been any prevalent disease in it … the children have always been the healthiest I have seen … it is admirably managed by the present head master and mistress. [It is still] substantially nothing but an old rough farm house, with small windows and whitewashed walls, a small and dark schoolroom, whose ceiling of rough boards and beams is only ten feet above a floor of coarse bricks, worn uneven by constant use.

Like the Stepney children at Limehouse, the children at the Wortham school were taught skills to help them find work on leaving, though rather than training for the sea, the Wortham boys were trained in agriculture. Bowyer added: 'I am convinced that this humble establishment has done as useful a work in rescuing the children educated in it from pauperism, as if it had been built in a more costly manner, and lavishly provided with all the conveniences to be found in the newest district schools.'

In 1844, to facilitate the separation between child and adult paupers, legislation allowed unions to combine to establish residential district schools to serve several unions. The Wortham school was relatively small, even when used by three unions, but other district schools, especially in the metropolitan area, could house over 1,000 pupils, hence the colloquial and pejorative term, barrack schools. The origins of district schools lay in the privately run establishments to which the metropolitan unions sent, or farmed out, their pupils both before and after the 1834 Act. Mr Drouet's school at Tooting, converted in 1825 into a school for pauper children from the London parishes, was particularly notorious. Between 1846 and 1848, Drouet almost doubled the number of children at the school, from about 720 to around 1,400. Tragedy struck in early 1849, when 180 children died in a cholera outbreak at the school.

At the inquest of four of the children, reported in the London newspaper *The Examiner* of 13 January 1849, the findings of the medical inspector, Mr Grainger, was given in evidence. He stated that, 'On the boys' side, there was a room containing eighteen beds nearly touching each other, in which were thirty-five boys ill with cholera, twenty-five being in bed (two in each bed) and ten sitting round the fire being convalescent. One boy had just died on my entrance.' Mr Grainger explained that only two nurses were on duty, one in the boys' wards and one in the girls', which was utterly insufficient given 'the nature of cholera, with the violent and most sudden evacuations, both by vomiting and purging'. He continued: 'I found that the children were continually vomiting in the beds and on the floor, and that consequently the sheets, bedding and floor were covered with the discharges, that no efficient aid was in a single case afforded to these suffering children.' Dickens took to print in *The Examiner* a week later and did not hold back:

The cholera, or some unusually malignant form of typhus assimilating itself to that disease, broke out in Mr Drouet's farm for children, because it was brutally conducted, vilely kept, preposterously inspected, dishonestly defended, a disgrace to a Christian community, and a stain upon a civilised land.[17]

Drouet appeared at the Central Criminal Court in February 1849 on a charge of manslaughter but on instruction from the judge, the jury found him not guilty. Drouet was dead by July, however, having been ill for some months.

Frederick Aubin opened his school in Norwood, south London, in 1821, and by 1838, there were 1,100 children aged under 15 housed there. The Norwood School buildings were taken over by the Central London School District as a poor law district school around 1849. It moved to new premises at Hanwell in the 1850s. Other district schools serving the London poor law unions followed, including those at Ashford near Staines and Sutton in Surrey. In the 1896 report of the Mundella Committee on the education and care of pauper children in the London area, it was noted that in the metropolitan area, there were three district schools housing over 500 children each, one with over 600 children, one with over 1,000 and one (Sutton) with 1,800 children resident.[18] There were large separate and district schools in other urban areas too, such as the Walsall and West Bromwich district school in the Midlands and Kirkdale in Liverpool. Like Wortham in Suffolk, some separate schools in more rural areas expanded into district schools by joining with other unions; in 1851, the Bridgnorth union in Shropshire took children from four other unions into its separate school at Quatt, with numbers rising from forty to 163 children.

District and separate schools successfully achieved the separation between adult and juvenile paupers, with the removal of the children from the workhouse site, although many would spend at least a short time in the workhouse itself. Another positive development was that adult paupers were not used in the schools; all staff were paid employees. Most district and separate schools were able to offer some form of employment training for both boys and girls, usually better quality than that offered in many workhouses, although still of limited value to the child. Despite these advantages over the workhouse, in the latter half of the century there were growing concerns about large district and separate schools, particularly the impact on the children's health, general welfare and emotional development when so many were housed and educated together. Davenport-Hill summed it up:

> As in the workhouse, the children almost invariably wear a uniform, bear the stigma of an outcast class, are herded together, are taught, fed, tended, and cared for wholesale … the 'ins and outs', with scant exceptions, mix with the permanent children without restraint. Under these circumstances it is not surprising to find many of the worst defects of workhouse life cropping up in the schools in spite of their large staffs and costly organisation.[19]

One of the consequences of putting so many children together was the loss of individuality; as one writer, quoted by Davenport-Hill, stated: 'The individual becomes a mere cog in an engine of many wheels, whereas in real life it has to be itself a many-wheeled engine.'[20] This lack of individuality led to anonymity – in the 1901 census for the Ashford schools, no place of birth was recorded for any of the 750 or so pauper children in residence. It was also difficult to support, or in some cases even to recognise, children with behaviour issues or special needs when so many were massed together. The Mundella Report noted that in one large workhouse, it took several months before a 3-year-old girl was identified as being dumb; the matron, though 'very kind', had sixty children to 'mother'; 'Now children are born, not in "sixties," but as individuals, and no one woman can mother 60 children.'[21]

Daisy Ball had been orphaned by the time she was 8 and after a brief time in the workhouse was sent to the district school at Wargrave, near Reading. The guardians referred her to the Waifs and Strays Society as she had 'developed habits of untruthfulness and stealing' and they felt as she was so young, she would benefit from care in a suitable home, where 'these propensities may be cured by special treatment', rather than remaining in the larger and more impersonal district school. Daisy was admitted to Rose Cottage in Dickleburgh in 1898, with Mrs Brandreth noting that she would need 'special supervision'.[22]

Although the children in pauper institutions may have had their basic needs met, together with education and basic medical care, even occasional treats, they had little love or joy in their lives. As Charlie Chaplin said of his time at Hanwell district school, 'it was a forlorn existence'.[23] By the 1870s, there were concerns that children in pauper institutions were not playing, even where there was the opportunity to do so. In the 1873/74 LGB annual report, a school inspector visiting the metropolitan district schools noted 'the great want of energy often displayed by the various children in the various playgrounds.' He felt that the children needed more encouragement to get involved in active play, as 'children often want to be taught to play as much as to work.' He suggested cricket, football and rounders for the boys and the provision of skipping ropes and hoops for the girls, with the adult staff joining in the games where possible.

Children, particularly girls, who remained for any length of time in the workhouse or poor law schools could quickly become institutionalised – they became dull, apathetic and unable to think for themselves. Some were classed as feeble-minded, although in many cases this may have been attributable to a traumatic or deprived childhood, lack of family life, institutional life away from the local community and school, and limited emotional development, rather than what today would be considered a learning disability or mental health condition. Such children tended to be unsuitable for domestic service, so often simply returned to the workhouse as adults as they were unable to support themselves.

Children in both the workhouse and pauper schools were usually employed in the institution when not in school, with boys doing gardening or industrial work such as shoemaking or tailoring, and girls carrying out domestic duties, ostensibly to train them for domestic service, although, in practice, they were mostly used as free labour. In the 1879/80 LGB annual report, Wyndham Holgate, inspector of poor law schools, wrote about the work of the girls in the schools:

Owing to the size of many of the buildings and the number of children collected in them, the three chief occupations of scrubbing, washing and mending become absolute drudgery, and lead ... to a perfunctory rather than satisfactory performance of the work, and arouse the worst point in the girls' characters, the sullen, obstinate and careless spirit peculiar to them.

Some twenty years later, Florence Davenport-Hill, giving evidence to the Mundella Committee, spoke of the 'monotony of the labour' with 'children, little things of 10 or 11 years of age, scrubbing the vast corridors and great dormitories'. She concluded that the industrial scale of the work in the institutions, 'preparing the vegetables wholesale, by the bushel', cleaning and using the industrial equipment in the kitchens and laundries, did nothing to prepare the girls for more refined domestic service in a single household. Even making and mending clothes in the institution was on an industrial scale.

Children in the larger institutions were vulnerable to disease, especially eye and skin conditions that seemed ever-present in most pauper schools. Ophthalmia could damage the eyesight permanently and in extreme cases could result in the loss of sight in one or both eyes. Edward Nettleship, an ophthalmologist, was commissioned by the LGB to enquire into the incidences of ophthalmia amongst the nearly 9,000 children in the metropolitan pauper schools. His report from the 1874 LGB annual report, quoted by Davenport-Hill, stated that only twenty per cent of the children had healthy eyelids, with fifteen per cent having active ophthalmia and nine per cent with permanently damaged sight.[24] Nettleship concluded: 'By far the larger share of ophthalmia in the schools, both as to number of cases, and as to obstinacy and serious results, is certainly due to school life.' Ophthalmia persisted, despite hygiene and sanitary improvements, reinforcing Nettleship's view that the disease was spread more by 'personal contagion, overcrowding, want of fresh air, and liberty, than ... defective or insufficient sanitary arrangements'. Most experts agreed that the best way to curb the highly contagious condition was to isolate the affected children and to reduce the number of children grouped together in the pauper schools, especially in large dormitories.

Ringworm and other infectious skin conditions were persistent problems in the pauper schools. To a young child, the ignominy of the resulting isolation and treatment was hard to bear. Charlie Chaplin cried uncontrollably when the nurse diagnosed ringworm, explaining, 'My head was shaved and iodined and I wore a handkerchief round it like a cotton-picker.'[25] There were also outbreaks of other diseases that could prove fatal to undernourished and weak pauper children. Wyndham Holgate reported on an outbreak of typhoid fever at the Ashford schools in 1885, which affected about forty-five per cent of the 660 children.[26] The dry summer had caused a shallow well that was used for drinking water to become contaminated with sewage. The various unions removed their children to convalescent homes at the seaside once they improved, but several children and members of staff died in the outbreak.

Cruelty and abuse towards children were widespread, although the central poor law authority supposedly regulated corporal punishment. Punishments were often excessive and random cruelty commonplace. William Hew Ross described one incident (probably at Sutton district school) involving the tailor Mr Allen, who Ross said had taken a dislike to him:

It was Sunday evening; the boys were standing in lines round the school singing hymns… . I must have been standing about 6 inches over the line. [Mr Allen] came walking down the school with his arms folded, walking very slowly. I was looking at him and singing; he pretended to be looking right straight in front of him. He marched just where I stood, and without appearing to take the slightest notice of me, I was felled to the floor with one of the most awful open-handed smacks I have ever had. I was taken up insensible and the blood spurting from my ear. I have never thoroughly got over it.[27]

Some instances of cruelty and abuse in poor law schools and workhouses were reported in the press and a few resulted in criminal convictions. In 1878, the Sheffield Guardians investigated a case of cruelty against the workhouse schoolmaster, Noah Payne. According to the *South London Press* on 2 March, 6-year-old Thomas Stephenson was found playing instead of being in school. Payne was alleged to have 'stripped him before all the boys, and thrashed him in a most savage and brutal manner with a cane. The lad's body was covered with wheals, and for two days he was unable to lie down.' Payne, who had allegedly previously been cautioned for a similar assault, resigned, but did not go quietly, writing to the *Birmingham Press*:

I hope you will allow me to contradict one part of the statement ... that the boy could not lie down in bed for two days – as nothing was said about it either by the guardians or the local Press. That all other statements were grossly exaggerated, I hope an impartial inquiry will shortly prove.[28]

An even more serious and sustained case of abuse was uncovered some twenty years later when Ella Gillespie, an infants nurse, was accused of cruelty to the children in her care at the Hackney union's schools at Brentwood, abuse which had apparently been going on for about ten years. Gillespie was immediately forced to resign and after hearing evidence from an internal investigating committee, the Hackney Guardians decided to prosecute. A warrant was issued for Gillespie's arrest, although it was over a fortnight before she was found and arrested.

The case against Gillespie was straightforward, with witness after witness, children and staff, testifying to the abuse she had administered, including to some children as young as 6. As reported in *The Essex Chronicle* on 1 June 1894, Mr Avery, prosecuting on behalf of the Hackney Guardians, outlined the alleged abuse she carried out:

Beating the children with stinging nettles, knocking their heads on the wall, cutting their heads with a bunch of keys, making the infants kneel with their bare knees on the wire guards over the hot water pipes, and keeping them there for a considerable time, forcibly immersing a child's head in a bucket of water and keeping it there, and beating children with a cane on their hands and feet.

It was also alleged that Gillespie kept the children short of drinking water and subjected them to 'basket drill'. Clara Good, aged 13, who had worked in the infants' dormitory under Nurse Gillespie, described the drill:

She used to make them get out of bed and carry their clothes baskets round on their heads... . The children only had their chemises or shirts on ... the drill took place in the evening ... after they had undressed ... and sometimes she would drag them out of bed and make them do it... . Sometimes they would drop their clothes or their baskets, and then Miss Gillespie would come out and hit them with the stick for it... . Anywhere she could. On their feet, heads, backs, or anywhere.

Ella Gillespie pleaded guilty at Chelmsford Assizes to the charges of child cruelty and was sentenced to five years' penal servitude. She was to serve her sentence at the Woking Female Convict Prison, but as it closed the following year, she was probably then transferred to Holloway.

With echoes of some modern child abuse cases, the case raised significant concerns about the length of time the abuse had been continuing without being reported and whether other staff were involved, or complicit, in the abuse, particularly Joseph and Rachel Hadwick, the superintendent and matron. *The Essex Chronicle* of 1 June reported that an internal enquiry divided the guardians, with some feeling that the Gillespie case had resulted in a loss of confidence in Mr and Mrs Hadwick, while another queried whether it was appropriate 'to take away the characters of Mr and Mrs Hadwick, who had served them so faithfully for over 20 years, on the evidence of three girls who had left the school, and had been searched out from the slums of Hackney on purpose to bear testimony against these old officers?'

Following the Gillespie prosecution and the suspension of Mr and Mrs Hadwick, an LGB inquiry opened to examine allegations against the management of the Brentwood schools. *The Essex Newsman* of 21 July 1894 reported on the inquiry which revealed that Mr and Mrs Hadwick had worked with Gillespie during her previous employment at a school in Leeds. It was also stated that Mrs Hadwick had been in correspondence with Gillespie after the warrant for her arrest was issued and had offered to give her a reference. Evidence from current and former staff and from child inmates indicated that the Hadwicks knew what Gillespie was doing and turned a blind eye, possibly because of a long-standing friendship between the two women. Mr Hadwick was robust in his defence, casting doubt on the truth of the children's evidence, saying that 'twenty-eight years' experience in the treatment of pauper children had convinced him that their two leading characteristics were lying and petty theft.' However, the Hadwicks were forced to resign and were replaced.

It seems that none of the inquiries investigated whether Gillespie had abused children in her care in any of her previous posts. In 1871, she was working as a teacher at Ripon Industrial School for Girls in Yorkshire which housed thirty-five girls aged between 9 and 15. In 1881, Gillespie was working as an officer at Leeds Moral and Industrial Training School, where Joseph and Rachel Hadwick were employed as master and matron. The investigations also did nothing to stop Gillespie from taking up posts working with children after she completed her prison sentence, although without the benefit of modern technology and schemes such as the Disclosure and Barring Service now in use, it is difficult to know how they could have achieved this. In 1901, following her release from prison after serving just over three-and-a-half years of her sentence, Gillespie was recorded as working as a matron at a training home apparently attached to an orphanage in Oxford.

The effect of cramming hundreds, if not thousands, of pauper children together in residential schools led some concerned with child welfare and poor law reform to consider different options based more on family life. In her report about the education and training of pauper girls included in the LGB annual report of 1873/74, Mrs Nassau Senior stated:

> One of the greatest objections to the plan of bringing up girls in large schools is that they are unable to get the cherishing care and individual attention that is of far more importance in the formation of a girl's character than anything else in the world ... what is wanted in the education of the girls is more *mothering*.

Mrs Senior suggested the establishment of separate schools for pauper children under the age of 8 or 9, and that these children should be further split into groups to 'return as far as possible to the natural order of families'. She added that 'each nurse [would] represent the head of a family, with a certain number of infants under her care, and a certain number of [pauper] girls in training under her orders, who would help her with the children, and learn all sorts of housework.' She also suggested that large wards could be partitioned to provide smaller rooms.

In 1878, F. J. Mouat and J. D. Bowley produced a report for the LGB on a number of village or grouped children's homes run by charitable or private organisations, based on similar approaches in Europe, in order to ascertain whether the system would be suitable for the education and training of children under the poor laws. Mouat and Bowley visited six establishments, all run along the family or cottage system, with the children divided into groups of limited size.[29] Around the same time as Senior and Mouat and Bowley were publishing their reports, several poor law unions across the country were experimenting with the grouped cottage homes system, although some of the earliest homes, such as those at Bolton, West Derby and West Ham, were on or adjacent to the main workhouse site.[30] Three Welsh unions, Bridgend and Cowbridge, Swansea, and Neath, together with two in England, Kensington and Chelsea, and Birmingham, were the first unions to establish grouped cottage homes away from the workhouse, some in rural surroundings outside the union. These grouped homes varied considerably in size, both in the overall capacity and the number of children in each cottage, and as the century progressed, more and more unions, especially the larger urban ones, saw grouped homes as a solution to the problems of housing and educating pauper children.

One of the largest, Kensington and Chelsea union's Banstead Homes in Surrey, opened in 1880, and by 1900 could house over 700 children from the age of 4. The homes were virtually self-sufficient with twenty-three cottages, two infirmaries (one serving as an isolation cottage), a school, bakery, chapel, laundry and shop, workshops, swimming pool, gymnasium, residential accommodation for the staff and administrative buildings. The union opened a separate probationary home in Hammersmith to limit the chances of infectious disease coming to the homes, and to try to weed out some of the 'ins and outs' who were often removed by their parents before they were ready for transfer to Banstead.

The grouped homes were an improvement on the big workhouse and district schools, with the children living in smaller groups in houses in the charge of house parents or a house mother and usually provided with better industrial training and education provision. The homes were often in the countryside, giving children space to play and exercise, and most importantly were away from the grim and harsh world of the workhouse and the possibility of corruption by adult paupers. Writing in 1889,

Davenport-Hill explained that there had been no cases of ophthalmia at the Banstead Homes since they opened and added:

> Nothing is spared to make a good and happy child of the little pauper; the chief supervision is of the very highest order, and the influence of this was apparent throughout the staff. This little colony is in the purest air and surrounded by beautiful country. Order, good organisation, and cleanliness are everywhere to be seen.[31]

However, as the century went on, there were concerns that grouped village homes were isolating for the children, as they were often self-contained with limited contact with the local community. The children grew up with children like themselves and had only their carers, teachers and trainers as adult models. Even Davenport-Hill added a rider to her praise of the Banstead Homes:

> Everywhere was the faint but unmistakeable impression of an artificial system; everywhere was the stamp of the poor law, the mark of the pauper. The Cottage Homes and their families were much too large for reality; their studied neatness and affected homeliness did not give the *feeling* of home, for its genuine conditions were wanting.

She also said that the children brought up in the homes had 'no right ever to return, either to find sympathy or to renew early affections and memories.' This was a significant difference between most poor law institutions and other forms of provision, such as certified homes and boarding-out schemes, which will be covered in later chapters, where children were generally welcomed back after they had left for employment.

In the 1890s, the Sheffield Guardians were the poor law pioneers in developing children's homes as we would know them today – keeping the idea of small units housing up to about thirty children in the charge of house parents, but instead of grouping the homes together in a separate complex, they were scattered around the community – borough or parish. Many voluntary societies and charitable organisations had provided individual small cottage homes for decades, but most had admissions policies so could restrict intake, whereas the poor law institutions had to take in any child that had settlement in its union who came through their doors. It is not surprising, therefore, that unions saw large institutions, whether single buildings or grouped homes, as the most cost-effective way of looking after pauper children.

By 1896, within three years of starting the scheme, the Sheffield Guardians had set up nine 'scattered homes' in the suburbs – ordinary rented properties each housing a small group of children in the care of a foster parent employed by the union. The scheme applied to all children over 3 years old in its care, not just orphaned or deserted children. In 1907, the union's Children's Homes Committee gave twelve benefits of the scheme, including providing homes approximating as closely as possible to the conditions of working class life; scattering homes around the city, so preventing the aggregation of any large number of children in one place and enabling children to attend elementary schools in small numbers to avoid their presence being especially noticeable. The scheme also gave the children the opportunity to attend evening classes, Bands of Hope, and other children's societies with other children; and enabled the children to mix with boys and girls of a superior social position as companions and friends.[32] In the early part of the twentieth century, many other urban unions across the country quickly followed Sheffield's lead, such as West Ham, Bath and Norwich. Some rural unions leased one or perhaps two houses within the union and set them up as children's homes, such as the Blything union in Suffolk which opened a home for boys and girls in the village of Yoxford. By 1913, about thirty children were resident.

Some poor law unions also used training ships as another, more specialised, institution for the care of pauper boys. The earliest training ships were run by the Marine Society from the late eighteenth century, with the Royal Navy's first training ship, HMS *Implacable*, opening in 1855 at Plymouth. Many more followed, often former 'wooden-walled' warships, run by private organisations and charities as well as the Royal Navy. Two training vessels, the *Goliath* and the *Exmouth*, were effectively floating district schools, providing pauper boys with an education and physical and seamanship training under naval-type discipline. The *Goliath* burned out at her moorings in December 1875, with the loss of twenty-three lives; her successor, TS *Exmouth*, was run by the Metropolitan Asylums Board and was moored off Grays, Essex.[33] The original *Exmouth* was replaced with a purpose-built steel ship (although designed to look like an old wooden-wall) in 1905.

In 1875, W. S. Bourchier, Captain Superintendent of TS *Goliath*, reported on sixty-five named boys from the London union of St George's who had been discharged from the ship between April 1871 and early February 1875. The report, which was included in the 1874/5 LGB annual report, noted that more than half the boys had gone to sea on leaving, with four enlisting in the Royal Navy and the remainder joining ships of the merchant service. Nineteen joined the Army, four went into other employment, three were taken by friends and one returned to his school. Six of the boys were serving in naval or military bands.

The remarks column provides more information about some of the boys, indicating that Captain Bourchier tried to keep tabs on his 'old boys', either directly or indirectly. Several boys visited their old training ship when on leave and others wrote letters telling him of their progress. Most boys were recorded as 'doing well' and only a few had been lost sight of. Francis Kemp had been sent to *Goliath*, 'as being of a very turbulent disposition', so it was probably with some satisfaction that Captain Bourchier noted that he had 'turned out a very fine boy, and is doing well'. Michael Maddigan, who had joined the ship *Snowden* in December 1871 had 'Grown a fine young man; he visited the ship; is doing well and serving his time.' Some were less successful: John Forbes ran away from his ship and was last heard of working as a shoe black in London, and although Oswald Simpson joined a merchant ship on leaving, he returned to the *Goliath*, 'as unsuitable from being too small and weak'.

Charlie Chaplin explained how he was left alone at the Hanwell district school when his older half-brother Sydney left at the age of 11 to join the *Exmouth*. Sydney's *Exmouth* record shows that he achieved second class standard in the cornet and first class in bugle and as Charlie said, 'now it was paying off' as when Sydney was 16, he got a job as a steward and bugler on a Donovan and Castle Line passenger boat sailing to Africa. As well as waiting at table, Sydney sounded the calls for meals.[34]

As with the *Goliath*, some *Exmouth* boys, such as Nathaniel Simmonds, left to join the Army. Nathaniel was orphaned by the time he was 10, and after spending a day in the Stepney workhouse in 1872, he was sent to the Forest Gate district school and then to TS *Goliath*. In 1876 after the destruction of the *Goliath*, Nathaniel, then 14, was admitted to the *Exmouth*. By the time he was discharged to the 5th Fusiliers some eighteen months later, he had gained an inch in height (to 4ft 6ins), 13lbs in weight and three quarters of an inch on his chest measurement. A few, such as 9-year-old James McCall and 11-year-old James Blanchard, were returned to the union as unfit for sea or for training. James Blanchard was discharged from the *Exmouth* in 1878 but by 1881, with no occupation recorded, he was living with his mother and stepfather, and his siblings in Poplar. Within a few months, Blanchard was dead, aged just 16. He died suddenly from heart disease.

Various charitable and private organisations, such as the Marine Society and the Philanthropic Society, made some provision from the eighteenth century onwards for juveniles at risk of offending, including those who had criminal parents, or whose parents could not control them. However, it was not until the 1850s that legislation formally introduced two types of certified juvenile institution to cater for such children and for those convicted in the courts of criminal offences. Firstly, reformatory schools were established for juvenile offenders and then, following an Act of 1857, industrial schools were introduced, initially aimed at children aged 7 to 14 who were convicted of vagrancy. Both types of institution were usually managed by voluntary organisations, but certified and inspected by the government. Some training ships were designated as reformatories, such as the *Akbar*, moored in the Mersey and the *Cornwall* on the Thames. Others were certified as industrial schools, including the *Southampton* at Hull, the *Formidable* at Portishead and the *Mars* at Dundee.

It is hardly surprising that John Neavecey of Lowestoft in Suffolk turned to crime at a young age. Over a period of forty-five years, his father James was convicted of numerous offences, mostly theft, and served over twenty-five years in prison. He was serving a seven-year sentence in Dartmoor in 1880 when, according to *The Lowestoft Journal* of 27 March that year, his 10-year-old son John was charged with stealing 4 stone of coal from the Great Eastern Railway Company. John said that his mother had threatened to punish him if he did not bring anything home. A month later, John was charged with stealing four pairs of stockings which he said he took to get bread. *The Lowestoft Journal* of 24 April 1880 reported the magistrate saying it was 'a sad case' and that though Neavecey was a 'mere child', he had appeared in court several times before and had been whipped. The paper continued: 'They felt the best thing they could do would be to send him to a Reformatory for five years, and he hoped that he would come out a good boy. He would, therefore, first be imprisoned for ten days, and afterwards removed to Thorndon.' The records of the Suffolk Reformatory at Thorndon, near Eye, show that John Neavecey emigrated to Canada after serving his sentence. The reformatory received excellent reports of the lad's progress and John himself wrote to the reformatory on at least two occasions.[35]

The certified industrial school was initially something of a hybrid institution, bridging the poor law, education and criminal justice systems. Children convicted of vagrancy, exhibiting challenging behaviour or living under immoral influences could be sentenced to a period at an industrial school, but voluntary cases were also admitted through either parents or the poor law unions. The timetable was strict, but there were, as with larger poor law schools, opportunities to join bands, even swimming lessons. Younger children would be in full time education, but the older ones, aged from about 11, would be half-timers, carrying out industrial work or training for part of the day, and school for the rest.

By the early twentieth century, the Buxton Industrial School (also known as the Red House Farm School) in Norfolk had its own farm of over 50 acres with stock including pigs and poultry, so many of the boys worked part time on the land, either farming or gardening. Other boys worked at bootmaking, tailoring, baking or carpentry. There were industrial schools for girls too, such as the certified home at Cold Ash in Berkshire run by the Waifs and Strays Society which housed about thirty girls, some sentenced by the courts, others voluntary admissions. Their industrial training was chiefly limited to domestic duties – needlework, cooking and laundry work. Industrial schools gradually became more linked with the criminal justice system than with the education system; in 1860 supervision passed to the Home Office from the Education Department. In time, and with changes to legislation concerning juvenile crime, many of the industrial schools were later reclassified as borstals or approved schools.

In 1908, eleven boys, aged from 10 to 15, were admitted as voluntary cases to the Buxton Industrial School from the West Ham Poor Law Union. It is likely that most of the boys had already been in the care of the West Ham Guardians for some time, either in the union schools or boarded out. St John Clues, born in about 1896, was almost certainly boarded out in Dickleburgh before coming to the school – his name appears on the village's First World War roll of honour and the industrial school log book states that on 19 August 1910, 'The boy St John Clues spent the day in Norwich at the invitation of the Rev Forbes Rector of Dickleboro who knew the boy before he came to the School.'[36] Harry Hearne was about 10 when he was admitted to the Buxton school, an illegitimate child with unknown parents. Unsurprisingly perhaps, he was suffering from 'urinary incontinence', presumably bed-wetting, and had a stutter. He left in 1914 and like many other boys from the school, including St John Clues, he joined the Royal Navy, perhaps encouraged by spending time working on the masts and rigging installed in the school grounds.[37] George Marks, who was 14 when he arrived at the Buxton school, absconded just ten days later. He disappeared early in the morning and, by nightfall, the weather was closing in, as recorded in the school log book: 'Quite a snow storm and blizzard tonight hope the foolish boy Marks will find shelter. No news of him as yet.' The snow continued the next day but Marks was picked up that evening at Great Yarmouth and on his return was whipped with six strokes of the tawse on his backside. Marks absconded again in November the following year, and was sentenced to be held at the reformatory training ship, *Cornwall*, until he was 19.

The state made slow, if steady, progress in providing appropriate accommodation, education and training for pauper children and others, such as juvenile offenders, in its care. Following the 1834 Poor Law Amendment Act, many quickly realised that the workhouse was no place for a child and experimented with various solutions – separate and district schools, training ships, certified and grouped homes – which all had some benefits for pauper children and were an improvement on the workhouse. However, it was not until the beginning of twentieth century that there was significant change, with a greater focus by the unions on small cottage homes and fostering, provision still used in the twenty-first century. Nevertheless, most of the older types of provision, including the workhouse itself, were still in use well into the twentieth century. Although state provision for pauper children during the period of the new poor law was often bleak, grim and inadequate, it was usually better than the alternative, as William Hew Ross explained:

> I had a great deal to be thankful for at the workhouse. I entered it like a little heathen. Before going there, I had roamed unchecked about Woolwich, learning all kinds of wickedness and vice. Had that life continued, with no one but my poor old grandmother to look after me, I should soon have been far beyond her control, and I believe must eventually have been sent to prison, and perhaps as a transport.[38]

The Rev Henry Brandreth and his wife, Louisa, who founded the children's charity in Dickleburgh in Norfolk, with their children Rosalind and Roland, c.1895. (*Dickleburgh Churchwardens and Parochial Church Council*)

Rose Cottage, Dickleburgh. *Our Waifs and Strays* magazine, March 1900. (*The Children's Society Archive*)

Children outside Rose Cottage, Dickleburgh. *Our Waifs and Strays* magazine, March 1900. (*The Children's Society Archive*)

Lee Cottage, Dickleburgh. *Our Waifs and Strays* magazine, February 1889. (*The Children's Society Archive*)

It is quite impossible to close this little account of Rose Cottage without paying a tribute of grateful appreciation to the lady who in the first instance started this Home more than twenty years ago (later on handing it over to the Waifs and Strays Society), and who has maintained an untiring interest in it, and taken a very practical part in its management. We withhold this lady's name out of consideration for her own wish, that she should not be brought prominently forward in the description of a work which was most truly to her a labour of love and a valued interest in her life for so many years; but to those who have known Dickleburgh and Rose Cottage, the names of her husband and herself will always be connected with the memory of the village and Home. The Matrons (whose conscientious work she highly valued) and the children sadly miss her constant visits now that circumstances have led to her leaving the place, and one knows that she misses them and the work to which she was so devoted; but we can feel sure that Rose Cottage and all connected with it, will always occupy a very warm place in her heart.

And so we leave Rose Cottage, with a feeling of deep thankfulness that it is only one of many training places throughout the country for poor friendless little ones; training-places which are well worthy of bearing the sweet name of *Home*.

Article about Rose Cottage, Dickleburgh, following the retirement of the Rev Henry and Mrs Louisa Brandreth from the parish, *Our Waifs and Strays* magazine, March 1900. (*The Children's Society Archive*)

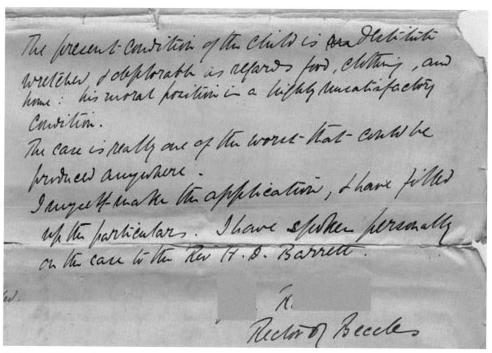

Waifs and Strays Society Application Form for Ernest Simmonds of Beccles, Suffolk, 1889, giving details about his home life. (*The Children's Society Archive, Case File No. 2258*)

Newscutting, undated [1901/2], on Victoria Tooke's Waifs and Strays Case File, referring to the conviction of her mother, Alice Tooke, for abandoning a male child in the countryside, near Norwich. (*The Children's Society Archive, Case File No. 7335*)

with her. This was done, and prisoner left with the child, Mrs. Utting giving prisoner a bottle of milk and some biscuits. When the child left it was suffering from bronchitis. From this time until that morning Mrs. Utting saw no more of the prisoner nor the baby. Shortly before twelve o'clock on the same night Police-constable Capon was passing by a field situate about 200 yards from the Windmill public-house, Aylsham-road, and belonging to Mr. Hannent, when he heard faint cries proceeding therefrom. He got through the hedge, and then found the baby, fully dressed, lying on its back on the bare ground, close to the fence. There was no gate near the spot, nor any gap in the fence, which was about twelve feet high from the ground level, and reached by a bank six feet high. The officer found on the top of the fence, just above where the child was lying, a plaid shawl and a red stocking cap. The child was cold and its eyes swollen, whilst the legs were partly bare. The night was a frosty one, and the ground hard and cold. On the lip of the child was a place that looked as if it had been caused by a fall. The child was taken to the Workhouse infirmary early on Tuesday morning. It was stated by a witness, named

Baptism Register, Dickleburgh, 1897, showing baptisms of several children who were boarded out in the village or resident in Rose Cottage. (*Norfolk Record Office, PD 704/10*)

Dickleburgh School, Class V, c.1910. Four of these children have been identified as being boarded out in Dickleburgh – Minnie Clarke (far right, back row), Agnes Clarke (second right, front row) and two unnamed boys – third from left, middle row and third from left, front row. (*Dickleburgh Church of England Primary Academy; Dickleburgh Village Society*)

Admissions Register, Dickleburgh School, 1907–1909, including admissions of seven boarded-out children and five residents of Rose Cottage. (*Dickleburgh Church of England Primary Academy*)

Former Burton-upon-Trent union workhouse, children's pavilions, 2000. (*Peter Higginbotham, www.workhouses.org*)

Former Depwade union workhouse, Pulham Market, Norfolk, 2013. (*Author's own*)

Former Depwade union workhouse chapel, Pulham Market, Norfolk, 2013. (*Author's own*)

Former West Ham union workhouse, Leyton, East London (formerly Essex), 2018. (*Author's own*)

Former West Ham union workhouse, boardroom block and chapel, Leyton, East London (formerly Essex), 2018. (*Author's own*)

Former Hartismere union separate/district school, Wortham, Suffolk, 2018. (*Author's own*)

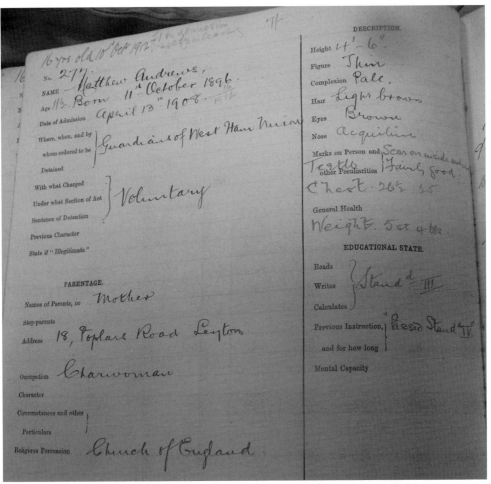

Admission and Progress Register, Buxton Industrial School, Norfolk, entry for Matthew Andrews. (*Norfolk Record Office, C/SS 8/33*)

ADJOURNED CASES.

The following are the particulars of a few of the cases of boys who are waiting for admission:—

J. H. G. C.—6 years. Father died of consumption; mother delicate; very respectable, neat, and tidy; cannot earn more than about 7s. a week; has one other child, a girl of 3; could manage if relieved of the care of this boy.

T. G. P.—4½ years. Father dead; mother left with five children under 8. Grandfather has taken one; no other relatives able to assist; very respectable.

H. H.—10 years. Illegitimate. Father deserted mother two years ago; she has since been in a Home; has now obtained situation, by means of which she can support younger child if this boy is provided for; her only hope of redeeming her character.

T. B.—9 years. Father dead; mother left with seven children: eldest daughter delicate, with a relative; two girls, 16 and 14, in service; relatives doing their best to help; mother works hard; respectable; could manage if one child were taken.

All the above cases have been thoroughly investigated.

List of four boys awaiting admission to the Waifs and Strays Society with details of their family circumstances, *Our Waifs and Strays* magazine, February 1885. (*The Children's Society Archive*)

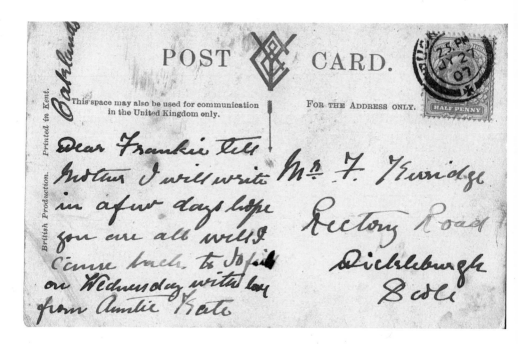

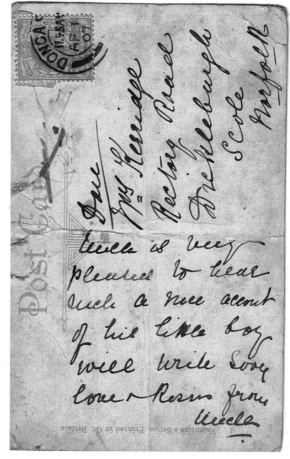

Postcards sent to Frank Mendham (born 1895) and Donald Jefferson (born 1902) while they were boarded out in Dickleburgh with Esther Kerridge, 1907. Both boys were illegitimate and were boarded out from a very young age. It is possible that 'Auntie Kate', who in other postcards signs herself K. Mendham, was Frank's birth mother. (*Private collection: Pauline Spinlove*)

Extract of Letter dated February 1910 from Ada Pine to Edward Rudolf, apologising for setting fire to bedding at the Dickleburgh home and pleading to remain in London so she could see her mother. (*The Children's Society Archive, Case File No. 14,841*)

Dickleburgh School Log Book, 1908, recording absence of boarded-out child, Emily Mallett, through chicken pox. Two other children, M. Roland and B. Punchard, were excluded from school as they were boarded out in the same house as Emily. (*Dickleburgh Church of England Primary Academy*)

Form of Undertaking by the Foster Parent for Caroline Simpson of Acton, Suffolk, in respect of Alice E. George, 1887. (*The Children's Society Archive, Case File No. 1024*)

Extract of Letter, dated 12 January 1898, probably from Miss Doughty of Lowestoft to Edward Rudolf, relating to the proposed adoption of Isabella Timperley by Mr and Mrs Smith of Lowestoft. (*The Children's Society Archive, Case File No. 4090*)

EMIGRATION HOME.

THE first portion of the Emigration scheme consisted, as our readers will probably remember, of the raising of a sum of one thousand pounds for the purchase of certain freehold property at Sherbrooke, in the province of Quebec, and for fitting up the premises thereon as a Girls' Reception Home. It was desired to obtain this amount if possible by the 1st January, when the purchase was to be completed.

With deep thankfulness, we are able to announce that the £1,000 has been obtained, and that the property passed into the hands of the Society about three weeks ago. Steps will at once be taken to adapt the premises, and provide the necessary furniture; and it is hoped that our first party of girl emigrants will leave England in April, in charge of Mr. Bridger.

It will be necessary, in order to complete our scheme, that a Boys' Home should be established as well as a Servants' Home, for those of our girls who may not be able to keep their situations. Next month we hope to be able to announce for which of these two objects it has been decided to issue an appeal.

E. DE M. RUDOLF, *Hon. Sec.*

Article in *Our Waifs and Strays* magazine, February 1885, describing the Waifs and Strays Society's successful purchase of a property in Sherbrooke, Quebec, Canada and plans to turn it into a girls' reception home. (*The Children's Society Archive*)

THE SHERBROOKE HOME.

The Sherbrooke Home, *Our Waifs and Strays* magazine, August 1885. (*The Children's Society Archive*)

Extract of Letter (c. 1895) from Edith Stiff in Canada to Mrs Brandreth of Dickleburgh explaining how 'lonesome' she is in Canada. (*The Children's Society Archive, Case File No. 1443*)

Copy   A letter from Edith Stiff   Bulwar   P. 2
to Mrs Brandreth of
Dickleburgh

My dear Godmother,
I am so sorry I have not wrote to you
before. I have left my place at Montreal because they wanted
a bigger girl than me. I went back to the Home till I
got another place, you asked me when you wrote to me if there
was a home to go back to yes. But this is the last time
I may go back to it I have got a place in the country at a farm
there is just Mr and Mrs Lindsey the other girl has not left yet
but I came because they are going to shut up the home the
Matron has had to leave it because she is to sick to look after
it any longer. the other girl says it is a very nice place here
she is very sorry to leave it but she is going to be married. I am
going to see how long I can stay here for I shall have nowhere to go
to if I leave here all the girls ho are 15 are not aloude to go back
to the home. they say I am 15 will you please wright and tell me my
right age. I have got your Lightness in my bedroom it is so nice to
think I have got a friend In the world could you please to give
me Mrs Manns Address I should like to have it. it is so lonesome
out here it makes me think of England how I do wish I had never
left you I often think it was my best home I had. they all say
that when I have been that all that is against me is I am Impertant
it does seem so hard for I feel as though I could help answering
back but I am going to try and not do so here. I think I shall like
being here very much. the reason I did not wrote to you before is they dont
alow us to wright when we are the home. I have been in the Home
nearley 3 months I was servant there but I made up my mind I would
try and wright as soon as I got out to a place. It is a tenbull place
out here the men are all the time after the girls I have had an afful
lot ask me to Marrie them. of course I have refused I try not to take
any notice of them all I can I tell you for I have no one else to tell
I will turn over a new leaf and try to be a better girl for I feel so
unhappy now I think this is all I have to say for I have got to go to

Fegans' emigration party, April 1913. Louis Fewings, who was boarded out in Dickleburgh, is believed to be amongst this party, but has not been identified. (*Fegans' Archive*)

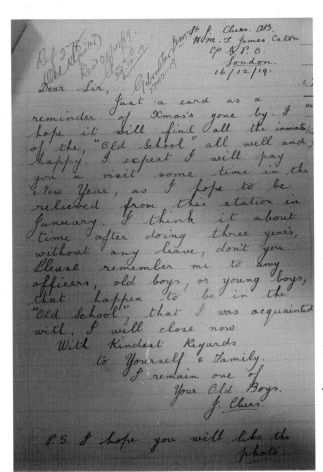

Waifs and Strays Society Case File for Eliza Shirley, recording her placements in various homes, 1892–1894, until her return to the workhouse at Burton-upon-Trent. (*The Children's Society Archive, Case File No. 3055*)

Letter (enclosed in Admissions and Progress Register) from St John Clues to staff at the Buxton Industrial School, Norfolk, 16 December 1919. Clues attended the school from 1908 to 1912, leaving to join the Royal Navy. (*Norfolk Record Office, C/SS 8/33*)

Children's graves, All Saints' churchyard, Dickleburgh. The stone Celtic cross behind the plot marks the graves of Henry and Louisa Brandreth. (*Author's own*)

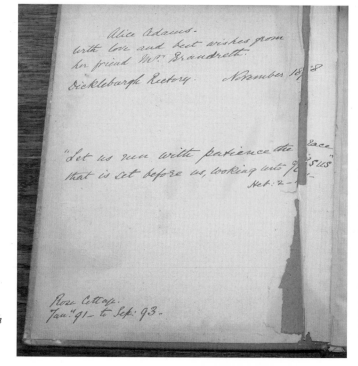

Inscription in a copy of *Pilgrim's Progress* given by Mrs Brandreth to Alice Adams in 1898, five years after Alice left Rose Cottage in Dickleburgh. (*Dickleburgh Village Society collection, by permission of Gwen Pooley*)

Chapter 6

The Charitable Response

Is it possible that in this great city there are others as young as this boy, as helpless, as ill prepared to meet the trials of cold and hunger and exposure of every kind? Is it possible ... that there are many such in this great city of London of ours – this city of wealth, of open Bibles, of Gospel preaching and of ragged schools?[1]

Thomas John Barnardo, c. 1870

For centuries, religious orders, churches, charitable organisations and individuals have given help to those in need, providing necessities such as shelter, food, blankets, coals and clothing, and sometimes other support, such as medical assistance and free schooling. Since the Reformation, this charitable help has run alongside state provision, and so it continues to this day. Early charities were often small and local, providing for the poor within a parish or town, but later charities might be more specialised or wider in geographical scope, resulting in the mix of national and local charities we see today, some of which have their origins 200 or more years ago.

From the medieval period, one of the commonest forms of charitable giving was through wills, with the testator bequeathing either a monetary payment or income from land to the use of the poor. Some benefactors set up schemes of apprenticeships for pauper children or charity schools. One of the first residential charity schools, Christ's Hospital, was established at Newgate Street, London to provide food, clothing, lodging and 'a little learning for fatherless children and other poor men's children' in November 1552 at the instigation of King Edward VI. It was granted a royal charter the following year and still exists today although it moved from its original site to Horsham, West Sussex in 1902. It was funded by subscriptions from the Church, businesses and householders in the City of London. Infants were sent out of London and cared for by nurses, who were paid a weekly allowance – an early version of fostering. Those of school age attended local day schools until they were about 10 when they returned to London to be educated. The school's distinctive uniform of a long blue coat, matching knee breeches, yellow socks and white neck bands gave rise to its colloquial name of the Blue Coat School.

Illegitimacy, abandoned babies and infanticide were major problems in eighteenth century England, with hundreds of babies abandoned on the streets of London each year. Thomas Coram was born in Lyme Regis in Dorset about 1668 and went to sea when he was 11. He was then apprenticed to a shipwright before setting up in business himself. Living in semi-retirement after a failed business venture in the American colonies and several unsuccessful philanthropic projects, Coram was moved to action by the sight of abandoned infants and street children in London and decided to establish a home to care for and educate foundlings and illegitimate babies. However, it took him seventeen years of persistent campaigning and canvassing for support and funds before his plan came to fruition. On 17 October 1739, George II signed the charter incorporating the hospital for the 'Maintenance and Education of Exposed and Deserted Children', a secular charity better known as the Foundling Hospital, but in 1741, Coram was ousted from the board and took no further part in the administration of the hospital he had worked so hard to establish.

In the early years, mothers bringing their babies for admission were guaranteed anonymity, with the governors issuing a public notice about the opening of the hospital in temporary premises in Hatton Garden: 'No questions whatsoever shall be asked of any person bringing a child, nor shall any servant of the Hospital presume to discover who such person is, on pain of being dismissed.' The entrance lights were extinguished to ensure the women could not be identified and by midnight on the first evening it opened, the hospital was full, with thirty children admitted. Others were turned away as the minutes of the hospital's daily committee reported the following day, 26 March 1741:

> The Gov[erno]rs observing seven or eight women with Children
> at the Door and more amongst the Crowd desired them that they
> woul'd not Drop any of their Children in the Streets where they

most probably must Perish but to take care of them till they could have an opportunity of putting them into the Hospital which was hoped to be very soon…On this Occasion the Expressions of Grief of the Women whose Children could not be admitted were Scarcely more observable than those of some of the Women who parted with their Children, so that a more moving Scene can't well be imagined.[2]

A permanent hospital was built a few years later, north of Bloomsbury in open fields, designed to house 192 girls and 192 boys in separate wings, in simple accommodation, two children to a bed. Every child was given a new name on admission, Christian and surname; sometimes named after a noted worthy associated with the hospital or given a typical foundling name such as Hope or Charity. A record of each child was kept, and many mothers left tokens or keepsakes that could be used to reunite mother and child if she returned to reclaim her child. Most babies were wet nursed in foster care, returning to the hospital aged between 3 and 5.

The hospital had various admission policies over the years, including admission by ballot and, between 1756 and 1760, 'general reception' when, as a condition of a government grant, the hospital had to accept all children presented for admission. From 1763, the mother had to submit a petition, pleading her case for the admission of her child, explaining the circumstances of its birth and why she could not care for it herself. Maria Colby, from Harleston in Norfolk, was living with her married sister, Mrs Elizabeth Baker, in Islington when the lodger Walter Cross (or Walter Frost as Maria named him on her application form) seduced her, as she explained in her accepted petition of 1868 to the Foundling Hospital:

While I was about to leave the room he caught hold of me and forced me upon the sofa. I struggled with him until I lost all power and he then effected his purpose. I was at that time in a very delicate state of health. I completely lost my senses. When I had recovered he had left the house. About a fortnight later … intercourse was repeated partly with my consent in his bed-room – he never promised marriage and never gave me money.[3]

Maria stated she was too ashamed to tell her sister what had happened, so it was another two months before Mrs Baker discovered her sister's pregnancy, by which time Walter Cross (or Frost) was long gone.

However, other papers on the same file indicate that Maria and her family conspired to deceive the Foundling Hospital about the real identity of the father of Maria's child. In an undated, anonymous letter to the hospital, the writer stated: 'I think the way they are trying to Impose upon your Noble Institution Shameful. the Father of the Child is Her Sisters Husband William Baker and a man that can well keep the Child.' There was a certain irony in this claim as James Twiddy, who had inquired into the case on behalf of the hospital, stated that Elizabeth Baker and her other sister, Hannah Brown (who lived in Kennington, south London) were covering the costs of childcare for Maria's baby (eight shillings a week) but could not do so for much longer as 'their respective husbands complain of this burden.'

William Foster White, who was the treasurer of St Bartholomew's Hospital (and presumably was part of the establishment of the Foundling Hospital), wrote to John Brownlow, the secretary of the Foundling Hospital about the case: 'If this is true, it is a great Shame ... for such a heap of lies must have been told by all parties... . I feel so vexed after all that has been done for this wretched Girl that she should so shamefully deceive us.' An undated letter from Elizabeth Baker, Maria's sister, possibly written to John Brownlow, provides strong credence to the anonymous writer's claim that William Baker, Maria's brother-in-law, was the father of the child:

> I do hope & beg of you to look over my untruthfulness the ...
> possition I was in is my only excuse it has nearly driven me mad, but
> I have great hopes that your kind and generous heart will forgive
> the moste unhappy creature that I am, and have been this last six
> months I do think if it last much longer I shall surely break down
> but I do hope and Trust come what will after the kindness you have
> shewn you will forgive and pity your moste misserable and Humble
> Servant
>
> I cannot write any more may god forgive me.

Whoever the father was, the matter did not end well. Maria's son was accepted into the care of the Foundling Hospital in September 1868 and was baptised as Edmund Randall, before being sent out be nursed in Chertsey, Surrey.[4] He died there on 25 October, aged just six months. His death certificate described him as a foundling and recorded 'Marasmus' (undernourishment), as the main cause of death. The informant was Elizabeth Humphrey, who was present at his death, possibly his foster mother. Edmund's birth mother, Maria Colby, had been in hospital with tuberculosis following his birth and after spending time at a convalescent home went to live with her other sister, Hannah Brown, in Kennington. By 1871, she had returned to Norfolk and resumed living with her parents in Harleston. She died there six years later, of 'pulmonary phthisis' (tuberculosis), with her mother present at her death.

Many other institutions for destitute children established at this time, especially those founded by religious organisations or individuals, would not accept illegitimate children, providing only for orphans or partial orphans of the respectable poor. Edward Pickard, pastor of the Carter Lane Meeting House in London, was the prime mover in the establishment of the Orphan Working School, supported by pastors and other members of the Protestant dissenting churches.[5] The orphanage opened in 1760 in Hoxton, London, for legitimate, orphaned boys of respectable parents who had not received parish relief. Facilities for girls were provided the following year and by 1769, there were fifty-three children resident, most from Protestant dissenting families. Like the Foundling Hospital, the Orphan Working School was highly structured; governors were appointed on payment of an annual fee or a lump sum for life and served on various committees. Initially, children aged 6 to 9 were admitted through the nomination of governors by rotation, although a child could be accepted immediately on payment of sixty guineas. From 1810, admission was through a ballot with governors having several votes, although it was still possible to purchase admission, at a cost of 120 guineas.

There was a strong emphasis on education and training in the orphanage – the children were to 'be carefully instructed in the principle and duties of the Christian religion ... taught to read and write, so far as may be necessary in any future station; and used to such labour and work as may be convenient and suitable.' Boys were employed in carpet weaving and spinning horsehair and girls in knitting and domestic duties. Shoemaking and netmaking were other industries available at the orphanage in later years. Children were apprenticed to a trade or service when they were aged 14 or upwards, with care being taken to find appropriate placements. In 1773, new premises opened in City Road, Islington and about 1850, the school moved to Haverstock Hill, north London. In 1949, the school amalgamated with another school to become the Royal Alexandra and Albert School, now located at Gatton Park, Reigate in Surrey.

The Rev Andrew Reed founded a similar institution in 1813, the East London Orphan Asylum, although it changed its name and location several times. Its aim was to provide for destitute orphans:

> To rescue them from the walks of vice and profligacy; to provide them [with] clothing and maintenance; to fix the habits of industry and frugality; to train them in the path of religion and virtue agreeably to the formularies of the Church of England and to place them out in situations where their principles shall not be endangered and the prospect of an honest livelihood shall be secured.[6]

The charity provided for children who had lost either both parents or their father, with the mother unable to provide for them and, like the Working Orphan School, favoured children from respectable families, as stated in the description in the 1861 census, by which time the establishment was based in Clapton: 'London Orphan Asylum, Clapton, for the Maintenance & Education of Fatherless Children who are respectably descended but destitute of means of support.' The website of its successor, Reed's School at Cobham, states: 'Inspired by the vision of our Founder, Andrew Reed, a central aim of Reed's School is to support children who have lost one or both parents.'

According to the 1857 annual report for the orphan asylum, Thomas Frederick Butler was admitted 'under free presentation as a war orphan' at the age of about 9.[7] His father, Samuel Butler, a paymaster sergeant in the 12th Lancers, died of cholera during the Crimean War and his mother, Elizabeth, was also dead by the time of Thomas's admission. Thomas left the orphanage in about 1863 and worked as a bricklayer but in 1867, aged

19, he followed in his father's footsteps and joined the Army.[8] He served in the West Yorkshire Regiment for nearly twenty-six years, including over seven years in India where he attained the rank of colour sergeant. His career took a downward turn on his return to England, being twice demoted to the ranks, but by the time of his marriage in 1883, he had been promoted back to colour sergeant and was discharged with a pension in 1893, aged 44.

The latter half of the nineteenth century saw a huge growth in private and charitable homes for orphaned and destitute children, not only in London and other cities and towns, but also in rural areas. As the consequences of poverty upon children became more apparent, there was an increasing focus on 'child rescue', plucking destitute children directly from the streets of London and elsewhere, as well as taking in children who were orphaned or abused, or where the family simply could not support them. It was often a philanthropic individual who helped initially, responding to the sight of destitute, orphaned and abandoned children on the streets, as Coram had a century earlier, although other charities were established by religious denominations or orders. Many philanthropists involved in child rescue were evangelical Christians, intent on leading the poor to salvation, such as George Müller, Thomas Barnardo, Thomas Bowman Stephenson and Edward Rudolf. Through their missionary work and teaching in ragged and Sunday schools, they realised that the poor, especially children, needed not just education and spiritual training, but also basic practical help – food, shelter and clothing. Some charities established at this time still exist today, sometimes under a different name, now working with statutory authorities to support families, children and young people, although the focus has moved away from institutional care to supporting young people within their families or the community.

George Müller was a Prussian immigrant who came to England in 1829, and by 1832 he was living in Bristol where he founded the Scriptural Knowledge Institution for Home and Abroad, focusing on Bible distribution and education. Müller decided that he would neither take a salary nor request funds for his ministry or mission work, instead relying on the power of prayer to provide all he needed. He opened his first orphanage for girls in a house in Wilson Street, Bristol in 1836 and over the next few years, rented further houses in the same street for the care of infants and boys. Dickens described how the infants' orphanage came about:

> Aided by gifts, little and large – fourpence, a gallon of dry peas, tippets, old clothes, bits of bacon, sugar, money, – the work went on, and before the end of the following November [1837], more than seven hundred pounds had been raised without one contribution having been asked for, in a direct way, by Müller himself, and the Infant Orphan-house was opened.[9]

In 1845, following complaints by other residents of Wilson Street about the presence of over 100 children in the street, Müller decided to establish a purpose-built orphanage outside the city. He remained true to his belief that God would provide and within two years over £11,000 had been donated to the project so building could start on the New Orphan House at Ashley Down, north of Bristol. It opened in June 1849 and by 1870, Müller had erected a further four houses on the site, with over 2,000 children resident. Müller always waited until the required funds were available before embarking on his projects; he never asked for funds and he never got into debt.

Walter Allen's father John, who ran the King's Head Inn in Holt in Norfolk, died when Walter was only about 18 months old. His mother, Frances, quickly married again, to William Coe, a traveller, ten years her junior. Frances and William and Frances's four young sons moved to Newcastle after the marriage but within three years, the family had been split apart when Frances Coe died aged just 39. The boys' stepfather, William Coe, probably deserted the Allen boys after their mother's death, and it seems likely that the poor law authorities had to step in. In 1871, the two oldest boys were boarding in Newcastle, William, aged 10, was a patient at Newcastle upon Tyne infirmary and the youngest, Walter, aged 6, was resident in the Ashley Down Orphanage in Bristol. Walter returned to Newcastle on leaving the orphanage, working variously as a clerk in a brass foundry and a clerk and storekeeper in a locomotive works.

In 1859, the Honourable Mrs Emmeline Way started a small home at Brockham in Surrey, with just two pauper girls. Shortly afterwards the home was certified by the Home Office under the Industrial Schools Act so the children admitted were state-funded, but as Florence Davenport-Hill explained, 'this gave it in some degree the character of a reformatory institution, which it was desirable to avoid, and was not indeed, fair to the inmates.'[10] Mrs Way lobbied for a change in the law to allow poor law unions to send their pauper children to private and charitable schools, and children's homes, at the union's expense as an alternative to poor law institutions and industrial schools. This was achieved with the Poor Law (Certified Schools) Act of 1862. Mrs Way's children's home was recertified under the Act and many other certified homes (which were subject to inspection by the poor law authorities) followed, such as the cottage homes in Dickleburgh in Norfolk. Some children were therefore in effect rescued twice – once from destitution, the loss of parents, homelessness or cruelty and then again from the harsh and bleak regime of the workhouse or district school.

Many of the earliest private homes opened after the 1862 Act were for pauper girls, but a few were established for boys, such as the home in Clapham Park Road, London for twenty boys. The boys worked in the house and looked after rabbits and chickens. They attended the local elementary school, and on reaching the required standard, were permitted to work half or full time. Around 1877, the home moved to Milton Bryant in Bedfordshire and was renamed the Inglis House Boys' Home, with the number of residents reduced to thirteen. Miss Hesba Stretton, quoted by Davenport-Hill, stated that the boys at the Inglis home produced their own fruit and vegetables, bread and butter. She added that 'they are outspoken manly lads' and contrasted 'the out-door healthy life of their well-controlled boyhood with that of the neglected children of the slums, or of the "ranks and rows" of institution boys, inevitably reduced to a machine-like existence.'[11]

It is perhaps appropriate that the charity founded by Thomas Barnardo 150 years ago still bears his name, as he operated as a 'one-man band' for many years, which brought its own problems. Thomas John Barnardo was born in Dublin in 1845 and underwent a spiritual conversion on 26 May 1862 when he was only 16. He started working with the poor in Dublin but moved to London in 1866 intending to train as a doctor prior to going overseas with the China Inland Mission. However, he was soon drawn into evangelical work with the poor in the East End. He was primarily an evangelical Christian, intent on saving souls, and though he is mainly remembered for his child rescue work, he also did much to help the adults of the East End, with a blurring of the edges between evangelical missionary work and social work. He saw at first hand the suffering during the cholera outbreak the year he came to London, saying, 'but for the cholera outbreak epidemic in 1866, I should never have known Stepney.'

In 1868, Barnardo opened the East End Juvenile Mission in rented cottages in Hope Place – a mix of a ragged school and a mission hall. George Holland, who had set up a ragged school mission in Whitechapel a few years earlier, wrote about his visit to Hope Place that year:

> To give some idea of the work going on, there are held weekly special services for children; Bible Classes for men, women and children, mothers' meetings, girls' sewing classes, a special service attended every week by 130 lads. A little church has also been formed, numbering to this date nearly 90 souls (adults). A day school is in formation and also a Refuge, to be nearly self-supporting, in which orphan lads in work will be boarded and lodged at a charge of three shillings weekly. The total weekly expenses are about £4 10s.[12]

Barnardo started rescuing children from destitution during the winter of 1869–70. The turning point was when he discovered Jim Jarvis, one of the boys in the ragged school, was sleeping rough on the streets. Jim took Barnardo to one of the 'lays' where homeless children spent the night, the iron roof of a shed in an old clothes market off Petticoat Lane, where they found eleven boys, in rags, lying up on the roof, with no covering of any sort, and huddled together for warmth. When Barnardo asked if there were other destitute boys like this, Jim replied, 'Oh yes sir, lots, 'eaps on em! More 'n I could count.'[13] From his later writings, it seems Barnardo saw the encounter with Jim Jarvis as a revelation from God, showing him that his future was in London rather than in China.

In December 1870, Barnardo opened his first children's home, initially for around fifty boys, in rented premises at Stepney Causeway. A short time after its opening, Barnardo's encounter with another destitute child,

John Somers, proved a further turning point in his mission, leading to the well-publicised policy of 'No destitute boy ever refused admission'. Somers, or Carrots as he was nicknamed because of his red hair, was one of a large group of children that Barnardo came across one night in the Billingsgate area. There was only space for five of the boys in the home, and Carrots was left behind. Shortly afterwards, the boy was found dead, having spent the night in a large sugar hogshead (barrel). He was just 11 years old and the coroner concluded the cause of death was from 'exhaustion, the result of frequent exposure and want of food'. In 1876, around the time the earliest state-run 'grouped homes' opened, Barnardo established a girls' village at Barkingside in Essex – individual cottage homes, with ten to twenty girls of varied ages in each, cared for by a house mother. By 1906, there were sixty-five cottages at Barkingside, with more planned, and eleven ancillary buildings. A school operated from the beginning with a new building opening in the village in 1893 and a school of embroidery in 1903.

Barnardo was a man of action; his heart often ruled his head; he could be quarrelsome and took a strong dislike to certain groups, especially Roman Catholics. He was autocratic, proudly running his charity, with substantial funds, single-handed, without the checks and balances provided by committees, treasurers or independent auditors. This approach put him in a vulnerable position and was to land him in trouble at various times. Like many great men, Barnardo ruffled feathers along the way but his achievements were huge, with a permanent legacy – a national charity that still bears his name and remains at the forefront of working with vulnerable children over a century and a half after he founded it. In his 1943 biography, A. E. Williams summed up Barnardo's life's work:

In the short space of forty years, starting without patronage or influence of any kind, this man had raised the sum of three and a quarter million pounds sterling, established a network of Homes of various kinds such as never existed before for the reception, care and training of homeless, needy and afflicted children, and had rescued no fewer than sixty thousand destitute boys and girls.

Edward de Montjoie Rudolf was another who responded to the plight of destitute children in London in the latter half of the nineteenth century, founding the Waifs and Strays Society in 1881, a charity that still exists, although now called The Children's Society. Edward Rudolf was born in Lambeth in 1852, the son of William Edward Rudolf, a former Army officer who was by then in his sixties, and his second wife, Susan. John Stroud stated that after William Rudolf's first wife Cordelia died in 1848 'in his loneliness and despair the major took unto himself a very young girl, sixteen-year-old Susan Amy Goodin, a child whose origins are obscure.'[14] Research shows that Susan Goodin, Edward Rudolf's mother, was born in 1832 in Islington, the third child of William Goodin, a shoemaker. It is likely that her parents had either died or had deserted the children by 1840, the year Susan was admitted to Islington workhouse, aged 7. She was discharged to 'Mr Wm Drouet's' (possibly Drouet's school in Tooting) eleven weeks later, although nothing more is known of her until her marriage to William Rudolf in 1854. It seems likely that Susan initially worked for William as a servant, as Stroud suggests.

It is not known whether Edward knew of his mother's early life or the circumstances of his birth, but his childhood and teenage years were rarely secure or particularly comfortable. His elderly father William had limited income and in 1865, when his father was 80 with failing sight, the young Edward, who had been educated with his younger brother Robert (Bob) at home by his father, took matters into own hands and applied for a job, although he was not quite 13 years old. He later wrote, 'I was successful and felt proud and grateful that I had commenced my working life.'[15]

Edward moved to a job at the Dutch Consulate on a higher salary and supplemented his wages with a wastepaper business as well as studying after work. In the late 1860s, amidst the family's difficulties, he started teaching at a popular educator class two evenings a week, helping young lads to improve themselves, while continuing his own education at the City of London College, reading Greek and Divinity, with a view to entering the ministry. In early 1871, William Rudolf died and within a week of his father's funeral, Edward had sanctioned his mother's admission to the Bethlem Hospital because of mania caused by 'the recent loss of her husband'.[16] Edward passed the Civil Service examination in early 1871 and took up a job as a clerk in the Office of Works, which helped to ease the financial burden on the family. His mother was discharged from hospital, as 'recovered', in August 1871.

Edward started a night school at St Philip's Church with his brother Bob and then in 1872, became superintendent of the Sunday School of St Anne's, South Lambeth. The turning point in Edward's life and work took place in 1880, when two brothers who regularly attended the Sunday school stopped coming. They were later found begging for food at a nearby gasworks. When Edward investigated further, he found that the boys' father had died, leaving seven children, but their mother would not go into the workhouse, so the two boys had to look out for themselves.[17]

Rudolf, a Church of England man through and through, was troubled that the only place that would take the brothers free of charge was a non-denominational home run by Thomas Barnardo; all the homes run by the Anglican Church required payment. Rudolf's time had come. Unlike Thomas Barnardo, who leapt into action when he saw a need and then dealt with the fallout afterwards, Edward Rudolf took a measured approach to his idea for a specific Church of England charity for destitute children, spending a year or so sounding people out, especially within the hierarchy of the Church. This paid off and the Archbishop of Canterbury agreed to be president of what was initially called the Church of England Central Home for Waifs and Strays. In 1893, its name changed to the Church of England Incorporated Society for Providing Homes for Waifs and Strays and in 1946 it was renamed the Church of England Children's Society. From 1982, it was called The Children's Society, as it is known today.[18] Things moved fast – the society rented and furnished a house in East Dulwich – an early example of a cottage home – opening its doors to children in early 1882. The charity rapidly expanded in terms of income, numbers of children accepted and the opening of new homes. It took over many privately run homes, including Mrs Brandreth's in Dickleburgh. Rudolf confirmed in evidence to the Mundella Committee in 1895, that the society was 'not merely a philanthropic institution, but distinctly a religious mission'. Christian instruction was a key element of life in the society's homes, and the Church of England network, with clergy and parishes across the country, proved invaluable in the promotion and growth of the society's work.

Most children's charities in the nineteenth century started by providing basic residential care, perhaps in a rented house or cottage, although some also established grouped cottage homes or larger institutional homes. The Waifs and Strays Society mainly used small cottage homes with perhaps up to thirty children in each, supervised by a matron and assistant matron or by a married couple in the boys' homes. The children usually attended the local school and church, but still much of their time was spent in the home, subject to a strict routine, including household chores, as this female former resident recalls: 'We all had our particular jobs to do. We were told, over and over again, that if we wanted anything in life we must work for it, and we accepted it.'[19] Some homes seemed more like poor law institutions, with strict discipline and even cruelty as this man recalled decades later about his childhood in a society home in Dover at the beginning of the twentieth century: '"Call *me* mother now!" That instruction still lingers in my memory. She and her husband were anything but mum and dad. They ruled by and seemed to delight in the use of strap and cane.'[20]

There were good times in the homes too though with lots of fun and presents at Christmas as well as occasional breaks from routine and day outings, as this memory of life in a children's home in 1910 shows – although the Liverpool trip sounds a rather strange choice for an outing for children:

We were allowed to stay up late to watch Halley's Comet pass in the sky… we had a very good view too, as the night was very clear. We were told to look very carefully as we probably should not see it again… . We had some nice outings, two which I remember were once to a cinema and another to see a convict ship at her berth in Liverpool.[21]

Inevitably, there were good and bad experiences of life in children's homes in the nineteenth and early twentieth centuries; much depended on those in charge of the home and the ethos of the charity that ran it, as well as the child's individual character and experiences before coming into care. Writing in 1971, Stroud quotes from one woman formerly in care who realised that even for children living with their families, life could be bleak:

My life, compared with present-day standards, was tough and well-disciplined but we had kindness, cleanliness and wholesome food, and a good Christian upbringing which has sustained us through hard times and for which I thank God. We attended the Church of England school so we met outside children who in many ways were far worse off than us. In fact we were envied by many as there was great poverty in those days.[22]

In contrast to the small cottage homes of the Waifs and Strays Society, Barnardo operated boys' homes more like the poor law barrack schools. In 1895, he reported to the Mundella Committee that there were 395 children in Stepney Causeway, 420 in Leopold House, 110 in Shepherd's Fold and the same number in Jersey House, as well 100 in the babies' home. In the 1860s and 1870s, some charities, as well as the poor law unions, established grouped homes based on the family system, with the children housed in small groups, usually ten to thirty, in separate cottages grouped together, often forming a self-contained village with all necessary services on site. At its peak, Barnardo's Village Home for Orphan, Destitute and Neglected Girls at Barkingside in Essex could take around 1,500 girls. Princess Mary's Village Home for Girls at Addlestone in Surrey opened in 1872, intended for girls with criminal mothers, those in danger of drifting into crime and female pauper children. When completed, it had capacity for 200 girls. Mouat and Bowley described the arrangements in their 1878 report:

The unit adopted for the family is 10.... . Each little household is complete in itself, with its general living room, its dormitory or dormitories, its kitchen, larder, and suitable out-offices.

Each is ruled over by a house mother, assisted by one of the elder girls; and all the ordinary household duties naturally involved in the charge of a family of 10 children are discharged by them. Every child as it advances in age and becomes fitted for the work, takes a part in the management of the household, and in the care and training of the younger children.

Thomas Bowman Stephenson established the Bonner Road children's home in Bethnal Green after the home outgrew its original premises in

Lambeth. Originally called the National Children's Home, the charity is now known as Action for Children. The Bonner Road home was run as a grouped homes complex and was housed in four ordinary terraced houses along the street, with playgrounds, schools, kitchen, laundry, chapel, swimming pool, industrial workshops and additional accommodation added at the back, in what had originally been a stone yard. By the time the home moved to purpose-built premises in Harpenden in 1913, it housed over 300 children. In 1878, Mouat and Bowley reported on the home:

> A distinguishing figure of this school as compared with the other institutions alluded to in this report is, that children of both sexes are admitted, and that while occupying separate houses, and being employed on different industrial pursuits, boys and girls receive school instruction together, and mix to a certain extent in the play-grounds.
>
> The boys' houses are in charge of a matron and two young men as assistants, the girls' houses are superintended by a matron and an assistant 'sister'. The children sleep and take all their meals in their respective houses, where also playrooms are provided for them. The meals are not cooked in the houses but in the general kitchen.

Like the larger poor law institutions, most of the charities aimed to provide some form of training for the children in their care – domestic work for the girls and a range of trades for the boys such as tailoring and bootmaking. Barnardo took this a step further, providing paid work for older boys while they were in his care, or accommodation for poor boys who were working but unable to find cheap lodgings. The first of Barnardo's commercial ventures was the wood-chopping brigade that he set up at the East End mission; others that followed included the shoeblack brigade and the city messenger service. In 1895, Barnardo explained to the Mundella Committee that although his Stepney home was large, he considered it was a 'modified illustration of the barrack system' because of the freedom the boys enjoyed through regular sports activities in public parks and the provision of a range of workshops at the home. He stated:

These industries bring my boys in constant touch with the public, and there are perhaps at least 100 of the boys always in and out of the streets, and in the city on messages, and these are regularly changed, and another 100 is selected … and there is also a great flow of the public through the institutions, and doors are always open and leave is given frequently.

The Waifs and Strays Society provided several industrial training homes for children, such as the home at Frome in Somerset where the boys produced most of the society's printing in its workshop. St Chad's Home at Far Headingly near Leeds provided factory-type training and work in its machine-knitting workshop for girls over school age who were unfit for domestic service, usually because of a physical disability. This was a commercial enterprise, selling knitted hosiery across the country, ranging from high quality silk and cashmere ladies' stockings to coarse socks for the inmates of reformatories, industrial schools and workhouses. The August 1890 edition of *Our Waifs and Strays* magazine, describes the work:

There are twenty girls at work… . There are nine machines under competent control. Each machine in busy hands can turn out seven pairs of stockings a day. The stockings are commenced and chiefly made by machine, and are then taken to the finishing-room to be 'toed', and finished by hand. Thence they go on to the pressers, who place them on blocks, and fit them, by means of heavy irons, into shape. Then they are paired and carded, and passed on to the forewoman for examination. The 'finishing' is so neatly done that it is difficult to say where machine work ends and hand work begins.

Several children were sent to St Chad's from Dickleburgh, including Rose and Esther Oakes. Esther was rather slow and dull and Rose had lost all her toes due to frostbite before she came to Rose Cottage. Esther, like her older sister Emma, went into service eventually, but the 1911 census shows Rose was boarding in a house in Ashtead, Surrey and working from home as a self-employed stocking knitter.

Nineteenth century children's charities were particularly concerned about children they believed were living in immoral surroundings or under criminal influences. There were fears that girls would become prostitutes and perhaps have illegitimate babies and that boys would turn to crime and drink. The charities were also anxious that such children might influence and taint the more respectable children in their care. The Waifs and Strays Society established several certified industrial schools for girls, some very young, who had been rescued from 'immoral surroundings' in the hope that they would be reformed through care and training. Boys might be sent to the Standon Farm School, a certified industrial school in Staffordshire. The charities identified many children requiring rescue, such as W. J. N. who was described in the February 1885 edition of *Our Waifs and Strays,* as 'Boy aged 4 years, illegitimate. Mother leads an immoral life. A case for rescue from surroundings of the utmost depravity.' The society's 1890 annual report lists the accepted cases for that year, including, 'Lizzie L., 8, illegitimate … the mother was immoral and a drunkard; Lizzie has lived with her grandfather, being generally in the street till near midnight.' Another is 'William V.; father dead, mother leads an immoral life; the boy has lived with his grandmother, who sends him out to beg, and he will no doubt fall into crime if not rescued; an elder brother is now in a Reformatory.' Some charities opened residential homes for blind and deaf children or for those with physical or mental disabilities, such as the St Nicholas Home for Crippled Children, opened by the Waifs and Strays Society in 1888. Many voluntary organisations turned to other forms of childcare as well as children's homes, such as boarding out, adoption and emigration, which will be covered in later chapters.

Finance was an issue for most of the children's charities, with occasional or even ongoing crises when there were insufficient funds available to maintain the numbers of children in their care. This could be a particular problem for Thomas Barnardo, who vowed never to turn away a destitute child, but the Waifs and Strays Society, which operated a more restrictive admissions policy, was not immune and had one such crisis in 1885, which the editor reported in the September issue of *Our Waifs and Strays*: 'The present receipts for General Purposes have for some time been insufficient for us to continue the payments for all the children who have been boarded out in our villages, and placed in other Church Homes, and at the same time to maintain our existing Homes.'

The society's governing body decided to withdraw some children from foster parents and other institutions but hoped that some could be taken into the society's own homes in England or could be emigrated to Canada. Without further funds, though, it was feared some children would be withdrawn from the society's care completely.

Subscriptions and private donations, in money or in goods or services, together with fundraising events, were the main source of income for most children's charities, although those that operated as certified industrial schools and homes received funding for children sent to their establishments by the courts or the poor law unions. The Waifs and Strays Society raised some funds from the sale of goods and services, such as 'Chutnee (real Indian)', text and bookmarkers, and knitted hosiery from St Chad's, and 'ear-trumpets (improved)' available from Pershore in Worcestershire. They also sold an interesting range of items from the Beckett Home at Meanwood, including matrons' caps and aprons, and sweets named 'Beckett Home Delight' and 'Meanwood Rock'.[23] George Müller was a rarity in relying on the power of prayer to attract financial and other support for his children's homes; most other charities had persistent and often inventive ways of promoting themselves and attracting funds and support. Barnardo was perhaps ahead of his time, producing 'before and after' admission photographs of the children for publicity to attract funds, though he was accused later of doctoring the 'before' photos to show the children in the worst possible light.

Many of the poor law children who came into the care of Mrs Brandreth's charity in Dickleburgh in its early days were partly funded by the relevant poor law union and partly by private subscription. According to the children's case files, most of the private subscriptions, usually 1s 6d a week for each child to match the 3s 6d offered by the poor law union, came from either personal friends of Mrs Brandreth, female members of the local gentry and landowning families, or the female relatives of the local clergy. More unusually, the 1s 6d weekly top-up funding for Leonora Sampson was collected 'in pence' from local children by Mrs Brandreth's daughter, Rosalind, who was then aged about 16. Occasionally Mrs Brandreth had to do some juggling to keep the finances straight. When a placement for Esther Burrell did not work out and Esther returned to the home in Dickleburgh, Mrs Brandreth not only had to persuade the guardians to restart their allowance, but also had to make arrangements to cover the private subscription of 1s 6d which had already been allocated to another child.

The Society of Waifs and Strays used its supporters' magazine, *Our Waifs and Strays*, to promote its work, to attract funds and to thank its donors and subscribers. Most issues contained requests for financial support for individual children, playing on the emotions of their readers, such as this entry from July 1888, requesting five shillings a week:

> To board out or place in one of our Homes, George W. C., aged eight, illegitimate; father unknown; 'mother has hitherto succeeded in paying for the child out of her wages as domestic servant, but trouble has destroyed her reason, and she is now in an asylum, apparently dying'.

There were numerous pleas for items for the homes, such as this courteous request from Mrs Brandreth in August 1890: 'We find that our children have so many kind friends willing to help them, that we venture to suggest that our scarlet blankets, many of which have been in use at Rose Cottage for fifteen years, are quite worn out, and we shall be thankful for a fresh supply before winter.' The same month, St Chad's Home needed funds to buy a large second-hand cupboard from a local joiner: 'The girls have had many gifts of books, and some of them are very fond of reading, but so far there has been no place to store them.' The range of gifts and the variety of donors, including children, are reflected in the lists in each edition of the magazine. In June 1884, the Harrow home recorded the following donations: 'Mrs Longley Mills, jam; Frank, Maurice, Anthony and Esther Barker, cakes; Mrs Ruault, buns; Mrs Stewart, books; Sunday-school children, clothing.' Gifts donated to the society's homes in 1884 and 1885 included a framed portrait of Queen Victoria, toys, books, skeins of wool, scripture pictures, cricket bats, a kettle, oranges, buns for Good Friday, bacon, vegetables, eggs, a daily supply of milk, seed potatoes, numerous parcels of clothing and underclothing, socks, quilts, pinafores, cuffs, hats and boots.

Local initiatives, such as bazaars, concerts, plays, drawing room meetings, sales of work, game stalls, special church services and magic lantern shows also raised funds. Many events were supported by the great and the good of local society. The 'Patronesses' listed in an advertisement for a bazaar to be held on 12 December 1885 in Nottingham in aid of the Waifs and Strays Society included one duchess, two countesses, two viscountesses and four other titled ladies. In October 1885, the magazine provided 'A Few Hints to Bazaar Holders', offering loans to set up such events and advising that 'the *best season for Bazaars just now is* BEFORE CHRISTMAS, when many people would go to get Christmas and New-Year presents who would not go later, and, indeed, could not afford it later; and the best time for Entertainments or Lectures would be *in the Christmas Holidays.*' Further suggestions included selling only one sort of thing on each stall, 'so as to have one stall say, for china, one for pin-cushions, one for clothes for poor people, one for dolls, etc: which makes far more show than mixed stalls and stall-holders.' Ever mindful of spreading the word as well as raising funds, the article suggested that 'Several gentlemen should be asked to take turns at taking the money at the door, and might have a packet of "Waifs and Strays" leaflets or Reports to give to each person on leaving.'

Most charities were established to help provide destitute children with residential care, boarding out, emigration, or often a combination of all three. However, two charities took different approaches, and in doing so, not only had significant influence on charitable work in the latter half of the nineteenth century, but also made a lasting contribution to the development of child welfare and protection. The Society for Organising Charitable Relief and Repressing Mendicity, known as the Charity Organisation Society (COS), was formed in 1869 and used a casework approach, targeting relief based on rigorous research into the nature of the problems facing those applying for help. It also aimed to bring together charitable organisations in London to work in tandem with the poor law authorities to create a more co-ordinated and efficient approach to relieving the poor. This sounds like the start of a modern and professional approach, as indeed it was, but the philosophy behind the organisation was rather different – the COS was described by one modern writer as 'professionally pioneering, but ideologically reactionary'.[24] The COS later established the first Citizens' Advice Bureaux and after changing its name to the Family Welfare Association in 1946 it was rebranded in 2008 as Family Action.

The COS supported the distinction between the deserving and the undeserving poor, and had no truck with the latter, considering that any help given to them would simply encourage fecklessness and dependency. It considered that such people were the responsibility of the poor law and should go into the workhouse. The COS was also in accord with the authorities that out-relief should be withdrawn, leaving charities to help the 'deserving poor' within the community. It aimed to help people return to independence and regain their self-respect, for instance by providing training and work tools to support employment. It was a harsh view, in line with the poor law, with self-help seen as a virtue, and reinforcing the prevailing view that poverty was a consequence of personal failing and not of economic and social conditions. The COS also took a high-handed view of morality and would only help those it regarded as morally upright. It was against indiscriminate almsgiving, and favoured loans rather than gifts, and so disapproved of charities such as The Salvation Army and Dr Barnardo's.

The COS provided the Waifs and Strays Society with information and sometimes advice on some of its cases, such as that of two sisters, Rachel, aged 9 and Emma, aged 7, whose father was dead, leaving their mother with seven children, which was highlighted in the July 1888 edition of *Our Waifs and Strays.* The Stepney COS committee reported:

> The father was a very respectable man; the widow had no trade but borrowed a machine from us and made a brave struggle to support the children, but her earnings are now only about six or seven shillings a week, and this with a shilling or two from her sisters constitutes her total income. The family has been such a respectable one that they shrink very much from throwing the children on the parish.

The case of Mary Varah who was resident in Rose Cottage in Dickleburgh shows another view of the COS. The Waifs and Strays Society requested references from the COS's Bethnal Green branch for Mary's mother, Mrs Berry, when she asked that Mary be allowed to return to the family home. According to Mary's Waifs and Strays case file, the COS had investigated the case in 1902, prior to her admission to the society and found it satisfactory. Surprisingly, the COS denied that they had recommended the case, in fact they stated they had a bad opinion of the mother and had suggested in 1902 that the guardians should take the children. The COS had clearly had no contact with the mother for many years but, with the help of the Waifs and Strays Society, they tracked her down to Clare Street in Bethnal Green. Their report described her circumstances and stated, with no supporting evidence, that they had never had a very good opinion of Mrs Berry, that she was untidy and not a very truthful woman. They also pointed out that William Berry was her third husband (she had been widowed twice by the age of 37). They felt the family lived in rather a rough street and suggested the society should itself try to get Mary apprenticed, as it would be better for her not to return to her mother's 'rather squalid house'. However, the Waifs and Strays Society did allow Mary to return home, having received other satisfactory references about her mother. This included one from a local lady who said that Mrs Berry 'seemed straightforward in what she said', adding that Mrs Berry was anxious to keep Mary at home for a month before getting her into a business to learn a trade. It seems Mrs Berry kept her word, as in 1911, Mary, aged 18, was employed as a book folder and was still working in the book trade when she married five years later.

The National Society for the Prevention of Cruelty to Children (NSPCC) has a long history not only of tackling child cruelty and bringing perpetrators to justice, but also of advocacy and campaigning for children's rights and protection. Although a society for the prevention of cruelty to animals was founded in England in 1824, becoming the Royal Society for the Prevention of Cruelty to Animals (RSPCA) some thirteen years later, it was over fifty years before a similar organisation to protect children was established. The Liverpool Society for the Prevention of Cruelty to Children was formed in 1883 and a similar society started in London the following year, as described in the January 1885 edition of *Our Waifs and Strays*:

On October 27 the Society for preventing Cruelty to Children opened a Shelter in Harpur Street, on the north of Theobald's Road, near Queen's Square. To this Shelter any children found homeless can be taken, and ill-used children can be here protected and cared for while their cases are under investigation. The Society, which was inaugurated in July ... may now be considered in full working order. But in these past three months it has not been idle. Over 150 cases have been brought before it: 36 of starvation, 51 of desertion, 14 of the infliction of wanton suffering and 51 others which it is difficult to describe. The Society invites everyone to co-operate in the work by contributing information, or giving time to investigate any cases. It is only by the united and persistent efforts of all that cruelty to children can be suppressed.

By 1889, thirty-one towns and cities had formed similar societies and in May that year, the London society combined with several others to form the NSPCC with Benjamin Waugh as its first director. Later that year, Parliament passed an Act for the Prevention of Cruelty to and Better Protection of Children. The NSPCC has been closely linked with the introduction of legislation to protect children from abuse and cruelty from the latter half of the nineteenth century.

Although many of the Dickleburgh children suffered some neglect and hardship prior to being taken into care, there were few examples of serious abuse, at least not that came to light on admission. One notable exception was the case of Isola Emms. Isola was physically disabled and had learning disabilities. After her mother died, her father remarried but six years later, when Isola was about 16, she was removed to a place of safety by the NSPCC because of severe physical abuse by her stepmother, Rebecca Emms. According to an undated news cutting on Isola's Waifs and Strays case file, the assaults included hitting her with her fist, holding her ears and twisting her round and round the table, shoving her against the copper, burning her arm and assaulting her with the buckle end of a strap. A witness heard the child being beaten in the house and someone saying, 'The sooner she is dead the better. She is worth more dead than alive.' The witness had heard the defendant say the child was insured and Inspector Starke of the NSPCC confirmed that he had seen a policy from the Prudential Assurance Company in the house. In 1893, Rebecca Emms was convicted of five counts of assaulting Isola and was sent to prison for twelve weeks, with hard labour.

The NSPCC was involved in several other Waifs and Strays Society cases of either neglect or abuse over the years, such as that noted in the society's annual report of 1893, concerning 9-year-old Esther from Castleford in Yorkshire, who was taken into the care of its cripples' home that year:

> Mother dead; the inspector of the Society for Prevention of Cruelty to Children found this child lying on a filthy bed, suffering from running wounds caused by hip disease. 'She was unable to wash herself, or her clothing which were mere rags.' There was but one bed in the house, upon which her father and an elder brother (in addition to herself) slept. The house was so filthy that the sanitary inspector caused it to be cleansed. For days during the winter, Esther had no fire, and but for the kindness of neighbours would have starved. The man was sentenced to a fine of 20/- with costs, or one month in prison … the father promises a small payment.

It is not clear from this entry in the accepted cases list what the father's circumstances were, other than that he had been widowed, but the comment about his promising a contribution to Esther's maintenance costs hints that this was a case of neglect caused by poverty and inability to cope, rather than deliberate abuse. The consequences for Esther, though, were still significant.

Charities and voluntary societies, both large and small, national and local, which were established in response to the plight of destitute, orphaned, neglected and abused children have had a significant and lasting impact on the way such children have been cared for over the past 150 years. At a simple, practical level, the establishment of numerous children's homes by charities and individuals across the country offered not only the opportunity to provide for more children but also an alternative, for some children at least, to the poor law institutions. Children in the voluntary societies' homes did not mix with adult paupers, unlike those housed in workhouses, where despite the rules of segregation it was virtually impossible for children not to encounter adult inmates. Although some charity-run children's homes might house as many children as the district schools, the aim of many charities, especially in the latter half of the nineteenth century, was to provide something more akin to family and community life through small individual cottage homes and boarding out, with the children attending the local school and mixing with other children in the community.

The charities were able to tap into a vast resource of philanthropic goodwill, especially amongst the ladies of the upper and middle classes, and the wives and female relatives of the clergy, who had the time and inclination to devote themselves to good works. Some of these women provided substantial financial support to the charities; others provided patronage, putting their names and influence behind the charity. Others – 'parish ladies' as Harriet Ward called them – formed a dedicated and effective volunteer force – organising fundraising events, encouraging subscriptions, referring children, visiting boarded-out children, acting as local secretaries and, in some cases, running children's homes and boarding-out committees.[25]

The voluntary sector also played a key role in the development of child welfare and protection policies in the nineteenth and early twentieth centuries, sharing good practice, giving evidence to many royal commissions and other enquiries and lobbying for changes to legislation. Several writers, including Derek Fraser and Harriet Ward, argue that the voluntary societies took a pioneering role in child welfare at this time and assert that the first seeds of professional social work could be seen in the work of the COS and some of the 'parish ladies'. Louisa Brandreth, who founded and managed two cottage homes and a boarding-out scheme in Dickleburgh, was a good example. The Waifs and Strays Society's case files and articles in the supporters' magazines indicate that not only was she an efficient administrator and case worker, but she treated the children under her care as individuals, with compassion and affection. She was perhaps not only a philanthropist but also what Ward would describe as a 'prototype for modern social workers'.[26]

Chapter 7

Family Life in Care –
Boarding Out and Adoption

We frequently find that children come down to us in a dazed condition. They do not seem to understand simple things of every-day life. It takes time to open their minds. The difference then becomes very great. There is a strange influence in 'our baby', or in 'our cat' or 'the cow which has to be seen in the meadow'. The child's brains seem to open, and his affections develop. The family ties are, I believe, of the greatest service.[1]

The Rev Frederick Green, Secretary of the
Denmead Boarding-Out Committee,1895

The establishment of grouped homes and small cottage or scattered homes, housing perhaps ten to twenty-five children in the charge of house parents or matrons, was an attempt to provide pauper children with care run on family lines, away from the harshness and taint of the workhouse or the size and anonymity of the district school. This was still institutional care though, run according to a strict regime and timetable, even though children usually received more individual attention than those in the larger institutions and many, especially those living in cottage homes, attended local schools. The main alternative, fostering (usually known as boarding out at this time), was a key feature of the Scottish poor law system, especially after the new poor law of 1845, but there was much slower take-up of fostering schemes by poor law authorities in England. Foster parents (or nurses as they were called in Scotland) were paid a weekly allowance for each child, sometimes with additional payments for clothing, school fees (prior to the introduction of free elementary education) and medical care.

There was a tradition of boarding out pauper children in Scotland in preference to institutional care even before the 1845 Poor Law

Amendment Act, which transferred administration of poor relief from the established Church of Scotland to lay parochial boards.[2] There were few poorhouses in rural areas under the old poor law so boarding out was a practical solution to the problem of deserted and orphaned children, but the system was also used in places that did have poorhouses such as Glasgow. In 1819, over 250 children were under the care of Town's Hospital in the city, of which only fifty-eight were resident; the remainder were boarded out.[3]

After the 1845 Act, which required parochial boards to appoint inspectors of poor, boarding out became increasingly popular in Scotland, especially with large urban parishes, as it was considered a cheaper option and better for the child than institutional care. The Act also created a central body to oversee the poor law system – the Board of Supervision for Scotland – but its powers were limited, and the parishes had a high degree of autonomy. George Greig, the inspector of poor for the City Parish in Edinburgh, explained in his 1864 report, quoted by Florence Davenport-Hill, that about eighteen years earlier the parish had started to board out its children in the country, 'where they might have the physical advantage of the country air, as well as the moral one of being separated from bad associates, and brought into contact with people of good character.' Greig stated that the children were boarded with 'cottagers, farm-servants, or tradespeople', supervised and visited regularly by the assistant inspector, and annually by the inspector or members of the Edinburgh parochial board. Greig stated:

> Preference is given to people of character who have a steady income apart from the allowance for the board of the children, and who will receive and treat them exactly as members of their own family; and it is found that when the children are sent out young, they learn to call the parties to whom they are sent father and mother. They acquire towards them the feelings of children, and the result generally is that the nurses acquire for them a parental affection.

Increasing concerns about the influence of parents on their own children when resident in the poorhouse led some Scottish parochial boards to separate pauper children from parents whom they deemed unfit, and board them out as in the same way as deserted and orphaned children, often many miles away. There were restrictions on the practice, however; for example, parochial boards had to ask permission of the parent to board the child and the parishes were not permitted to keep the child if its parents requested its return. Parishes were particularly concerned about illegitimate children as the inspector of poor in Paisley, Mr James Brown, stated in 1869:

> We do not like to separate the mother from the child; we keep such cases (there are but few of them) in the poorhouse until we despair of the mother doing any good in the way of supporting herself and the child; when once we are satisfied that that is hopeless, we then ask permission of the mother for her children to be sent out into the country, she herself remaining in the house.[4]

In the early 1850s, the Board of Supervision for Scotland raised concerns about the practice of boarding out after details of a case of neglect and inadequate supervision surfaced, but concluded that even though there might be occasional cases of neglect or mismanagement, 'in the vast majority of cases, the children appear to be treated with kindness, and often with tenderness.'[5] Significantly, given its aim to break the cycle of pauperism, the board added that by becoming members of the family and placed in a similar position to that of the children of independent labourers, boarded-out children were 'speedily absorbed and lost sight of in the mass of the labouring population in which they have been brought up, to take their place naturally, and … side by side with the members of the family in which they have been reared.'

Parishes in England and, after 1834, poor law unions, might resolve the issue of their pauper children by binding them as apprentices to tradesmen, or to mill or colliery owners in the industrial parts of the country. Those sent to the mills and mines were often housed together in 'apprentice houses', but those apprenticed to tradesmen, whether local or from further afield, would usually board with their masters or mistresses. Although there were some exceptional masters, such as Robert Owen at New Lanark in Scotland, all apprentices were expected to work, sometimes from a very young age. Many were neglected and abused and some died. Some fictional examples can be found in the literature of the time. In his epic poem of 1810, *The Borough,* George Crabbe recounts the story of Peter Grimes, the drunken and lawless Suffolk fisherman who wanted an apprentice:

> He wished for one to trouble and control;
> He wanted some obedient boy to stand
> And bear the blow of his outrageous hand;
> And hoped to find in some propitious hour
> A feeling creature subject to his power.
>
> Peter had heard there were in London then —
> Still have they being! — workhouse-clearing men,
> Who, undisturbed by feelings just or kind,
> Would parish boys to needy tradesmen bind;
> They in their want a trifling sum would take,
> And toiling slaves of piteous orphans make.

Despite warnings, Peter Grimes took on three apprentices – the first was found dead in his bed, the second fell from the mast and the third died at sea when Grimes sailed for London. In Charles Dickens' novel, Oliver Twist was apprenticed to Mr Sowerberry, an undertaker, and on his first night, after giving him some 'coarse broken victuals' which had been left for 'Trip' (presumably the dog), Mrs Sowerberry showed him where he was to sleep: 'Your bed's under the counter. You don't mind sleeping among the coffins, I suppose? But it doesn't much matter whether you do or don't, for you can't sleep anywhere else.'

Under Gilbert's Act of 1782, 'all infant Children of tender Years, and who, from Accident or Misfortune, shall become chargeable to the Parish' should either be admitted to the poorhouse or boarded out with 'some reputable person or persons' in or near the child's place of settlement, for an agreed weekly allowance, until they were of an age to be apprenticed or placed in service. The Act also encouraged relations or 'any other responsible person' to foster these children. However, Dorothy Wordsworth, the sister of poet William, indicated that the parish children in Grasmere in Westmorland were often boarded out to the lowest bidders, who were probably least able to care for them properly, adding that sometimes these children 'are hardly used, and sometimes all moral and religious instruction is utterly neglected.'[6]

However, there were examples of boarding out being used as a more genuine form of child welfare in England in the eighteenth and early nineteenth centuries. Both Christ's Hospital and the Foundling Hospital fostered babies and young children away from the main institution until they returned to start their main education and training in the hospital itself. There were also communities or individuals who took destitute children into their homes, either to avoid them going into the workhouse or to provide better care than the parish could afford. In March 1808, eight children under the age of 16 were orphaned when their parents, George and Sarah Green, died on the fells above Grasmere trying to return to their cottage after spending a day at a country sale in Langdale.[7] The two oldest girls were already working, and one of the younger boys was taken in by a relative, leaving five destitute children to the care of the parish. Perhaps influenced by their misgivings about the boarding out of pauper children in the parish, the Wordsworths determined to raise money to supplement the two shillings a week allowed by the parish for each of the five younger children to ensure that they were placed in respectable homes, supplied with good clothing, were properly schooled and placed in service or apprenticed. Just over £500 was raised for the children and a local committee formed to manage the funds and supervise the fostering arrangements. When the youngest child, Hannah, came of age in 1828, the trust had spent nearly £400 on the children's care over twenty years, but prudent investment meant that there was still over £500 in the accounts, so each child was given a lump sum of £60. Community care at its best!

According to a memoir of her life, Kitty Wilkinson of Liverpool, who is remembered primarily as the originator of baths and wash-houses for the poor, was apprenticed as a child in a cotton mill in Lancashire, although she had a happy enough childhood living in the apprentice house.[8] She started to take in foster children in the 1820s after a neighbour whom she nursed died, leaving four children orphaned and homeless. At various times over the next twelve years or so (the *Memoir* ends in 1835),

Kitty took in at least another fourteen children, ranging from babies to teenagers. She nursed the babies, arranged for apprenticeships and work placements for the older children, negotiated with parents, and juggled the household budget, at the same time caring for her own family, including her own blind and 'deranged' mother for some years.

A few enlightened individuals and poor law unions experimented with boarding-out schemes in England from the 1840s, such as Warminster in about 1849, Sandbach about 1852 and Ringwood about 1857. The Rev J. Armitstead, the local vicar, started the Sandbach scheme, 'taking pauper orphans by two or three at a time from the workhouse, and placing them with respectable dames in their own district: the dames being under the superintendence of the clergyman, the guardians and the relieving officer.'[9] Rev Armitstead emphasised the emotional benefits of foster care:

> Experience has proved that strong domestic attachments arise out of such relations. The well-selected household guardian usually becomes a lasting friend. The child dressed in no workhouse clothes, and its relation to the workhouse almost unknown to itself, goes to the national school, in due time goes out to work with a fair chance of getting good situations, and when out of work, the orphan girl knows where to find a chimney-corner where she may look for a welcome.

In 1861, Mrs Hannah Archer, the wife of the chairman of the Highworth and Swindon Board of Guardians in Wiltshire, published a pamphlet entitled *A Scheme for Befriending Orphan Pauper Girls*. Extensive extracts were published in *The Englishwoman's Review* some five years later.[10] Hannah wrote of the orphaned girls in the workhouses:

> Theirs is a dull life from year to year, without a ray of hope to brighten up their prospects. They have nothing in the world to cling to. The Workhouse schoolmistress can not do a mother's part to the many little girls of all ages, from three to fourteen, placed under her charge. The thing is impossible. She can teach them all to read and work; she can keep them clean and make them orderly in their conduct; but to sympathise with them, to respond to the

wistful look of those who feel their desolation, to soothe them in their sorrow – holding out a hope of happier days in store – this she cannot do. She can be gentle with them, as a shepherd with a flock of lambs; but they are to her as a mass of human life, and one rule must answer for all.

Her solution was to invite the 'Gentlewomen of the Church of England' to organise themselves into local committees 'for the purpose of befriending ... and taking the oversight of' workhouse girls, liaising with the poor law guardians to place them with 'trustworthy cottagers' in their own unions, with the children attending local elementary schools. She believed that under the care of foster parents and 'living in a well-ordered domestic circle', the orphan girls would learn 'the home duties so necessary in a girl's education' and have 'the opportunity of gaining a proper knowledge of life before being thrown on their own resources', as well as acquiring friends along the way. Although Mrs Archer may have had a rather rose-tinted view of the lives of the labouring poor, her idea of voluntary committees, including some parish ladies, liaising with the poor law authorities to arrange foster care for pauper children was the route followed in England after 1870.

In 1869, the English Poor Law Board commissioned one of its inspectors, J. J. Henley, to investigate the Scottish system of boarding out of pauper children, with a view to deciding whether to adopt a similar system in England. Despite having some difficulty in understanding and being understood because of the 'want of a common dialect' and the short period of time available to him, Henley carried out extensive research in Scotland, visiting parochial officials, poorhouses, schools and foster homes and interviewing a range of people involved in the care of pauper children. Henley's report, published in 1870, contains a wealth of detail about individual children and foster parents as well as a careful critique of how the system worked in Scotland, with the warning that, 'Those who are not well acquainted with the different habits and modes of life in the working classes of both countries must be careful not to draw a too hasty conclusion that what is good in one country must necessarily be so in the other.'[11] He presented a balanced view, quoting from those who objected to the boarding-out system as well as those who favoured it. Objections often focused on the morals and habits of the children from the urban poorhouses and the perceived detrimental effect on the country communities that received the children.

Henley emphasised that the selection of suitable foster parents was the key to the success of the Scottish system, stating that, 'The house of the crofter with his bit of land and cow is the best place for a child.' He carefully observed the children's attitude towards their foster parents or nurses as they were termed in Scotland: 'The younger children seemed to rush to them as their protectors. They often called the nurse "mother", and when school was over the children hastened home, and entered without fear.' Some foster mothers worked hard to reverse the effects of the poorhouse on the children. Mrs Ellen Kay, a widow from Lockar Briggs, near Dumfries stated that the three girls she was fostering had been in the Dumfries poorhouse 'awhiles': 'When the bairns came to me from the poorhouse their heads were full of beasts and muckle scabs, a kind o'scurvy like over their heads and bodies; I wrought on with them the whole summer with sulphur, saltpetre, and Harrogate salts, and brought them out of it.' Henley confirmed the treatment was successful as the children were healthy when he visited them, though whether the children appreciated it is a different matter.

Henley was also generally impressed by the commitment of the foster parents in sending the children to school. While visiting in the Aberdeenshire countryside, he was told that all the boarded-out children had gone to school, despite deep snow:

> I followed the track of one little girl who had gone to a school one-and-a-half or two miles distant; her route was across country, and as I followed her steps over the stone walls, under which the snow was drifted, I reflected that this was not bad training for a life of labour.

However, he did have some concerns about the level of supervision of children boarded out in remote areas, where the paid inspectors might only visit infrequently. He gave an example of a 70-year-old foster mother on parish relief who was out when Henley visited, leaving her 2-year-old foster child in the charge of a young woman who, by her own account, lived at an infamous house:

The old woman's one room is very high up a narrow corkscrew staircase, is about seven feet square, with one window that will not open. The room at the time of visit was in disorder and very dirty. The only bed was on the floor with very dirty coverings. The child was behind the door playing with a filthy cinder pail, and was a mass of black.

In November 1870, following Henley's report into the Scottish boarding-out system, the English Poor Law Board issued a Boarding-Out Order which allowed English unions to board children outside the boundaries of their own unions under the care of voluntary certified committees.[12] Only orphaned and, with some caveats, deserted children could be boarded out, and the order and accompanying explanatory letter stipulated various conditions, including regular visits to the children by members of the committee and quarterly reports on each child from the local school teacher. To ensure the boarded-out children did not stand out, they were to be provided with 'good ordinary clothing' and 'anything resembling a "workhouse uniform" should be most carefully avoided.' Further regulatory orders followed and in 1885, the LGB appointed an inspector, Miss Marianne Mason, to inspect and supervise the work of these out-of-union boarding-out committees.

In the 1870s, the issue of baby farming came to a head with the trial of sisters Margaret Waters and Sarah Ellis. These women, and many more like them, advertised for babies and children, either to foster or to care for while their mothers went out to work, in either case money was paid over to the women. In many cases, the children were neglected and often died; indeed, many of the mothers were aware that was what would happen. It was often a 'no questions asked' way of getting rid of an unwanted child, or one they simply could not care for. Ten children were found in the care of Waters and Ellis, of which about half were severely neglected, and four of the youngest died shortly afterwards. Waters was executed for murder in 1870 and Ellis was convicted of accepting money under false pretences and sentenced to eighteen months in prison. Following a select committee report, the Act for the Better Protection of Infant Life was passed in 1872, requiring professional foster mothers to register with the local authority. In addition, notice had to be given to the coroner of the death of any child who was in the care of such foster parents, usually followed by an inquest. Other legislation followed, including an Act in 1897 that gave greater powers of inspection and raised the age of children subject to protection from 1 to 5 years.

In her report in the LGB annual report for 1891–92, Miss Mason, the inspector for boarded-out children stated:

> Boarding out is, according to my experience, if well carried out, the best of systems, and if badly, the worst ... and I sometimes find scandalous cases of ill-treatment, neglect and cruelty... . The guarantee for the system lies, not in the absence of such cases, but in the fact that they will be discovered and reported.

Marianne Mason took her duties supervising the supervisors very seriously, travelling the country visiting foster homes, seeing the boarded-out children at home or at school and meeting the committees, often taking committee members out with her on her visits, to show them how to check the children properly for signs of neglect or abuse. In the same report she explained her approach to inspecting the children:

> The feet are a better guide than anything else to the treatment of a child, for it is in the hollows of the ankles that strata of dirt accumulate most visibly; and having now seen some thousands of children's feet, I am generally able, by taking off one stocking, to tell the date of the last bath to a week, if it is only weeks since... . The removal of a stocking also often reveals broken chilblains, blisters, and sores, nails uncut, and broken below the quick, or growing into the foot. The neck, shoulders, and upper part of the arms also show dirt, bites, and marks of vermin, skin complaints and blows. Beating is generally begun on the upper part of the arms. I sometimes find bruises there, evidently made by sticks; and where this is the case I undress the child as much further as necessary. I have thus now and then found a child covered with bruises.

Miss Mason was an efficient and dedicated inspector, but she was also kind, compassionate and mindful that the boarding-out committees were made up of volunteers, reporting in 1892: 'It does not seem to me kind to report the deficiencies of persons voluntarily engaged in troublesome work without showing them how to improve.' Similarly, with the foster parents; when she found a child in clean condition during her inspection, she would record this 'to the foster parents' credit' and if she found 'dirt of months' standing [but with] no other trace of neglect or ill-treatment', she would work with the local committee to remedy the matter, 'because I draw a distinction between the dirt of mere ignorant custom and that of wilful neglect. It cannot therefore be said that I am unduly severe towards the foster parents, or that I do not make allowance for the habits of labouring people.' In her evidence to the Mundella Committee in 1895, Mason related in detail how she carried out her inspections in the various districts and then explained the key to the whole scheme, although the last sentence suggests there was some self-interest in her methods:

> The grease that moves the wheels of the whole department are these sugar mice; I give one to every child and ... [one] to every child in the same home where the boarded out children are, so as to make no difference.... . If the child ... is pleased, the foster-parent is pleased, and if the foster-parent is pleased, the committees are pleased ... and if the committees are pleased then they do not worry us with troublesome communications.

Mason may have been considerate in the way she treated all those involved in the scheme, but she would not allow excuses for poor management, particularly if it affected the welfare of a child. In 1891, the NSPCC successfully prosecuted Adam and Eliza Collins for cruelly ill-treating Jessie Bolton, a 4-year-old girl boarded out with them by the Bristol union. The case came to light when a neighbour heard terrible screaming coming from the Collins' house for over an hour, shortly after Jessie had been taken home by Eliza Collins. The child was subsequently removed and was discovered to have a wound on her left leg caused by a buckle, two wounds on her back, a large cut on her head that was bleeding, severe bruises on her legs and her right thumb was cut to the bone.[13] Adam Collins admitted tying the child to the bedstead by her thumbs and beating her with a stick, with his wife present, and the couple were imprisoned for three months and one month respectively, with hard labour. According to Miss Mason's report to the LGB in 1892, locals, including the curate in charge and a churchwarden, saw the couple as 'thoroughly trustworthy and respectable people, and eminently suitable to take charge of a boarded-out child' and 'thought Collins was one of the very last men to have been guilty of such cruelty'. The secretary of Axminster boarding-out committee stated, 'The matter seems to be one of those accidents which nobody can foresee, and which will occasionally occur in spite of all precautions.' Miss Mason disagreed, 'for the ill-treatment might easily have been discovered, if the child had been now and then partly undressed. Matters need never have come to this pass.' She added that subsequent to her removal from the Collins' house, Jessie's body, under her clothes, was found to be 'covered with weals and marks of ill-usage of various dates, which gave evidence that she must have been ill-treated not once, but continuously.'

Despite rigorous regulation in England, or perhaps because of it, the English poor law authorities never embraced the boarding-out system in the same way as the Scottish parochial boards, although it was a key feature of provision for several of the major voluntary societies in England, such as the Waifs and Strays Society and Dr Barnardo's. Children boarded out by the Waifs and Strays Society were supervised locally by a committee, or by the clergy or clergy wives such as Mrs Brandreth at Dickleburgh, but as fostering expanded, the society followed the lead of the LGB and appointed a female inspector to supervise the supervisors. Miss A. L. Lee seemed even more formidable than the LGB's inspector Miss Mason, and a little less forgiving about dirt. Writing in the society's magazine, *Our Waifs and Strays*, in May 1892, she said about boarded-out children:

Frequently they are kept for week after week, and for month after month, unwashed, with the exception of the hands and face. For months together the underclothing is left ragged and dirty, and unrenewed; constantly it is seriously deficient in quality and quantity. Boots are worn which are too small, too tight, and too short; the feet are consequently cramped and injured, and sometimes permanently misshapen. Often the children are infected with vermin, more especially in the hair.

Miss Lee was concerned, like Miss Mason, that the supervisors did not inspect the children thoroughly enough:

> Clean pinafores are sometimes put on a child when the ladies are expected to visit. I saw one woman thus preparing a very dirty child for a visit.
>   'Won't you wash the child?' I said... .
>   'A pinafore,' she answered, whilst tying it on, 'covers a deal of dirt.'

Miss Lee stressed the need for the supervisors to educate the foster parents in the care of the children, suggesting that presents 'such as brushes, toothcombs, tubs, towels, sponges, nail-scissors etc will offer some inducement to carefulness and cleanliness.' Miss Lee was not prepared to take the answers she was given at face value, so when she was assured by the child himself, the foster parent and the supervisor that the boy was washed every Saturday, she asked him, 'Why then is your neck so dirty? "It wasn't necks last Saturday," he said. "It was feet, and it's necks next Saturday."'

Both the poor law authorities and the charities looked for foster parents from the 'respectable' working class, excluding any who were in receipt of poor relief. Some boarding-out committees preferred married couples, while others were happy to board children with widows or single women. Committees usually judged each application to board children individually, but most avoided applicants who saw fostering primarily as a means of acquiring additional income.

Over forty-five couples or individuals have been identified through census returns and the Waifs and Strays Society case files as fostering children in the Norfolk village of Dickleburgh, or the neighbouring communities of Langmere and Shimpling, between 1881 and about 1912. Occupations included farmers and agricultural labourers, boot and shoemakers, wheelwright, grocer, butcher, newsagent and dressmaker. In 1911, two of the foster mothers were recorded as old age pensioners. The ages of the foster parents were equally varied; the youngest were Chester and Edith Bartrum, with Edith just 22 with an 8-month-old son when they fostered two boys from West Ham. Ten years later, the couple were still fostering, by then with two children of their own. At the other end of the age scale there were seven foster families where one or both parents were in their seventies or eighties. Joseph and Ann Baldwin fostered at least seven children over an eighteen-year period, and both were over 80 in 1911 when they were looking after 14-year-old Catherine Kemp, although their unmarried daughter Emily, in her forties, was also resident. The foster parents were mainly married couples, but there were at least nine widows and four single women. Eliza Fish was one of the most prolific foster carers. She was a single woman in her early fifties when she was first noted as taking in foster children and fostered at least eight girls over thirteen years.

In Dickleburgh, short-term foster care was occasionally provided for girls from Rose or Lee cottages either because of behaviour issues or illness – especially contagious illness – although it sometimes turned into a permanent arrangement. Robert and Mary Lacy, of the neighbouring hamlet of Langmere, took several such cases, including Frances Field, who had St Vitus' dance. Elizabeth Smith, a widow, looked after Winifred Price when she was suffering badly with ringworm, although as the Rose Cottage matron visited and some of the older girls took Winifred out for walks, perhaps she did not feel too isolated. Widow Sewell took in Agnes Sampson who was moved out of Rose Cottage because she was suffering from consumption; she later died at Widow Sewell's house.

Committees might move children to different foster homes within the community for a range of reasons, not only because of neglect or ill-treatment. Willie Bartram, who came under the Dickleburgh committee, had epilepsy and his foster mother, Mrs Cook, thought it undesirable to keep him with her little girl, so he and his brother were moved to a different home in the village with no other children resident. Percy Mallett did not get on with his foster mother's son, so was transferred from Mrs Chenery to her parents, Joseph and Ann Baldwin, still in Dickleburgh, an arrangement that seemed to suit everyone. However, within a few months, Percy was sent to the society's certified home in Frome, as he had missed twenty-two school attendances in one quarter and his foster parents were finding him 'very difficult to manage.'[14]

The correspondence files of the Depwade Poor Law Union Boarding out Committee give further insights into the fostering arrangements in Dickleburgh and the surrounding area and include communications with existing and potential foster parents as well as local supervisors.[15] In 1911, Mrs Osborne of Starston wrote requesting a little girl to board out as company for her own girl. She did not mind how old the child was, but made it clear she did not want a boy. Some three months earlier, she and her husband Charles had asked that a child boarding with them, James Alexander, be removed as he had been 'misconducting himself', so her unwillingness to take in another boy was understandable.

Sometimes there were disputes over maintenance payments. In early 1911, the Depwade Guardians threatened Mrs Rosanna Hubbard with legal action if she did not return a cheque for 13s 8d which the guardians had sent to her in error. Mrs Hubbard had cashed the cheque, assuming the money was to cover the cost of buying items for her foster child, who had just left her care. The clerk wrote back, 'You were of course perfectly aware that you were not entitled to the money and should have returned the cheque for correction', but Mrs Hubbard had clearly spent or committed the money and explained that it was impossible to return it that week as she 'had other Pays to make.' She hoped to pay it back the following week or as soon as she could. The clerk, perhaps trying to shift the blame for his own error, responded, 'Whatever other payments you may have to make it is certainly your first duty to return money which does not belong to you and which has come into your hands by mistake.' Three days later, Mrs Hubbard returned the money to the guardians, saying she was sorry to have kept them waiting.

There is detailed information available about boarding out in nineteenth and early twentieth century England in official reports and evidence provided to various enquiries, including examples of individual cases, good and bad, from across the country. Details can also be found amongst charity records and in any surviving records of local boarding-out committees, but there are few first-hand accounts of fostering by the children themselves, even after they reached adulthood. This may be, as Stroud suggests, because if fostering is successful, there is nothing much to say: 'The children, integrated into the families and merged into the life of the community, lead peaceful, uneventful, ordinary lives, dramatic only in the contrast with what might otherwise have happened to them.'[16] The few accounts that do exist provide examples of both good and bad experiences. A boy who was fostered in Devon between 1910 and 1918 had to walk three miles each way to school and was expected to be home by 5 pm, three quarters of an hour after finishing school. One day he stayed late in school and, arriving home five minutes late, was beaten with a horse whip.[17] By contrast, this Waifs and Strays girl enjoyed a contented childhood in Suffolk, attending the local school with her brother and singing in the church choir:

> We were taught to help in the house and all water had to be fetched from the village pump and milk from the dairy, lighting was by oil lamps, it was a truly rural life! As I look back I realise it was almost a normal childhood, our foster-mother was a wonderful person and although there were no luxuries there was much love.[18]

Stroud quotes a woman who in 1910 was taken in by 'a loving Christian foster-mother, Miss E. Edwards' who fostered nineteen children over time. She wrote, 'We were cared for and loved, often more than a real mother could do.'[19] Other reports showed how some children kept in touch with their foster parents after leaving care. Giving evidence to the Mundella Committee in 1895, the Rev Frederick Green, Vicar of Denmead in Hampshire, and secretary of its boarding-out committee stated that children turn to 'mother', not the workhouse, in time of difficulty and need or when they are unemployed out of situation. 'When in a situation, and a holiday is possible, again the old home is sought. We so often hear the remark, "So-and-So is coming for Easter" or "for Christmas" or "can manage to get here for a week in the summer."' Occasionally, the care or love of the foster child for the foster parent is mentioned. Donald Jefferson, an illegitimate child born in Norwich in 1902, was boarded out in Dickleburgh from a very young age with the widowed Mrs Kerridge and remained in the Dickleburgh area for most of his life. According to Donald's daughter, her parents cared for Mrs Kerridge until her death in 1931, aged 83.

Ernest Simmonds was boarded out by the Waifs and Strays Society in Carleton Rode, near Attleborough in Norfolk, when he was 6, because of the appalling conditions he was living in with his mother in Beccles in the neighbouring county of Suffolk. His mother tried to snatch him from the school playground a few years later but was thwarted by the rector's wife, who threatened her with the police. However, legally the mother was within her rights and the society reluctantly returned the child to her. His foster father, Henry Pegnall, a farmer, was very upset by the boy's removal, and was reported as saying that he 'loves the boy as if he were his own, & would gladly keep him for nothing if he could afford it.' The story had a happy ending, though. About a year later, Ernest was back living with his foster parents in Carleton Rode, and he was still boarding there eighteen years later, in 1911, then aged 27, working as a bricklayer, although his foster father, Henry, had died some three years earlier.

Boarding out, properly managed, could provide children with some form of family life and something approaching a normal childhood, but they were usually still under the care of the poor law union or a charity, and subject to official visits and inspections, however kindly they were carried out. Foster carers had no parental rights over the boarded-out children and the children were not legally part of the foster parents' family. Adoption offered a more radical solution to the issue of the deprived or unwanted child, with the adoptive parent or parents taking responsibility for the child on a permanent basis and the child becoming part of the family, at least in theory. However, Britain was slow to legislate for the adoption of children, so most adoptions prior to the 1930s were informal with little or no paperwork, and with no legal standing.

Guardians of the poor were able legally to adopt children in their care under certain conditions from 1889. Matilda Bruty of Clare in Suffolk was one of the Dickleburgh children in care who was adopted by the state. According to her Waifs and Strays case file, her mother, Elizabeth, deserted her children because of the 'naughty conduct' of Matilda's stepfather, Charles Balls. He was described as a quarrelsome man of intemperate habits and when he was drunk, he was 'a nuisance to all around him so not likely to get constant employment.' Matilda was resident in Kedington workhouse when the chaplain of the Risbridge union wrote on her application to the Waifs and Strays Society on 17 September 1896:

I consider this a case well worthy of recommendation. The influence of the child's father is so pernicious that it would be well that she should be removed altogether from his charge. The girl is one who will do her best to learn what is taught her & will no doubt make an excellent servant in time.

The following day the Risbridge Guardians formally adopted Matilda. It was probably just as well that they did – nothing more was heard of Matilda's mother and five years later, her stepfather and her youngest brother Arthur were in Kedington workhouse, possibly having been there for some years.

It was not until the 1926 Adoption of Children Act that general adoption was brought within a legal and regulatory framework in England and Wales. The legislation was permissive rather than mandatory, however, so informal adoptions continued until the 1930s, alongside those sanctioned through the courts. Children adopted informally were covered by any existing legislation, such as laws relating to murder and, from the 1870s, to infant life protection and cruelty to children. However, with no regulatory framework for adoption or formal vetting process for adoptive parents, there was no guarantee that any abuse would be identified. Another issue with private or informal adoptions was that adoptive parents had no rights to the child or recourse to the law if the birth parents came back to claim their child. Although there were probably many successful unofficial adoptions, the lack of legislation also opened the way to abuse, such as baby farming and the sale of babies for adoption.

Despite these issues, there were many informal adoptions prior to the 1930s, although research is hindered by the lack of formal records and the secrecy surrounding many adoptions, particularly if illegitimacy was involved, as it frequently was. However, poor law union records, census returns, and the records of charities can help to identify adopted children and sometimes provide details about their adoptions. Informal adoptions through family and friends have taken place for centuries, providing care for illegitimate, deserted or orphaned children related or known to them. Charles Aickman from King's Lynn in Norfolk was adopted by his uncle and aunt, Thomas and Jean Spurr, after the deaths of his parents. In

1881, Charles, aged 9, was living with the Spurr family in King's Lynn, described both as 'nephew' and 'adopted'. Edith Aickman, Charles's older sister, was taken into the care of another aunt, Lydia Preston, in Birstall in Yorkshire, although in the 1881 census she was described as 'niece' with no indication that she had been adopted. Charles' older brother, Fordyce Aickman, was baptised in Birstall in 1881 with his sister, Edith, so it seems likely that he too was in the care of his aunt Lydia, before he left for employment.

For poor law guardians and charities, informal adoption could be the ideal solution to the problem of how to care for destitute, orphaned and deserted children, as it relieved them of all financial, and sometimes welfare, responsibility for the child. Some family adoptions were facilitated through the guardians, as in the case of Harry and Leonard Leeder of Thelveton in Norfolk, the illegitimate twin sons of Kate Leeder. In 1901, the two boys, aged 5, were resident in the local workhouse, recorded as 'deserted' while their single mother, described as a domestic laundress, was boarding in Hampton, Middlesex with her 5-month-old daughter, Ethel, born in Surrey. It would seem Kate Leeder had 'fallen' twice, which was considered a great sin by society and the Church. Harry and Leonard were then taken in by their grandparents, William and Salome Leeder, who had had sixteen children of their own, and on 23 October 1909 William 'fully adopted' his grandchildren.[20] In 1911, the two boys, then aged 15, were still living in Thelveton with their grandparents; Harry was working as a house painter and Leonard as a farm labourer.

Arthur Garland, a farmer and cattle dealer from Dickleburgh, and his wife Charlotte adopted at least two children, Alberta Ford and Florence Garland. In 1881, Alberta was living in the village with the Garlands as their adopted child; twenty years later, Alberta's eldest son, George Murrell, aged 7, was living with or visiting Arthur and Charlotte Garland, described as 'grandson', suggesting that Alberta had been truly adopted by the Garlands. Fourteen-year-old Florence D. Garland, born in London, was also living with Arthur and Charlotte in 1901, described as their adopted daughter, but it is not clear whether Florence was related to the couple or whether she was a destitute child who took their name on adoption.

At least three children who came to Dickleburgh under the auspices of the Waifs and Strays Society were adopted after spending time in care in the village. Isabella Timperley's young parents from Hulme near Manchester died when she was less than 2 years old. She came to Dickleburgh from Withington workhouse schools in 1894 aged 8, moving to the Lowestoft home the following year when Lee Cottage in Dickleburgh closed. Isabella's Waifs and Strays case file records that in 1898, James and Maria Smith, a couple in their fifties from Lowestoft, offered to adopt her. The Smiths had lost their only daughter some years earlier. James was a railway labourer and his wife took in lodgers during the summer season. The vetting of the Smiths was quite thorough, including references and an unannounced visit by a member of the local Waifs and Strays committee who found the house 'clean & in order' adding that 'Mr and Mrs Smith looked respectable and kind'. The Waifs and Strays Society recommended that the Chorlton Guardians agree to the adoption, with Edward Rudolf writing, 'I think myself it is an exceptionally good offer.' This was echoed by a member of the Lowestoft committee who wrote, 'It seems like boarding out at exceptionally favourable circumstances & in this case without expense' and would make room for another 'unfortunate child'. In 1901, Isabella was still living with her adopted family, but within the space of three years all evidence of her origins had disappeared – she had taken her parents' name of Smith, was noted as their daughter, not adopted daughter, and her birthplace was given as Lowestoft, the same as the rest of the family, although she was born in Manchester.

There was also an example of a failed adoption. Esther Burrell, an illegitimate child from Aldeburgh in Suffolk, was admitted into the Wickham Market workhouse after her mother and grandparents died, before coming to Dickleburgh aged 9. When Esther was just 11, Mrs Brandreth sent her to a Mrs Ward of Asenby, near Thirsk in Yorkshire who had offered to adopt a child through the Waifs and Strays Society. Mrs Brandreth took up references for Mrs Ward from the local clergyman and said she had had 'satisfactory letters' from Mrs Ward herself. Esther was taken to Peterborough and then sent on to York, possibly on her own. Two months later the poor girl was returned like an unwanted package to the home at Dickleburgh. Apparently little Esther was unable to take charge of the house when Mrs Ward was ill in bed. Clearly Mrs Ward was looking for a servant, not a child to adopt. The matter was probably rather embarrassing for Mrs Brandreth as not only had she sent an 11-year-old girl over 200 miles to adoptive parents she had never met, but when Esther left the home, her funding ceased. She managed to sort everything out though, with a final comment on the matter to Edward Rudolf that Esther would be far better at the home than with Mrs Ward in Thirsk.

The stigma, shame and consequent secrecy attached to illegitimacy, as well as the limitations the child would bring on the mother's ability to earn her living, meant an unsupported single mother often had a stark choice between deserting her child, entering the workhouse or disposing of it in some way. Adoption might have seemed the most acceptable of these choices, but this often meant using the services of a baby farmer or even the mother trying to sell her own baby. Many cases of baby farming across the country were reported in the press long after the scandal of Margaret Waters, including the notorious case of Amelia Dyer who was charged with murdering a female child, whose body was found in the River Thames on 30 March 1896. *The Huddersfield Daily Chronicle* of 20 April reported on the police court case when the child's mother, Evelina Marnon, a single woman from Cheltenham, gave evidence as to how her daughter had been placed in Dyer's custody:

Correspondence took place through an agency after seeing an advertisement in a Bristol newspaper. Witness called herself Mrs Scott, and the female prisoner [Amelia Dyer] signed her letters Mrs Harding. In these communications 'Mrs Harding' discussed the terms upon which she would adopt the child. Ten pound was the sum agreed upon, and the writer spoke of her readiness to act the part of a mother to 'Dear little Doris'.

Mrs Harding [Dyer] collected the child from her mother and wrote reporting her safe arrival at her home in Reading. Miss Marnon later wrote asking how her daughter was, but received no reply, and did not see her again until she was shown her body in the mortuary. Miss Marnon identified the child's pelisse and other articles that were produced in court in a cardboard box.[21] Amelia Dyer was found guilty and was hanged at Newgate on 10 June that year.

Well into the twentieth century, newspapers carried private advertisements from people offering children for adoption as well as from those wishing to adopt. These three advertisements in the 'Miscellaneous Wants' column of *The Leeds and Yorkshire Mercury* of 27 October 1905 are typical, though rather bizarrely are followed by advertisements for cast-off clothing and old artificial teeth.

> Adoption – Would kind, motherly person Adopt healthy Baby Boy; no premium.
>
> Lady, no children, desires to ADOPT CHILD; good birth, premium.
>
> Lady desires to ADOPT BABY; moderate premium.

The 1926 Adoption Act unfortunately did not end the practice of baby farming. *The Scotsman* of 9 June 1928 reported the case of a council dustman, Edward Lamb, and his wife Emily, from Withernsea in Yorkshire who were convicted of neglecting four children aged between 11 months and 5 years, one of whom was unnamed and unregistered. The children were not related to Mr and Mrs Lamb and two of the children had come from local nursing homes, possibly mother and baby homes. The children were starved, and it was alleged that this was a case of baby farming. The Lambs' landlady, Mrs Challans, had clearly been duped into renting the property to them, believing them to be a respectable family with two children, until she called on them one day and found the house in a state and the four neglected children living in a room with the Lambs' adult son.[22]

Single mothers were also vulnerable to approaches from unscrupulous people offering to take the baby off their hands, promising them rich rewards, such as the case reported in the supplement to the *Manchester Courier and Lancashire General Advertiser* on 3 November 1883 when May Morley or Cross, aged 25, was charged with taking away 7-month-old George Geary, the child of single woman, Eliza Geary. George's mother had been tempted by Morley's promises of money and of continuing visits to George to hand him over for adoption by a rich, married lady who wanted to make him heir to all her property. Eliza handed over the child to the defendant at a London railway station though did have the foresight to get Morley to sign a paper that stated 'I, May Morley, receive this child from Eliza Geary to deliver up faithfully to the said lady, and that she shall in future hear from me.' Morley gave Eliza £5 and promised to pass on the adoptive mother's address. A few days later Eliza received a telegram from Morley reporting the safe arrival of the child and that a long letter would follow. Unsurprisingly, there was no 'rich married lady' and Eliza never heard from Morley again, but the police eventually traced her to Maidenhead where George Geary was found safe and well.

Adoption agencies began to appear towards the end of the nineteenth century, such as the oddly named Baby Exchange set up around 1890 by W. J. Stead, who advertised babies for adoption through *The Review of Reviews*, a journal he had co-founded.[23] Mrs Janet Ransome Wallis founded the Haven of Hope for Homeless Little Ones in 1893, later known as the Mission of Hope, a home for unmarried mothers and their children that specialised in adoptions, and by 1926, Mrs Ransome Wallis had arranged over 2,000 adoptions.[24] There was a large increase in the number of illegitimate births in England and Wales during the First World War and in the number of orphaned children, because of both the war and the Spanish influenza epidemic. The mortality rate of illegitimate infants was substantially higher than for children born in wedlock, so after the war there were growing concerns about the welfare of illegitimate children and their mothers. Organisations such as the newly formed National Children's Adoption Association, which operated a mother and baby hostel in Kensington and arranged many adoptions in the early 1920s, and the National Council for the Unmarried Mother and her Child (now the single parent family charity Gingerbread) started campaigning for adoption to be regulated by law. However, it took at least two committee reports and several failed attempts before the 1926 Adoption Act was passed. It was just the first step in regulating the adoption system, and gave full parental rights to adoptive parents, but only for those who chose to follow the formal route through the courts.

Fostering and adoption remain two key planks of the child welfare system today, but the journey towards full legally regulated systems was slow and, in the case of adoption particularly, marked by the secrecy and shame surrounding illegitimacy, even into the second half of the twentieth century. The Poor Law Board in England published its first regulatory order concerning boarding out by poor law unions in 1870, providing a partnership between local voluntary committees, poor law unions and the central poor law authority. Some charities, such as the Waifs and Strays Society, later adopted the regulations for their own use, so before the end of the nineteenth century, boarding out schemes in England and Wales were generally well-regulated and there was some consistency across the country, especially after the appointment of Miss Mason as the government inspector of boarded-out children. Unfortunately, both boarding out and adoption were tainted by the issue of baby farming; the lack of any regulation of adoption until 1926 enabled unscrupulous people openly to advertise for babies for adoption and allowed would-be adoptive parents to adopt a child with little or no consideration of their suitability. However, many of the informal family adoptions and those arranged through reputable children's charities or adoption agencies prior to the 1926 Act took the children out of the poor law system and gave them a chance of a normal family life, as well as offering a practical solution for unmarried mothers and childless couples.

Chapter 8

New Lives, A World Away – Child Migration

I am one of those emigrant boys that came to Canada in 1907 on the
White Star Line ... I was wondering how you got to even thinking
of such people as us. I thought we were long forgotten as we were
only Home boys and it didn't matter much about what happened to
us. We were of no importance.[1]

George Mackie, Pembroke, Ontario, c. 1970

Sending unaccompanied pauper children to far-flung parts of the
British Empire, such as South Africa, Canada, New Zealand
and Australia, was perhaps the most contentious of the different
methods of providing for destitute and orphaned children in the
nineteenth and twentieth centuries. Child migration schemes have existed
in various forms for around 350 years, although not used continuously
throughout that period, with the last unaccompanied child migrants sent
to Australia as late as 1967. The earliest known examples date from the
early seventeenth century but the practice appears to have declined by
the following century. In the first half of the nineteenth century, several
philanthropists established refuges for delinquent and vagrant children
in Britain, focusing on training and rehabilitation, with some of the
children emigrating, particularly to South Africa.[2] In 1869, Maria Rye's
scheme to emigrate pauper children, with Annie Macpherson starting a
similar scheme the following year, signalled the start of almost a century
of child migration, primarily to Canada and later to Australia, interrupted
only by the two world wars. The transportation of convicted juveniles
has been covered in chapter four and the evacuation of children during
the Second World War falls outside the scope of this book.

In 1618, the Virginia Company took a group of 100 street children –
orphaned or destitute – from London to Virginia in America as labour
for the plantation owners. Some were as young as 10. More went the

following year and in 1622, the Council for New England also asked the City of London for pauper children to be sent to them. These children were regarded as a nuisance, a burden on taxpayers and were even thought to be spreading the plague. Emigration seemed the perfect way of getting rid of them and providing labour for the colonies, although it is arguable how much use a 10-year-old child would be.

The Society for the Suppression of Juvenile Vagrancy, or as it later became known, the Children's Friend Society, was founded in 1830 by Edward Pelham Brenton, a retired Royal Navy captain. A social reformer, Brenton was greatly concerned about the treatment of juvenile delinquents and vagrants, especially the conditions and regime on board the hulk *Euryalus,* moored off Chatham, which was used as a floating juvenile prison. He stated, 'I denounce this system as atrociously extravagant, cruel and vindictive.'[3] He petitioned Parliament, requesting that convicted children of either sex under the age of 16 'may no longer be committed to the common prisons of the land, but be carefully guarded and educated and kindly disposed of, either at home or in colonies of His Majesty.'[4]

Brenton opened an asylum for vagrant boys and those on the periphery of crime, followed by a similar institution for girls. After a period of training, the children were apprenticed or employed, but Brenton soon turned to emigration as the solution. The first group of children was sent to the Cape of Good Hope in 1832 and by the following year, they were being sent to Australia and Canada too. The society was short-lived and closed a few years later. However, shortly before Brenton's death, his campaigning came to fruition with the opening of the first boys' prison, Parkhurst on the Isle of Wight, in 1838. Following training, nearly 1,500 'apprentices', as the inmates were called, were transported to Australia, Van Diemen's Land or New Zealand between 1842 and 1853, when juvenile transportation ended.

The Philanthropic Society was founded in 1788 to reform boys convicted of petty crimes. Initially opening a refuge in Southwark, London, the society then purchased a farm in Redhill, Surrey in 1849, which served as a rehabilitation centre where the boys learned farming skills. After the Reformatory School Act of 1854, many boys were sent directly to Redhill by the courts, where they were often trained in preparation for emigrating to the colonies.

After 1870, numerous charities, emigration agencies and poor law unions enthusiastically followed the lead of Maria Rye and Annie Macpherson by sending parties of pauper and street children across the Atlantic to Canada. In Canada, the children were often called – usually disparagingly – 'Home Children', as most had spent some time in an institution in Britain or in Canada. By this time in Britain, small charities and enlightened unions were already experimenting with more family-oriented schemes, such as boarding out and cottage homes, so child migration schemes seemed 'out of step' with more progressive thinking on the care of pauper children.[5] Emigration was particularly attractive to the poor law unions though, as once they had paid for the voyage and kitted out the children, they were relieved of all future responsibility, financial or otherwise, for those children. For both charities and unions, emigration provided a practical solution to the problem of the seemingly endless number of pauper children requiring care, by creating space for more destitute children to move into the workhouses, children's homes and foster homes. There was also the view that emigration to the wide open spaces of the young country of Canada would give the children a fresh start away from poverty and crime, which would be good for the nation as much as for the children themselves. This extract from a long poem entitled *The Departure of the Innocents* which appeared in the Waifs and Strays Society's magazine, *Our Waifs and Strays* in August 1887, was typical of the attitude of Victorian children's charities towards emigration:

> Take them away! Take them away!
> Out of the gutter, the ooze, and slime,
> Where the little vermin paddle and crawl,
> Till they grow and ripen into crime,
>
> Take them away! Away! Away!
> The bountiful earth is wide and free,
> The New shall repair the wrongs of the Old –
> Take them away o'er the rolling sea!

Emigration was a policy of severance, usually separating the child not only from any friends or surviving family – friends and siblings who emigrated together were often parted on arrival in Canada – but also from familiar surroundings, activities and schools, even the British climate. At a time when steady progress had been made in this country in regulating child labour and providing access to elementary education for children of the labouring poor, pauper children who emigrated to Canada could be apprenticed at the age of 10, sent out to isolated farms with limited or no access to education, and subject to the whims and tempers of harsh masters and mistresses. There was some regulation and inspection, although vetting of potential employers and foster parents was limited, but given the vast expanse of Canada, the remoteness of many farmsteads and the limited local supervision, it probably did little to prevent abuse. However, the stories of the children show that while many were abused and suffered emotionally, the more resilient children or those fortunate in their placements flourished, welcoming the chance to become part of the emergent nation of Canada.

Maria Rye was born in 1829, the daughter of a London solicitor. She became involved in helping middle-class women find work in England, but with limited suitable employment available and numerous applicants, she turned to emigration as a solution. During the 1860s, she arranged the emigration of parties of women to the colonies, initially middle-class women, but when she realised that the demand was for domestic servants rather than for educated women as teachers and governesses, she focused on working-class women. Rye was a formidable character. She had the ear of the Archbishop of Canterbury and others in the establishment and was adept at using her influence and the press to further her causes. She was a strong, committed leader, liked to be in control and reacted very strongly to criticism.

Inspired by the work of the Rev W. C. Van Meter in New York, who rescued city street children and placed them in foster care in the country, Rye wrote a letter to *The Times*, published on 29 March 1869, describing the success of Van Meter's scheme and indicating that she wanted to 'attempt the same thing for the "gutter children" of London, Manchester, Birmingham, Bristol, Liverpool'. Rather than sending the British urban street children to country homes in Britain, Rye planned to ship them over to North America, extolling the virtues of Canada as 'a land … where a million men only occupy territories larger than the whole of Great Britain.' She anticipated that her idea might be challenged:

It will be said, no doubt, 'But if you take those children abroad what guarantee can you give us that they will be kindly treated, or even receive common justice from the people with whom you leave them?'

Interestingly, given the later criticism of her work, she replied with another question, indicating that whatever treatment the children received abroad, it could not be worse than their present lives:

What treatment will they receive from the cold, the starvation, the temptation they meet with in our gutters; what justice will they receive from our hands when the police, the gaol, the hospital, and the Magdalen receive them? Can anything I introduce them to in Canada or America be worse than that to which they are doomed if we leave them where they are now?

Those she met while travelling in North America were encouraging and painted a rosy picture of what the young British immigrants might find. They said:

We have no money to give you … but such as we have we give you – a bed at the side, a seat at the fire, the church, the school, with our own children, and, in time, a handle at the plough, and a good share of the increase of a land where the measure is always full and running over.

Not everyone was so keen. In 1869, George Cruikshank published a pamphlet entitled *Our Gutter Children,* echoing the title of Rye's letter, with an illustration showing the gutter children being swept up into a cart, with a woman, clearly caricaturing Maria Rye, saying:

I am greatly obliged to you Christian ladies and gentlemen for your help and as soon as you have filled the cart I'll drive off to pitch the little dears aboard of a ship and take them thousands of miles away from their native land so they may never see any of their relatives again.

Maria Rye set up an emigration home in Peckham, London and purchased the old courthouse and gaol which stood amongst two acres at Niagara-on-the-Lake, south of Toronto in Canada, converting it into a receiving home for the children, known as 'Our Western Home'. She took her first party of children over to Canada on 30 October 1869. The following month, *The Illustrated London News* ran an article on Rye's scheme, stating that the girls would be housed in the home and trained for domestic service until the age of 15 when they would be sent out to service with 'respectable families'. In practice, the girls at Our Western Home received no training and were very quickly sent out to families or employment, leaving room for the next contingent arriving from England. Rye took very few 'gutter children' to Canada; most were girls from workhouses and industrial schools, paid for by the guardians, so had already been removed from their poor circumstances and surroundings. By the early 1870s, thirty-six unions were using her services. When Maria Rye retired in 1895, she handed over Our Western Home and her Peckham emigration home to the Waifs and Strays Society.

Annie Macpherson was a very different character from Maria Rye and although the two names are often linked as they started similar emigration schemes around the same time, the two women came from different backgrounds and never worked together. Macpherson was born in Scotland to Helen and James Macpherson, who was a teacher and a Quaker. The family came to England on the death of Annie's father and some years later, when in her late twenties, she attended a Christian revival meeting in London which sowed the seeds of her later charitable work. She moved to London in 1865, some four years later, and became involved in the evangelical movement and helping the poor in the East End. Macpherson was particularly concerned about the plight of children, especially those employed making matchboxes, and she subsequently opened several homes for destitute children in London, including the Home of Industry in the old cholera hospital in Spitalfields. It was the

sheer size of the problem that made Macpherson turn to emigration as
a solution:

> Boys came to us for shelter instead of going to empty barrels, railway
> arches, and stairways. We found they were grateful for all that was
> done for them. The simple gospel lesson was our lever to lift them
> into new thoughts and desires... . But our walls had limits, and our
> failures in finding employment for many away from their old haunts
> became a great difficulty, and the God-opened way of emigration to
> Canada was pressed upon us.[6]

Macpherson had not set up a receiving or distribution home in Canada
by the time her first party of children arrived in Quebec City on board
the *Peruvian* in May 1870, but she remedied that and took a house
called Marchmont, at Belleville in Ontario later that year. The original
Marchmont was destroyed by fire in 1872, as was the second of that name
a few years later. The third Marchmont Home in Belleville has now been
converted into apartments. Macpherson opened several other homes and
a farm in Canada to house and train the children and seemed to have
a genuine concern about their welfare. She wrote: 'From the time that
we ... had a Home from which to distribute them, we followed out our
original idea of becoming parents to these rescued children rather than
simple emigration agents to supply the labour market.'[7]

By the mid-1870s, there were some concerns about child migration
schemes, especially Maria Rye's activities, with suggestions that she was
making excessive profits from the business and was not exercising proper
supervision of the children once they had been sent to homes or work
placements in Canada. In 1874, Mr Allendale Grainger, the husband of a
former employee whom Rye had dismissed, complained to the Islington
Board of Guardians about her, claiming, amongst other things, that
she was profiteering at the ratepayers' expense and that her checking
of potential employers and protection of the children were totally
inadequate.[8] Typically Rye responded robustly. She gave the names of
many prominent supporters and offered to present her accounts and
open her work to inspection. Her final comment was a masterpiece of
self-aggrandisement: 'And I thank God this day, and say it without fear

of contradiction, that my work is a glorious success and has in many ways exceeded my most sanguine expectations.'[9]

Maria Rye might have regretted her willingness to open her activities to inspection, as the LGB decided the same year to investigate the system of emigration of pauper children to Canada under the supervision of both herself and Annie Macpherson. Andrew Doyle, a poor law inspector for over twenty-five years, in his mid-sixties, was appointed to make the enquiry. Doyle travelled to Canada in June 1874, visited the receiving homes, met Maria Rye and Annie Macpherson and others involved in the schemes, then went out across Canada, alone, to visit 400 children and their employers or adoptive parents. He returned home in October and his report was published in February 1875.[10]

Doyle cautiously accepted that under certain circumstances and with stringent regulation and inspection, the emigration of pauper children to Canada could be an appropriate way of resolving the problem of overcrowded workhouses and poor law schools, and could provide children with opportunities to make something of their lives in a new country. He thought emigration was best suited to very young children who could be adopted into families and to boys who could take advantage of the pioneering opportunities in Canada. He praised Macpherson and Rye, though rather sparingly, stating that, 'Many persons in their disapproval of individual cases of hardship and neglect might fail to make allowance for the difficulties that these ladies have had to encounter, or to do justice to the good that they have undoubtedly effected.' However, Doyle's report was highly critical of most aspects of the child emigration schemes and it upset and angered many, particularly Canadian government officials and Maria Rye. One of Doyle's key recommendations was that there should be a proper emigration scheme agreed between the British poor law unions and the Canadian provincial governments 'for the reception, training, placing out, and supervision of the young emigrants'.

Although Doyle's brief related to the pauper children who were sent to Canada under the auspices of the guardians, he also saw many of the street children (or 'arab' children as he called them) that Macpherson, and to a lesser extent Rye, brought over and said, 'If I had visited only the pauper children I should have missed many very striking examples of success.' However, Doyle was concerned that many of the children sent out were 'of the very lowest class – the semi-criminals of our large cities and towns', which affected the Canadians' willingness to accept the children; they were looking for labourers, not criminals. Doyle explained:

> The managers of the Homes are familiar with numerous cases of complaints of insubordination, falsehoods, petty thefts, and of still graver offences. I confess I was surprised to find how frequently such complaints were repeated by employers during my visits, and how often I heard the determination expressed 'never to take another'. I do not say that such complaints apply exclusively or even more to what are called the 'arab' children than to workhouse children, but they are made, and in too many cases I found them to be well founded.

Doyle observed how quickly the children were moved out of the distributing homes into employment, staying just a few weeks, or in some cases a few days, giving no opportunity for any training or for the staff to assess the suitability of the children for placements. It seems that the LGB was unaware of this. Doyle quoted a letter from the LGB to HM Secretary for the Colonies in April 1873 about Rye and Macpherson's schemes: 'The children emigrating under this system are, as the Board understand, placed in the first instance in training establishments, where they are maintained and fitted for situations afterwards provided for them.' Doyle wryly added, 'This no doubt is what ought to be done, but what is not and never has been done.' He was also concerned that none of the homes had proper facilities for those, often older children, who came back to the home after leaving or being dismissed from a placement. Rather than seeing the home as a refuge, some seemed to be afraid to return.

Doyle commented that both Rye and Macpherson relied on 'adoption' as a means of placing the children in homes in Canada, but only a small percentage of children were placed with families as an adoptive son or daughter. The great majority, some very young, were sent out under an 'indenture of adoption', which was simply apprenticeship by another name. One 'intelligent shrewd girl' aged about 16 expressed the view:

'Doption, sir, is when folks gets a girl to work without wages.' Doyle added:

> I cannot help thinking that in a country in which wages are so high, and the cost of living, for a child in a family at least, so low, the terms of service are for the children less favourable than they ought to be. No one can wonder at the restlessness and dissatisfaction of boys and girls of fifteen and sixteen who find themselves 'adopted,' that is, bound to serve without wages, merely for their maintenance, and clothing, until they are eighteen.

He did, however, give unqualified approval to the adoption of young children into families, whether of 'gentlefolks' or 'small hard-working farmers'. 'From the very circumstances that lead to their adoption, to fill an empty place in the family, they are objects, as might be expected, of unusual affection,' he said, adding, 'Miss Rye and Miss Macpherson deserve the highest credit for originating such a method of placing out very young children.'

One of Doyle's concerns was that despite assurances to the LGB about the 'satisfactory arrangements made by these ladies, not only for proper superintendence during the voyage but also for the support and treatment of the children on their arrival in the colony, where suitable situations are found for them', the reality was very different. Doyle suggested that the work had 'rapidly outgrown the means provided for carrying it on, assuming that the means were sufficient at the outset.' He was particularly concerned by what he saw as inadequate and haphazard arrangements by both women for selecting homes for the children and for providing proper supervision of them after they had left the distributing home, writing:

> 'The homes should be seen,' but they are not seen.... . Miss Macpherson trusts to agencies that are wholly inadequate for obtaining requisite information; Miss Rye trusts to the accident of being able to find persons in different districts who will relieve her from the responsibility not only of finding suitable homes but of looking after the children when they are placed in them. As to the

'recommends' that are required their value is not much. A farmer's wife who had one of these children observed, 'My minister may know that ours is a respectable family, but I guess he can know very little about my being fit to bring up a child.'

It was though the lack of supervision of the children after apprenticeship or adoption that particularly alarmed Doyle; some children simply disappeared – changing situations or running away – with the distributing homes having no knowledge of their whereabouts. Rye had no plan for visiting the children at all, relying on correspondence, and Macpherson's system was inadequate, so neither had much idea how most of the children were doing, even if they knew where they were. Macpherson relied heavily on an agent, Mr Thom, to visit children in the Belleville and Galt districts, but as Doyle pointed out, 'however great may be the zeal and activity of Mr. Thom, and he is very zealous and very active, it is impossible that he can do more than pay an occasional visit to some of the children.'

Although Rye took him to see several children who seemed in a satisfactory or good state, many others had slipped through the net:

Not sure whether C. L. is in last reported situation.

A. L's. present address not known.

A. G., after being in seven different places, and in the House of Refuge at Rock Port in the United States, has been lost sight of.

J. F., who has had seven or eight different places, is said to be in the neighbourhood of 'Our Western Home' and 'believed' to be doing respectably, but address not known.

Doyle gave examples of issues with Macpherson's children too, such as the 13-year-old boy who was said to have been placed out in Montreal 'the day after landing' but nothing had been heard of him in over two years. A girl from Southampton workhouse who came to Canada in 1871, aged about 14, was in and out of situations and eventually the home was informed that she 'had lost her character' (that is, was pregnant) and needed clothes. Her child died and Doyle traced her to a 'low lodging-house' where she seemed bitter and resentful, not only about her life in Canada but about her treatment by the home, although she provided little evidence to Doyle to support her claims.

Doyle did not come across any examples of what he termed 'gross cruelty' but did find many cases of 'ill-treatment and hardship', including a 13-year-old girl being horse-whipped, a boy being beaten across the shoulders and a girl being kept on bread and water for three days for refusing to admit that she had stolen five cents. The common theme running through the children's responses to Doyle's question about why they had left their last place suggested that, for many, their childhood was blighted by unhappiness and a sense that they did not belong: 'The answer would very often be to the effect, if not in so many words, "I couldn't manage to please them; they were always scolding me; they used to beat me; I was very unhappy."'

Doyle's report was very critical, but his concern was less about the principle of child migration than about Rye and Macpherson's practical arrangements to deliver the schemes. He suggested that the work had outgrown their ability to manage it effectively (although he was perhaps not convinced that Rye's arrangements were ever satisfactory) and that the juvenile migration system needed an overhaul. Responding to Annie Macpherson's comment that it would 'be easy to set the little emigrant adrift, and, as it were, let him "paddle his own canoe" on the ocean of life, inquiring no further as to his welfare; but rather would we undertake a smaller work and carry out the healthful supervision of employers and employed', Doyle stated:

> But this, unhappily, is just what has been done. The little emigrants have been set afloat, and too many of them let to 'paddle their own canoes' until, as Miss Macpherson might express it, some of them have gone over the rapids, and others are already lost sight of in the great human tide of the Western cities.

Doyle was perhaps ahead of his time in his understanding of the children's emotional needs as well as issues of safety, abuse, and exploitation, so what were the outcomes of this ground-breaking report? In March 1875, the LGB suspended the emigration of children by the poor law unions and, around the same time, the Canadian government convened a select committee on immigration which heard evidence from Rye and Macpherson and staff at the homes, as well as from many witnesses from Canada involved in the two emigration schemes.[11] Witness after witness praised Macpherson and Rye's work and roundly criticised Doyle's report, and Doyle himself. Two said they had personal knowledge of the work done by the two women in their respective neighbourhoods, and that 'it was highly advantageous to all concerned' and an MP from Ottawa who was personally acquainted with Miss Rye's work in the neighbourhood of Chatham, Ontario, 'could not but give that lady credit for doing very much good, for which she was richly entitled to the thanks of the children committed to her charge'. A senator who had audited Macpherson's accounts and who had placed several of her children in various trades locally, stated 'the work was one not only calculated to benefit the children, but to be of service to the country'.

One MP, clearly incensed by Doyle's criticisms of Rye and Macpherson's work, believed that 'it was the desire of the Committee to obtain the fullest possible information on the subject, and allow the blame to fall upon those to whom it belonged.' Responding, another MP pointed out that Doyle was not on trial before the committee and that their aim was 'to ascertain the success of the enterprise.' Witnesses described Doyle's report as 'erroneous and unjust in its conclusions', 'unfair' and 'full of misapprehension and mistake'. Doyle was also accused of persistently presenting 'the dark side of the subject' and that his assertion that £200 was spent annually on each distributing home 'was utterly and absurdly incorrect'.

Annie Macpherson responded to the committee's questions in a measured way, providing factual answers and explaining any differences between Doyle's account and her own. Typically, however, Maria Rye showed no such restraint, saying she had come before the committee 'to protest against Mr. Doyle's unjust, ungenerous, and most inaccurate report.' She gave a prepared statement to the committee, rebutting most, if not all, of Doyle's criticisms, with some lengthy explanations and quite a few swipes at Doyle. She attached numerous testimonials about her work and the success of the children's placements and her detailed page-by-page notes on Doyle's report were also included in the committee's report at her request.

Doyle's report struck a nerve with the Canadians. As well as rebutting many of his observations, the committee report was critical of the poor law system in England, with one witness rejecting Doyle's idea of industrial training schools in Canada as an 'extension into this country of the English workhouse system, altogether unsuited to the ideas and condition of the people of this country.' Another claimed the street or 'arab' children sent out to Canada were 'less liable to be sulky; have more self-reliance; [were] less idle, and ... equal in every way except in education' to the union children. The Canadian press rapidly jumped on the bandwagon, including this view by *The Globe*:

> Any drearier or more forlorn prospect than what lies before a pauper child or guttersnipe in England is not easily imagined... . Anyone who knows the character of the great majority of Canadian homes ... would feel insulted by any lengthened or grave discussion of the question, whether or not it be for the advantage of such to leave England.[12]

Maria Rye continued her dispute with Andrew Doyle for some years through the English press and an exchange of correspondence with the LGB. In a letter to *The Times* published on 23 April 1875, she explained why so many children were returned to the distributing home:

> So great is the dislike of Canadians to inflict even necessary correction, and so become a by-word to their neighbours, that many persons are afraid to take these children on this one ground alone ... all the rebellious, obstinate and unmanageable children are returned to us [the Western Home] for discipline and management. I have had more than 200 such children returned to me within the last five years, for whom I have had to find 700 places ... which I venture, however, to say has taken up more of our time, our ingenuity, and our patience than all the work in England and crossing the Atlantic put together.

Rye insisted that the children in Canada did not require inspection in the same way as their counterparts in England because of the 'tremendous difference between the position of the persons taking the children in the two countries'. She claimed that in Canada, most children were taken by a 'substantial, orderly, comfortable, and well-established class of people' who lived on their own properties, whereas in England children were boarded out with poor cottagers who relied heavily on the child's maintenance payments and who, should 'any unforeseen trifle' put them out of work, would find very great difficulty in keeping the child at all.[13] She failed to note the other key difference, though, that the children in Canada were mainly lodged with employers under apprenticeship terms, whereas the children in England were boarded out with foster parents as part of the family. These comments, together with her failure to explain why twenty-eight children under the age of 15 had absconded without anyone knowing where they had gone, and how she had failed to prevent a number of girls having illegitimate children after emigrating, suggested that she was blind to the failings of her work.

Other charitable organisations quickly got involved in child migration, especially after the LGB lifted its suspension on the emigration of pauper children. These included Annie Macpherson's sister, Louisa Birt, of the Liverpool Sheltering Homes; Catholic priest Father James Nugent; Bowman Stephenson of the National Children's Home; John Middlemore; James Fegan; William Quarrier of Glasgow; Thomas Barnardo; the Waifs and Strays Society; the Church Army; the Catholic Emigration Association; and a host of smaller emigration agencies. Some initially used Macpherson or Rye's services, but many quickly set up their own distributing homes and made all the arrangements themselves, both in Britain and Canada. In 1882, the Canadian Government agreed to inspect the migrant poor law children annually through the Canadian immigration agents and in 1899 it created the post of Inspector of British Immigrant Children and Receiving Homes. George Bogue Smart was the only holder of this office, from 1899 until his retirement in 1933.

Significantly, neither the Canadian committee nor Maria Rye asked the children how they felt about their lives in Canada, unlike Doyle who interviewed about 400 'Home Children' on his travels across Canada. Rye was inclined to blame the children themselves for any failings, especially the former workhouse girls, and was indignant that Doyle had based his assertions in one case on 'the mere word of the girl herself' without asking Rye about her character. However, many first-hand accounts of the lives of the Home Children do exist, some contemporary, such as letters to family or charities back home, others from interviews, correspondence or reminiscences when the children had become adults, often in old age, looking back seventy or so years across their lifetime. Both are often very moving, from the immediacy of a young child's emotions and feelings in a strange country to the mature adult, looking back with pride on what they had made of their lives, or with bitterness and regret at how they were treated.

Older pauper children were supposed to give their consent to emigration before two magistrates, and most charities notionally, at least, sought the agreement of the child's parent or guardian, but in practice many did not or relied on enticing the child to emigrate with the promise of an exciting new life. In 1894, William Quarrier, visiting his Bridge of Weir orphan homes to identify children who wanted to go to Canada, told John Churcher what a wonderful place it was and that he already had a sister living in Ontario. As John explained in a letter written when he was in his mid-eighties: 'You can imagine the thrill, the excitement, the enthusiasm of such a prospect: to cross the mighty ocean, travel miles by train to meet an unknown sister, see new people and new lands. It was all too much for a 10-year-old-boy to contain so I said "Yes".'[14] Thomas Barnardo, who was perhaps the most frequent exponent of 'philanthropic abduction', a phrase he himself coined, was quite happy to leave parents in the dark about the emigration of their children, as this account by Helen Gough, who emigrated about 1912, shows:

> I wrote and told my mother I was going to Canada (our letters were censored) and I was told to write another letter and not to mention going to Canada. The night before we got on board the ship we were told we could write a loving letter home. I guess it didn't matter what we said as we would be on the sea when the word was received by mother.[15]

For the children, the voyage across the Atlantic was a strange new experience – sometimes frightening and sometimes wondrous. Few though escaped seasickness. Jim Eccleston, a young emigrant from the

Middlemore Home, had an uncomfortable voyage to Canada in May 1910 on the *Mongolian*. He shared a cabin in steerage with five other boys, but as he explained:

> The clank of the steering gear together with the whine of the propeller shaft, the smell of hot oil and steam, and no ventilation, drove me out. I spent my nights hidden in a corner on deck against a ventilator shaft for warmth.[16]

This unnamed 81-year-old lady recalled her voyage to Canada under the auspices of the Waifs and Strays Society when she was 9 years old: 'I remember the kindness of the ladies in charge. They made sure we saw the beautiful icebergs, and in the evening we were allowed to watch the Italian people dancing and singing on the lower deck.'[17]

After passing through immigration, the children faced a long and tiring inland journey, much of it by train. Colin Taylor, a Fegans' boy, showed what difference a little kindness could make to the young migrants. James Fegan, or 'The Governor' as he was called by the boys, not only accompanied Colin's party of children on the voyage to Canada but stayed with them on the train journey from Halifax to Toronto. Writing some sixty years after he emigrated at the age of 11, Colin recalled that one day the train stopped for a long time, so the boys were allowed to get out for a break: 'As we left the car, Mr Fegan stood at the outlet with a basin of warm water, some soap, a wash cloth and a towel. Each boy was given a refreshing rub over the hands and face and a kindly word from "The Governor".'[18]

Doyle was concerned that Rye and Macpherson sent the children out to their new homes or placements far too quickly, but decades later, this still seemed to be happening, with many children staying just a short time at the distributing home before going to their new addresses. Doyle also objected to children being paraded in front of 'employers' for selection, and although that may not have happened later in the century, prospective foster parents were certainly invited to the distributing homes to choose the younger children. One woman recalled decades later how, as a 9 year old, she had lined up with a couple of other girls at the home in front of a Mrs Beamer, who had come to choose a foster child, and was selected because she had blue eyes. She explained that she had had a 'good kind home' and was educated in the one-room country school, writing, 'What small things decide our lives!'[19] Pollie Jones had a similar experience in 1910. She had only been at the home at Knowlton, Quebec for a day when a single woman, Sarah Jane Williams, came to choose a girl: 'There were 12 of us in line like stairs. I was the shortest and the oldest one and she picked me.'[20]

For those children who were placed on remote farmsteads, the final stage of their journey from the distributing home to their new home was usually made alone, with only a railway guard to tell them where to get off the train. Mostly, the children were met at the station by the farmer with a buggy, but some like Percy White, a Barnardo's boy aged 14, were not so lucky. There was no one there to meet him when he got off the train, so he set off walking, eventually finding the farm after asking for help. The farmer promptly sent him back to the station a mile away with a wheelbarrow to collect his trunk, and on his return set him to work to bring in the cows![21]

Inevitably, the Home Children's own accounts of their lives in Canada indicate a mixed bag of experience. Many were ill-treated or abused or suffered emotional cruelty at various levels, although as in the case of Hugh Caesar, a Barnardo's boy, some of the charities did extricate children from bad employers:

> In Canada I was in and out of farms all the time. At one farm I accidentally let the pigs out on a Sunday. I got a terrible beating with a buggy whip. So I wrote to the Home and they sent me a ticket to go back to the Toronto Home. Later, Mr Owen got a letter from that farmer asking for another Home boy. He asked me, 'Does this man deserve another Home boy?' 'No, sir,' I answered.[22]

Life was not easy for the girls either – they might suffer physical or sexual abuse, or both. One girl who went out in 1912 said:

> I got more beatings in Canada than I [had] ever got. I was punished for things I didn't know what for sometimes. One spring we were rounding up the cattle and the cattle didn't get in the right place

between me and the farmer. He took the bamboo rod to me, not only then but several times. I have a spine injury and I blame it on that man.[23]

Mary Warriner went to Canada around 1910 and had a tough time to begin with, though she eventually settled on a farm with a childless couple whom she called 'Mom and Dad'. She said: 'I was not happy in my placements. The first place the son on the farm tried to take advantage of me and I fought him off and slapped him. The next place I just got tired of being their slave. So back to the Home.'[24]

For other children, Canada fulfilled all their hopes and dreams, giving them working and travel opportunities and for many, a happy family life. One boy, who discovered eventually that his brother had emigrated too and was on a farm only fifteen miles away said: 'Well, after we served our term as Barnardo boys we both got itchy feet and took to the road travelling across this great country, always finding work on the railway, in road construction, harvesting, lumbering. We were happy. Canada was God's country!'[25] Pollie Jones lived with her adoptive mother, Miss Sarah Williams, in Dunham, Ontario, from 1910 until Pollie married in 1929. In 1918, Miss Williams' brother, Luke, who farmed the land at Dunham, paid for Pollie's 13-year-old brother, John, to come over from England to join her, and the 1921 census reveals that Pollie, described as a domestic, and John, a farm labourer, were living in Dunham, Quebec with Sarah and Luke Williams. This was clearly more than an employer/employee relationship; after her marriage, Pollie visited Miss Williams weekly and nursed her through her final illness. After Miss Williams' death, Pollie discovered that her foster mother had left everything to her in her will: 'I never repaid Miss Williams for what she did for me. I did all I could for her.... . I am one in a good many Home children who can say they had a real good home. None better.[26]

Walter Longyear found true contentment and happiness in Canada, having emigrated in 1914, aged about 13, with his younger brother George. The little kindnesses in this strange new land made such a difference to Walter, the son of a Portsmouth cab driver:

I remember going for the cows in the pasture and I was so scared and took the farmer's hand. When I worked at the woodpile, Grandma would bring me cookies in her apron pocket. At breakfast they asked if I wanted cream on my porridge and I wondered what that was.[27]

Looking back at his life, Walter wrote:

I was really lucky to have a farm home where I was treated like a son, although I was never officially adopted. I worked on the farm with my employer until I was married and I finally bought the farm from the kind family where I had spent my first five years in Canada. Our sons have their own farms and I have lovely grandchildren. I am grateful to Dr Barnardo's Homes for taking such an interest in the boys and girls of England by bringing them to Canada where they could start rich new lives.

Some children were grateful for the opportunity for a new life in Canada because life in England was so bad. As a child, Mary Wallace Blake, née Woodhall, was living with a woman in Birmingham (presumably not a relation), helping her to sew hooks and eyes onto cards in return for food and clothing. She was rescued from this miserable life when she was 8 and placed in a home in Liverpool, where for the first time she went to school, before emigrating to Canada in 1910. Mary had a happy childhood in Canada with a Mr and Mrs Wallace, writing some sixty years later: 'They were real parents to me and I was very happy. They thought as much of me as they did of their own… . I thought as much of them as if they had been my own flesh and blood.'[28] Mary remembered nothing about her parents and never wished to return to England. Mary Wunder was about 9 years old when she came to Canada just before the First World War and wrote when in her sixties that she had never wanted to return to England, 'for I have no sweet memories of anything or anyone.'[29]

Schooling, or rather the lack of it, was a problem for many of the Home Children. The agency or charity placing the children usually required the foster parents or employer to ensure the child received regular schooling, although not necessarily all year round, given the demands of the farming year. However, many of the children's employers regarded education for their young charges as unnecessary. Some children, such as John Churcher, received only a partial education, despite a written agreement between the Quarrier Homes and his foster parents. John had a happy childhood in Canada, but resented being taken out of school early, writing later that his foster parents 'didn't put much value on education.'[30]

Percy White was even less fortunate: 'The farmer was very strict. I worked from daylight to dark. I was supposed to go to school every winter. No. Never sent to school, or to church or Sunday School. Never went any place.'[31] John Atkinson's experience was very different. He was about 10 when he emigrated and stayed happily in his first placement until he joined the Army in 1916 when he was about 16. He attended school every winter for six years, reaching the highest grade.[32]

What comes over from many of these accounts though, even from children who were not physically abused, is the constant hard work, the aching loneliness, the anxiety and the lack of either friends of their own age or a trusted adult close by in times of difficulty. Edith Stiff was one of the few Dickleburgh children who emigrated, sailing for Canada in 1892 when she was about 13. She was born in a London workhouse and had been a difficult and troubled child while in care in England, although both Mrs Brandreth and the matron at the Dickleburgh home were fond of her and felt she had many good qualities, despite being 'quarrelsome and irritable'.

In a moving letter to Mrs Brandreth, some three years after she emigrated, a copy of which is now on her Waifs and Strays case file, Edith wrote, 'It is so lonesome out here it makes me think of England how I do wish I had never left you.' She added, 'It is a teribull place out here the men are all the time after the girls I have had an affal lot ask me to Marrie them. Of course I have refused. I try not to take any notice of them all.' Edith was particularly anxious about her future:

I have left my place at Montral because they wanted a bigger girl than me. I went back to the Home 'till I got another place, you asked me when you wrote to me if there was a home to go back to yes. But this is the last time I may go back to it. I have got a place in the country at a farm... . I shall have nowhere to go to if I leave here all the girls ho are 15 are not aloude to go back to the home. they say I am 15 will you please wright and tell me my right age.

Edith was aware that her own behaviour was not helping her to keep her situations and wrote, 'I can … tell you for I have no one else to tell I will turn over a new leaf and try to be a better girl for I feel so unhappy.' Mrs Brandreth was very concerned and asked Edward Rudolf of the Waifs and Strays Society if it would be possible to put Edith under some form of care if she could not return to the home again as she was 'at a very dangerous age for any young girl to be homeless and friendless in Canada'. Alice Hall, who also spent time at Dickleburgh before emigrating, wrote in a letter to Rudolf, now on her case file, 'I am very lonesome out here I am so far away from the Home I do not see any body that I know.'

Apart from the very young children who were adopted into families, the Home Children quickly realised that they were there to work. A 12 year old in Canada detailed his daily labour on a 100-acre farm:

We would get up anywhere around 4.30 am and we would go to the barn, milk the cows and separate the milk and then have breakfast, groom the horses, put them on a wagon and mow the hay or cut the grain. Eleven o'clock would be our dinner time and then out to the fields again and then at 4 pm it was supper time. Then we worked on bringing the grain in… . By the time the horses were in, you fell into bed.[33]

The harsh Canadian winters came as a huge shock to the Home Children, especially those from the towns and cities in England. A 14 year old on a farm in Ontario suffered badly with the cold:

The first year here, the temperature was round forty to forty-five degrees below zero … and we had a pole outside and marked eleven foot of snow on it … the water froze and the wind was dreadful. I had been out here three or four months, when my two big toes swelled up so bad and so painful, I had to split new shoes in order to wear them… . It was so tender, when a cat ran over my foot under the table, I cried. I would sit down in the middle of the yard and massage my feet and cry with pain.[34]

For many young immigrants, the experience of being treated as a Home Child scarred them emotionally for life. Some were treated as less than servants; a 14-year-old girl recalled hearing a conversation between her mistress and a man, as she stabled the horse. 'The man said, "Who is that you have standing there?" And she said, "That's just the girl from the Home." And he said, "They're pretty poor trash, ain't they?" And she said, "Yes, they are."'[35] Some, such as Clinton Webb, were troubled throughout their lives: 'My background of life has given me a very insecure and restless nature.'[36] Others, such as Mary Wunder, spent a lifetime wondering why they had been sent to Canada and whether they had any relatives back in England: 'I never heard of anyone I belonged to. I've cried many a night because I had no one to call my mother... . Surely in England I must have someone.'[37]

The last forty years of the child emigration movement, from the 1920s to the 1960s, mainly falls outside the scope of this book but was perhaps one of the darkest periods in the history of children in care in this country. Details have only come to light in the last thirty years, particularly due to the dogged determination of Margaret Humphreys, a British social worker, to reveal the truth and to unite former child migrants with their birth families through the Child Migrants' Trust which she established in 1987. During this period, local authorities and charities sent children from children's homes in Britain and Ireland to orphanages and farm schools, particularly in Australia, including those run by the Big Brother Movement, Fairbridge Farm Schools and the Catholic Christian Brothers, as well as those of charities such as Barnardo's. Joy Melville and Phillip Bean summed it up: 'The history of child migration in Australia is in many ways a history of cruelty, lies and deceit. For instance, children were told their parents were dead; that they came from deprived backgrounds; that they had been "rescued" and should be grateful.'[38] Similarly, parents who believed their children had been adopted or were in children's homes in England were not asked to give their consent to emigration or even told that their children had left the country. One woman sent to Australia at the age of 4 later said:

I subsequently found out from my aunt that neither my mother, aunts or uncles knew I had gone to Australia. They had been told I was adopted in Ireland and although they had wondered about me and wanted to see me, they did not want to interfere. My aunt and uncle were shocked to hear I had been shipped to Australia.[39]

Many Australian child migrants are still alive and are now telling their stories, which sadly tell of mental and physical cruelty and sexual abuse. Over the past ten years or so, mainly due to Margaret Humphreys, there has finally been some action concerning the abuse of child migrants in the twentieth century, with investigations, apologies and compensation. The Independent Inquiry into Child Sexual Abuse, under the chairmanship of Professor Alexis Jay, published its report on the child migrant programmes on 1 March 2018, with Professor Jay stating:

Child migration was a deeply flawed government policy that was badly implemented by numerous organisations which sent children as young as five years old abroad. Successive British governments failed to ensure there were sufficient measures in place to protect children from all forms of abuse, including sexual abuse. The policy was allowed to continue despite evidence over many years showing that children were suffering. We hope that this report offers acknowledgement to those who experienced abuse resulting from the child migration programmes.

It is now clear that the Australian child migration schemes in the twentieth century involved deception by local authorities and charities, institutional abuse and failure to inspect sufficiently the institutions to which the children were sent. But what of the agencies that took children to Canada such as Rye, Macpherson, Barnardo, the Waifs and Strays Society and Fegans? Were they wrong, misguided or doing their best to help the destitute children in their care? There is no easy answer. And not all the agencies were the same. Rye certainly appeared to have little interest in the welfare of the children after they reached Canada, but many other charities set up proper visiting and inspection schemes to safeguard the children. For some children, migration proved the making of them, for others it brought misery and abuse. Perhaps it was simply a lottery, largely dependent on the character of the foster parent or employer, and the resilience of the child. Gail Corbett raises another key issue about the child migration schemes, sometimes overlooked – the Home Children's contribution to the growth and development of Canada. She writes in the preface to her book *Nation Builders: Barnardo Children in Canada*: 'Yesterday the children journeyed alone, seeking the promise of the New World. Today their numbers are legion and they are counted amongst our most courageous and successful nation builders.'

Chapter 9

Life After Care

When I look back I wonder what I might have been if I had had a normal childhood. Actually I ceased to be a child at the age of 10, No one can understand my feelings of loneliness and despair unless they have lived through it.[1]

William Tonkin, British Home Child

Children who were admitted to the workhouse or children's homes run by voluntary societies, or who emigrated to Canada, had inevitably already experienced some form of trauma, emotional or physical, such as the death of their parents, desertion, abuse, illness, injury, disability, malnutrition or homelessness. The poor law authorities and the voluntary societies in Britain provided the children in their charge with food, shelter, clothing, education and training, with the expectation that they would leave care aged about 14 to earn their own living, ultimately becoming independent adults. The aim was to break the cycle of poverty, so neither the children, nor their descendants, would return to the workhouse or care system. Fostering and small cottage homes run on family lines gave some children in care a more 'normal' childhood than life in the workhouse or the district school could provide, but there was very limited understanding of the emotional needs of deprived and vulnerable children at that time. Many children in care, especially in the large institutions and those who migrated to Canada, received little or no help to deal with the emotional impact of their early childhood, or support and encouragement to ensure that they went on to lead happy and fulfilling lives and to realise their potential as adults. Many succeeded though, despite the lack of support, through their own hard work, perseverance and resilience.

There are some published first-hand accounts of life in care, some written while the children were still in care, but most when they were adults, reflecting on their childhood. Some, such as the accounts by the Home Children in Gail Corbett's book and Phyllis Harrison's *The Home Children: Their Personal Stories*, give a flavour of what life was like after care too – marriage, children, employment or military service – and may reveal the physical and emotional consequences of spending time in the workhouse, in foster care or of being part of the child migration programme. Similarly, published autobiographies of public figures who spent time in the workhouse, such as Charlie Chaplin, Charles Shaw and Will Crooks, help us to understand the impact not only of institutional life on a child and the effect of the crisis which brought them to that point, but also the strength of family ties. However, for most children who spent time in care during the period of the new poor law, there are, at best, just family memories or correspondence, unpublished diaries, occasional entries in case files or more recent family history research to show what became of them in later life. The shame of being in care, especially the workhouse, meant that some never spoke of their childhood, even to spouses or children, so their stories may now be lost. Some children spent only a short time in care, perhaps returning to their families or dying young. Others experienced more than one type of care during their young lives, such as those who were returned to the workhouse as they were considered 'unsuitable' to live in small cottage homes such as Rose Cottage in Dickleburgh.

This chapter draws on some published accounts and on research into the lives of some of the 300 or so children in care in Dickleburgh after they had left, either prematurely or at the usual age of about 14. The research into the Dickleburgh children has been taken from the Waifs and Strays case files and genealogical and biographical sources mostly in the public domain, although the descendants of some of the children have also kindly provided memories and photographs. Although it is difficult to draw any conclusions about the impact of a deprived childhood and time spent in care on the children's later lives from this research, some patterns emerge, particularly relating to employment.

Training children for suitable employment was critical for both the poor law authorities and the voluntary societies, although expectations for the children were not high and were usually in line with the prevailing view about the labouring class's place in society. When the Depwade

Guardians in Norfolk discussed the new plan for a new district school over the county border in Wortham in Suffolk in the late 1870s, Sir Edward Kerrison, who attended by special invitation, spoke strongly about:

> Only teaching the necessary industries of the district labour on the land for the boys, and domestic service for the girls, and not endeavouring to advance them in trades and stations in life above those in which the honest self-supporting poor could place their children.[2]

Most of the Dickleburgh girls went into domestic service, with Mrs Brandreth finding 'situations' for them. Some, such as Rosa Garnham, settled quickly into service, remaining with one employer for many years. Rosa, who was one of the first children taken into Rose Cottage in the mid-1870s, explained in a letter in the February 1889 edition of *Our Waifs and* Strays: 'At the age of fourteen and a-half I went to service, as a general servant, at Norwich, where I have been for five and a-half years, and still hope to stay on.' In 1891, Rosa was staying at Rose Cottage as a visitor, described as a general domestic servant, and ten years later was recorded in service with a widowed lady in Norwich. In 1911, Rosa was still in service, but was away visiting again, this time staying in Sidcup with Belinda Beaman, the former matron of Rose Cottage. Rosa died unmarried aged 85 and although she was described as an invalid in the 1939 register, she seems to have had a contented life, grateful for being taken out of destitution and trained for service, and retaining her links with the old home in Dickleburgh in adult life.

Some of the Dickleburgh girls, such as Florence Mayes, had difficulty holding down a job and spent time in the society's home at Clapham Park for 'Girls out of Situation'. Florence's Waifs and Strays case file records that between November 1911 and July 1918 she went out to service on at least fifteen occasions, returning to the Clapham Park home between each job. The case file rarely explains the reason for her return, though after Florence came back to the home 'unwell', in January 1915, the matron, Miss Lockwood, remarked in a letter: 'She does not seem to want to earn her living just now.' Florence seemed to steady after this for a while, keeping her place with a Mrs Bauer in Wandsworth Common for about fifteen months, and then four months with a Mrs Stroud until she was 'summarily dismissed' and in November 1916 returned yet again to the Clapham Park home, before being sent out to service three or four more times.

In 1920, Florence wrote to the Waifs and Strays Society, possibly to Edward Rudolf, although he had retired from active work with the society the previous year, thanking him for his Christmas card and adding, perhaps with a touch of wry humour, 'I daresay you will be glad to hear that I am getting married in the month of April 1921, if I am spared by then.' She also asked for the address of Miss Lockwood, the former matron at the Clapham Park home, saying she would like to write to her, being 'one of her old Girls'. She requested a portrait of the recipient of the letter, 'as I have been in my present place two years and a half, should like one to keep in remembrance of you as you have always been a good friend to me Sir, when I was in the home's care.' Like Rosa Garnham, Florence seemed to want to keep in touch with those who had helped her through the difficulties of her early life.

For one Dickleburgh girl, Daisy Ball, going into service gave her a chance of a new life. She went out to service at 14, and by 1911 was working as housemaid in the household of Thomas Turkentine, a chartered accountant, in Kingston upon Thames. Daisy must have been busy, as it was a twelve-roomed house and the only other servant was the cook. Thomas's wife, Helen, was born in America, although a British subject by parentage, so it may have been through her that Daisy was offered a post in America at £52 a year including board and lodging. Mrs Brandreth informed Edward Rudolf that she would be sailing to New York on 22 November 1911, adding, 'She has worked herself up in service & been quite trustworthy for many years' and asking him if the society had an agency in New York so Daisy had a contact point if in difficulties. Rudolf replied that he was glad that she had obtained such a good situation and progressed so satisfactorily, suggesting that Mrs Brandreth contact the Girls Friendly Society, which he thought had a New York branch. He then wrote to the Reading Guardians stating, 'one of our lady workers has kept in touch with Daisy since leaving Rose

Cottage and proper arrangements will be made to ensure her welfare across the Atlantic.'

Some girls considered unsuitable or not yet ready for domestic service, such as those with behaviour problems, were sent by the Waifs and Strays Society for further training either to a laundry home or an industrial training home such as the Trewint Industrial Home in Hampstead. The Trewint home was certified as an industrial school in 1889 and provided residential training for girls aged 14 and over who were:

> naughty, tiresome, and unmanageable by their friends, and who are unable to keep small situations in which they have been placed, from having committed petty theft, proved themselves deceitful, or untrustworthy, untaught concerning the household duties they ought to be able to fulfil, or who are in danger of bad companions.[3]

The research into the Dickleburgh children suggests that most of the more troublesome, or troubled, girls had either an underlying mental health condition or learning difficulties, which became more apparent as the children reached their teenage years. There were limited options for such children after they were discharged from the care of the guardians, even if their mental health issues were acknowledged. The workhouse or asylum was often the only place available if they could not care for themselves, although some might return to their families or be supported through a charity, such as the Waifs and Strays Society, but funding could be an issue.

Deborah Samuelson was brought over from South Africa after the death of her parents by her aunt and uncle, Mr and Mrs Rigg, and stayed with them in Suffolk for a few years before being admitted to Rose Cottage at the age of 12. Her case file shows she was unable to settle in service, being in and out of Lee Cottage between jobs, and by the time she was 18, she was boarding with a woman locally, still supervised by the Brandreths, but not capable of useful work. There was increasing concern about Deborah's moral welfare, with Mrs Brandreth suggesting that she might come to harm as she regularly walked by herself to Diss across the common on errands, when the boys teased her, 'knowing her weakness'. Mrs Brandreth was concerned that Deborah did not know how to look after herself and that she needed specialist training for 'deficient girls', if she was ever going to earn her own living.

Deborah was eventually admitted to Church Stile House at Cobham, a Home of Rest for Women and Ladies, which took girls of 'weak intellect' to work in the home and laundry. She remained there for about a year, doing quite well, though her behaviour was variable; one report said that Deborah was strong and healthy but uncertain and although she could work very well at times, she could be obstinate and have crying fits for one or two days and do nothing. In 1897, there was an attempt to return Deborah, who was nearly 19, to her family, but both sets of relations refused to take her. Her uncle, Jacob Rice, had taken his own mother into his home some years earlier so he would 'not think of having anything to do with Deborah', adding he had 'more trouble with Mother than I know what to do with'. Edward Rudolf and Mrs Brandreth arranged to send Deborah to Mr and Mrs Rigg, her other relatives, but it seems they did not first get the couple's agreement to the move as Henrietta Rigg sent a telegram to Rudolf saying, 'Don't send Samuelson'. Mrs Rigg wrote the same day saying she thought Deborah 'was in some place for life' when she signed the society forms for her six years earlier and that her husband refused to have her as she was no relation of his. Deborah, by then described as 'girl of feeble intellect', did return to her aunt shortly afterwards, but by 1901, she was working as a laundress in St Michael's Convent in Waterlooville, Hampshire, which operated an industrial laundry. By 1939, Deborah was resident at the Knowle Mental Hospital a few miles away and she died of heart failure in February 1950 in hospital at Crondall, aged 71 and unmarried. Her permanent address was given as the Great House, Stockbridge, Hampshire, ironically a former union workhouse, which by then was a hospital for the chronically sick. It is likely that Deborah spent much of her life in institutional care.

Ellen (or May) Jackson was admitted to Rose Cottage in Dickleburgh from the West Ham union schools, but within a few months Mrs Brandreth wrote of her concerns about Ellen's behaviour to the Waifs and Strays Society and suggested that she should be transferred to a newly opened certified home for feeble-minded girls from workhouses in Ipswich as her behaviour showed at times that she was 'not always responsible':

She is a quick girl but has so little self-control that she will require very special care & training. She is very hysterical & throws herself about & screams & it is not suitable for her to be with others. Our Matrons like the poor child & she is very happy – but sure she will not learn to earn her living if left at Rose Cottage.

There were no vacancies at the Ipswich home, so Ellen was boarded out locally, but after eighteen months her foster mother requested her removal. According to Mrs Brandreth, Ellen who was then 14, was 'clever & bright, but very excitable & with a violent temper'. The West Ham Guardians transferred Ellen to a training home in London and she was discharged from the society's care.

In 1904, Mrs Brandreth met Ellen in London by chance and contacted Edward Rudolf about her. She said she seemed much improved and had done well in service as a kitchen maid, but the weak ankles she had as a child had deteriorated so much that she had to leave her situation. She had had surgical boots made but they did not fit properly and Ellen was unable to get a new job until the matter was resolved, so was staying with her married sister in the meantime. Edward Rudolf arranged for Ellen to attend the Royal Orthopaedic Hospital in London as an outpatient and Mrs Brandreth promised to find her a new situation when she was fit again. In 1911, Ellen was one of two domestic servants in the household of the manager of a steel works in Llanelly, Carmarthenshire.

Emma Brooks was noted as 'deficient in intellect' on her case file when she came to Dickleburgh from the local workhouse at the age of 11. When she was about 17, Emma was transferred to St Chad's Home, near Leeds where it was hoped she would learn machine knitting so she could support herself when older. By 1893, St Chad's felt they could no longer keep her because of her deteriorating mental health and destructive tendencies, and she returned to Lee Cottage in Dickleburgh. Mrs Brandreth clearly wanted to keep her out of the workhouse, writing, 'she came into my care in 83 & has always been a good & obedient girl & I should be very sorry to send her there – unless she gives trouble.' Emma was found a position in service, though probably in mangling or sewing work rather than domestic service, and the guardians continued to fund her, even though she was now over 20. She returned to Dickleburgh some fifteen months later and spent some time in Rose Cottage under supervision, but it was felt that she would never be fit for domestic service, so was temporarily boarded out with Miss Eliza Fish in the village, under Mrs Brandreth's supervision. A few months later, she was sent to a laundry home in Birmingham. The home reported:

> She is perfectly happy and does her best as regards her work: but her 'best' will we fear never be up to the average of our girls: for I find the matrons are almost despairing of being able to teach her any of the work by which the inmates earn part of their maintenance.

It seems likely that Emma returned to the Depwade workhouse a few months later, when her funding ceased – she would have been about 25 years old. She was resident in the workhouse at the time of both the 1901 and 1911 censuses, and in 1911 was recorded as 'a certified imbecile'. Emma's life had sadly come full circle.

Some other Dickleburgh girls were trained as machinists or dressmakers. In 1906, Mary Fewings and her younger brother Louis were boarded out in the Dickleburgh area by the guardians. The Dickleburgh boarding-out committee contacted the West Ham Guardians in early 1911, advising that Miss Catchpole, Mary Fewings' foster mother, was willing to take Mary on as an apprentice to the dressmaking trade.[4] After some negotiation, it was agreed that the guardians would pay Miss Catchpole eight shillings a week for twelve months, and that she would pay Mary one shilling, two shillings and three shillings a week in the three respective years of the apprenticeship. This was confirmed by a formal sealed apprenticeship indenture.

There was a wider range of occupations available for boys on leaving care, although they too sometimes struggled with employment. Some went into domestic service as grooms or gardeners, or worked on the land. According to his Waifs and Strays case file, Willie Bartram was about 9 years old when he and his younger brother Horace were fostered with Mrs Cook in Langmere, a hamlet bordering Dickleburgh. Willie was quite frail and subject to epileptic fits and within about a year of his admission, the Burton-upon-Trent Guardians offered to take him back, but the Dickleburgh boarding-out committee considered that 'the poor little fellow' had a better chance of growing stronger if he stayed in the country, so he remained in care in Norfolk. In 1903, the Burton Guardians sent Willie to the Home School for Delicate Children in Margate for six months on the advice of the Dickleburgh medical officer who said that he was not yet fit for employment and should be sent to the seaside where he could get sea bathing and extra nourishment to improve his health.[5] Six months later, the Burton committee agreed that Willie should return to Dickleburgh and asked the committee there to find him a job with a tailor or shoemaker as recommended by the schoolmaster at the Margate home. However, there was no suitable work in Dickleburgh, so Willie returned to the Burton workhouse while the guardians tried to find him employment.

By August 1910, Willie had left the farm near Swansea where he was employed as a farm labourer to try to get better paid work as a 'boots' or an ostler, but 'he was not equal to it, tramping, in & out of work for months'. Mrs Brandreth, by then widowed and living in Wanstead in Essex, helped Willie to get back his old job on the farm writing to Edward Rudolf that he 'will not again try to "better" himself for he has a good home, he is a little deaf and is not sharp.' The following April, Willie was again looking for a better job as he was only earning three shillings a week beyond his board and lodging. This time Rosalind Brandreth contacted Rudolf for help, writing, 'he is not brilliant, or strong, and his sight is not good, but he is a young man for whom we have reason to feel great respect.' Rudolf advised that he contact the Church Army. It is possible that Willie returned to Norfolk, marrying Mary Barrett in the Docking area in 1915.

The poor law authorities and voluntary societies saw Canada as a land of opportunity for the Home Children, especially for the boys who they thought would use their farm service as a stepping stone to branching out on their own, working the land to create farmsteads from the wilderness. William Gwilliam came to Canada in 1902 aged 14 and after leaving farm service, worked in the silver mines and spent a winter at a lumbering camp, before taking charge of his own destiny. He saved up to buy his first farm, then, as his daughter, Joyce, explained: 'The golden opportunity for adventure and advancement ... prompted him to sell his farm and go to Moose Jaw, Saskatchewan, where he homesteaded and did very well.'[6]

During the 1930s he sold up and bought a farm near Perth, Ontario. Joyce recalled: 'Father had a driving ambition. He purchased several farms in the area and built up a fine herd of Holstein Friesian cattle.' However, her father was disappointed that none of his sons took over the family farming business; after trying their hand at farming, they followed different careers.

Some Home Boys went travelling across the country after serving their term on the farm, turning their hand to a range of jobs, eventually perhaps marrying, settling down and finding regular employment. Others turned their backs on farming completely such as Jim Eccleston who went into the electrical trade and retired as district superintendent of an area of Saskatchewan, writing, 'farming was not for me'.[7] The accounts in Phyllis Harrison's book show that Home Boys worked in a range of occupations and industries – railways, the post office, factories, engineering, hospitals, construction, transportation; one joined the Royal Canadian Mounted Police, and another became a pastor. Many remained with the same company or organisation for decades.

Conscription was introduced in Canada in August 1917, but many Home Boys joined the Canadian forces earlier in the First World War, such as Louis Fewings who was fostered in Dickleburgh. Louis left his farm service, where he had received glowing reports from the Fegans' visitor, to enlist, although he was still only 17. He sailed for Britain with his unit in July 1916, arriving in Liverpool, the port he had left some three years earlier as part of Mr Fegan's emigration party.[8] He remained in Britain for some months, presumably because he was found to be underage, and was posted to France on 24 February 1917 with the 4th Battalion Canadian Railway Troop when he was a few weeks short of his nineteenth birthday. A few days before he left for France, he made a will, leaving all his possessions to his sister, Mary. In February 1918, he was granted a fortnight's leave in the UK, perhaps visiting Mary, who was still living in the Dickleburgh area. Louis returned to England in January 1919 and departed for Canada on 19 March, spending his twenty-first birthday at sea.[9]

Many boys leaving care in England joined the armed forces or the mercantile marine in their early teens, such as William Cash from Burton-upon-Trent who joined the Royal Navy when he was about 15 after leaving foster care in Dickleburgh. The Dickleburgh committee wrote to the Burton boarding-out committee stating that William had gone to HMS *Ganges* to start his training: 'He was quite determined to do his very best and there was every promise of the lad doing well.'[10] William was a deserted child taken into care when he was about 3 and was in foster care in Dickleburgh for about nine years from the age of 5, so it is not surprising, if quite touching, that in 1911, when William was serving on HMS *Inflexible* as an able seaman, he gave his birthplace as Dickleburgh.

Others joined the Army as boy soldiers, such as Harry Hales, who was probably fostered in Dickleburgh with the Lockett family and who was recorded as a boy musician, aged 17, with the Royal Munster Fusiliers at Kneller Hall (the Army School of Music) in 1911. Many other boys enlisted in the first years of the First World War or were conscripted from 1916 onwards. The roll of honour in All Saints' Church, Dickleburgh lists those from the village who served in the Great War, including several of the poor law boys who were boarded out in the village. Although most had left Dickleburgh some years earlier, it seems there were still people in the area who kept in touch with them, perhaps their foster parents or the rector, or in the case of Louis Fewings, his older sister, Mary.

Although many served, only two of those boarded out in Dickleburgh are known to have died during the First World War – Harry Hales and Lawrence Bishop. They were both regular soldiers, although only Hales' name appears on the Dickleburgh War Memorial. Harry Hales was still serving with the Royal Munster Fusiliers at the outbreak of war, by then an acting sergeant, and he arrived in France on 13 August 1914. He was killed at La Bassée on 21 December 1914 and is commemorated on the Le Touret Memorial to the Missing. The only clue to Harry being boarded out in the village, other than his name inscribed on the war memorial, is the entry in the soldiers' effects register. He names Mrs Ellen Lockett as his sole legatee, presumably his foster mother in Dickleburgh who, with her husband Edward, fostered at least two other boys around that time.[11]

Lawrence Bishop and his brother Albert were in foster care with Fred and Charlotte Snelling in Dickleburgh in 1901, but by 1911 they were back living with their birth family in Kilburn, London, which is perhaps why Lawrence is not commemorated on the Dickleburgh War Memorial.

He enlisted in the Scots Guards in 1913 and embarked for France on 11 August 1914, a week after the outbreak of war. He was returning to England, presumably having been wounded, on board the hospital ship, *Anglia,* when, just after midday on 17 November 1915, she struck a mine about a mile east of Folkestone Gate. Lawrence was posted missing, presumed drowned, and is commemorated on the Hollybrook Memorial in Southampton.

The records of Buxton Industrial School in Norfolk provide some useful insights into the lives of the boys after they left the school, such as details of work placements, military service and later contact with the school, both through visits and correspondence. Using the school's admission and progress register and log book together with military and other online records, it has been possible to track the later lives, especially during the First World War, of most of the eleven boys from the West Ham union who were admitted to the school in 1908.[12]

Seven of the boys went into farm service or similar, one went to work for a tailor, and one was sent to the reformatory training ship *Cornwall* after absconding twice from the school. The other two boys, St John Clues, who had probably been boarded out in Dickleburgh, and Walter Kellam, left the school aged about 15 to join the Navy, starting their training at HMS *Ganges,* by then the largely shore-based establishment at Shotley Gate in Suffolk. Two of the other boys enlisted in the forces prior to the First World War after initially going into other employment; Horace Bishop joined the Navy as a stoker and John Allcroft signed up with the Leicestershire Regiment. The admission register indicates that five more of the eleven boys enlisted after the outbreak of war, but little is known about the other two. No further details were recorded about Albert Turner after 1911 when he was still in farm service and although there is an indication that George Marks emigrated to Canada in 1914 and returned to Britain in early 1915, possibly undergoing military training, no Canadian or British military records have been located to confirm Marks' military service.

Four of the nine West Ham boys known to have served in the war died or were killed during the conflict. Walter Kellam, who enlisted as a boy in the Royal Navy in 1911 had a somewhat chequered career during the war. The school admission register records that he had left his ship while on the China Station in 1914 and had not returned, and his seamen's service records indicated that he served at least six sentences of between five and fourteen days in the cells before his last offence, desertion in Greenwich in 1918, for which he was sentenced to forty-two days' detention. Walter died on 6 July 1918 at the Haslar Hospital in Gosport of pneumonia, aged 23, and is buried in the Haslar Royal Naval Cemetery. Tom Wicks joined the Devonshire Regiment in December 1914 but a year later was hospitalised in Versailles with frostbitten feet. He returned to England and came to the school for two weeks' convalescence in the spring of 1916, before returning to the Western Front. He died on 1 July 1916, the first day of the Battle of the Somme, and is commemorated on the Thiepval Memorial to the Missing of the Somme.

The school heard about John Allcroft's progress from his old employers, Mr and Mrs Harris of Diseworth in Derbyshire, who had once written to the school complaining about the boy's 'fits of temper' in the first few months of his employment with them. John was wounded towards the end of December 1914 and returned to England to a hospital in Bristol but the following June, Mrs Harris wrote to the school informing them that John had died of wounds following an operation at a hospital near Folkestone. John Allcroft lived just five miles away from Diseworth and he was buried there with military honours on 6 June 1915, suggesting that Mr and Mrs Harris had become surrogate parents to the orphaned boy from West Ham.

Matthew Andrews was born in 1896 in Newington, London, one of twelve children of Joseph, a 'fish poulterer', and his wife, Amelia. Joseph died in 1900 when Matthew was only 3 and it seems likely that Amelia was unable to cope, despite taking in boarders, as by 1911 the two youngest children were in care – Matthew was resident at the industrial school in Norfolk and his younger sister Florence was boarded out in Leytonstone.

Matthew went out to farm service just before his sixteenth birthday, but within a few months, his employers were complaining to the school about him and his work, adding that his flat foot did not seem to be improving and was 'made the excuse for much'. Matthew worked as a ship's steward and had plans to emigrate to Australia, but the outbreak of war changed all that. In January 1916, Matthew's mother wrote to the school to advise that Matthew had been killed at the Battle of Loos, serving with the

Royal Sussex Regiment, having enlisted under the name James Maynard. Further research revealed that Matthew enlisted in the 21st Lancers on 15 August 1914 under his own name, claiming to be exactly 19 years old, though he was still only 17, but was discharged on 2 November that year as unfit for service because of a flat foot.[13] A month later, Matthew enlisted in the Royal Sussex Regiment as James Maynard, claiming his age as 19 years and 53 days.[14] He served in France from 8 May 1915, presumably having passed the medical this time. He died of a gunshot wound to the abdomen on 27 September 1915 and was buried at Noeux-Les-Mines Communal Cemetery. Although Matthew served and died as James Maynard (his sister's married name was Maynard), his mother was given as his next of kin, and he is recorded in the Commonwealth War Graves Commission records as the son of Joseph and Amelia Andrews, with his correct age of 18.[15]

The Buxton Industrial School records also reveal that the school kept in touch with the boys after they had left, sending Christmas cards, visiting them in their workplaces, resolving employment issues and occasionally sending books or postal orders. The boys often reciprocated, visiting the school, especially when on leave from the forces, writing letters and sending photographs of themselves. St John Clues made several visits and corresponded with the school at intervals during his fifteen years in the Navy. In a letter of April 1920, he wrote that he was planning to visit the school during his leave, sending regards to the recipient's family and the officers, and signing off 'With Kind Regards, From One of the Boys, Jack Clues.' His visit was noted in his record a few days later: 'Came to spend few days here, looks very well, a fine fellow.' Horace Bishop, who joined the Navy around 1912, spent his Easter leave at the school in 1914 and when he was discharged from the Navy after the war, wrote to the school about finding employment as a training instructor in drill and swimming in an industrial school. In October 1919, he wrote, 'being one of your old Boy's [*sic*] I ask you if you will let me know of a vacancy at the Old School with you, as I wish to give my service to that School I owe so much for my Past life I feel it a Duty to ask you.'

Ten Dickleburgh children died while in care, including two older girls, Ethelind Mills, aged 19, and 22-year-old Margaret Ford, who were both still under the general supervision of the Waifs and Strays Society because of their disabilities. All were buried at Dickleburgh, except Alice Copeman who died at St Chad's Home in Leeds and was buried there. In 1894, in the Dickleburgh churchyard, there were 'five graves, with neat stone crosses, each marking the resting-place of a child who died in the Homes. Every week these graves are visited by the Home children, who place crosses of fresh flowers on the mounds.'[16] The graves, except that of Margaret Ford, now lie together in a large plot to the west of the church, bounded by a kerb inscribed with the children's names and ages. There are no longer any individual crosses.

All these children died of illness, often tubercular-related conditions, including three sisters, Agnes, Richenda and Leonora Sampson. On the death of the third sister, Mrs Brandreth wrote to Edward Rudolf: 'All three sisters have passed away & we cannot regret it, for they would never have been strong enough for service. They have been dear, good children always.' Mrs Brandreth's comment also shows how the children were expected to enter employment on leaving care, and there is a hint of the difficulties that might be caused by children who were unfit for work and might need continuing care.

Several other Dickleburgh children died when they were in their teens or early twenties after they had left for employment. Annie Boulter was transferred to the Lowestoft home when Lee Cottage closed in 1895 and went out to service in Chiswick a few years later, but in December 1898, she accidentally set fire to her clothes with a candle at her employer's house and died within hours. She was just 15 years old. A memorial notice in *Our Waifs and Strays* in February 1899 stated: 'Her mistress writes that "we all liked poor Annie very much, and she was, I know, very happy here. I had her with me every Sunday afternoon to read with me." She went out from the Lowestoft Home, where she had earned an excellent character.'

Perhaps the most unusual death recorded was for Florence Dunnett who may have been the girl of that name who was admitted to Rose Cottage in Dickleburgh in 1882. In 1896, Florence was in service in Highbury, London when she dropped down dead in the street. The verdict of the inquest was that 'Death was consequent upon asphyxia, following congestion of the liver' and the report in the *Dover Express* of 6 November 1896, with the headline 'Tight Lacing', tells the sad tale:

Deceased rode on top of an omnibus, and when the vehicle had reached King's-cross she descended, and suddenly fell backward as though in a fit. She remained unconscious, and was conveyed in a cab to the Royal Free Hospital, where she was found to be dead. Dr Calvert said that not only were the stays of deceased very tightly laced, but all the garments fastened round her waist were fitted tightly to the body and much difficulty was experienced in removing them.... . Elizabeth Dyer, fellow servant of the deceased, said Dunnett used to ask why 'she didn't tighten a little more'. Witness's reply was that 'she didn't study such things.'

Some girls had illegitimate children after leaving care, such as Alice Matthews, described as 'deficient', who came to Dickleburgh in 1886 from the local workhouse after the deaths of her parents. Mrs Brandreth explained to Rudolf that after leaving care, Alice 'got into trouble at Harleston', the small town in Norfolk where she was brought up, just a few miles from Dickleburgh. In 1891, Alice, aged 17, was employed as a housemaid in a boarding house for young drapers' assistants in the town; three of the ten boarders were young men in their late teens or early twenties, so perhaps the temptation of living under the same roof as a young woman was too much for one of them. However, worse was to come, with Mrs Brandreth reporting in a letter to Rudolf in early 1893, that both Alice and her child had died. She wrote: 'I am thankful that she was under kind care in London in a Small Home at 31 Arbour Square, Commercial Road for the last 5 months of her life.' The home where Alice died was a small establishment for servants out of situation in the East End of London.

Rosa, or Rose, Gardner, one of the first children taken into care by Mrs Brandreth, gave birth to an illegitimate boy, William Henry, on 6 August 1889 at Queen Charlotte's Hospital in London, a maternity hospital founded in the eighteenth century. William was baptised two days later at St Mark's Church, Marylebone with thirteen other babies, six of whom, like William, had been born to single women at the hospital. According to William's granddaughter, he was taken into care by the Waifs and Strays Society, and his case file shows he was fostered with a couple in Hertfordshire when only a month old, so the pattern of care continued into the next generation.

Occasionally, the Waifs and Strays Society reluctantly returned a child to the poor law authorities because of behaviour problems or a mental health condition. Maisey Clark lost an eye in an accident before she came into care and wore a glass one. She was described as 'a very good, bright intelligent child' by the superintendent of the West Ham union schools when she came to Dickleburgh, but by the time she was 12, her case file shows there were concerns about her mental health and her future. She was considered unfit for domestic service and too young to be sent to one of the society's industrial training homes, so Rudolf wrote to the West Ham Guardians requesting Maisey's removal, citing her mental health and poor eyesight, adding, 'It is needless to say that everything possible has been done for the poor girl, but having regard to her mental weakness, the time has now arrived, when we must ask you to relieve the Society of the case.'

Rudolf also wrote to the matron at Rose Cottage: 'I am sorry the above course should have to be adopted but the fact unfortunately remains that there must be a certain number of children who are unsuitable for our Homes through some cause or other.' The matron replied that Maisey was ready to go to London at any time, asking whether they needed to send her with more than she was wearing and adding, 'She will have all her little treasures herself.' Four years later, Mrs Brandreth, by then living in Wanstead, Essex, wrote to Rudolf asking if the society could help Maisey, then aged 16, to get a new glass eye, saying she was 'quite friendless' and had difficulty maintaining herself, not being very bright and with very low wages. By January 1908, Maisey Clark was resident in the Lewisham workhouse, described as deficient.

Alice (or Ada) and Dorothy Pine came to Dickleburgh from the Westminster workhouse in December 1909 after they had been in and out of various London workhouses following the imprisonment of their father, Charles Pine, for his involvement in a warehouse robbery in Charing Cross Road earlier that year. However, Alice was sent back to the workhouse within three months of her admission to Rose Cottage because of an incident at the home; a newspaper cutting on her case file explained what happened:

One of the Union's girls, aged 13 years, having been guilty of arson, had had to be removed from their certified Home at Dickleburgh, Norfolk, to another of the Society's Homes.[17] It appears the girl set fire to some bed clothes, and the only reason she could give for the act was that she wanted to see her mother, and she thought she could accomplish her desire this way.

The matron discovered the fire, and no significant harm was done but Alice was removed promptly from Dickleburgh to the Clapham Park home as a temporary measure. From there, she wrote a very contrite letter to Mr Rudolf:

My dear sir just a few lines to let you know why I did such a wicked and wrong thing. I did set lite to the towels and beding for the purpose because I wanted to be sent away from the home I did so want to come back to london. I hope you will forgive me. I am very sorry I have been so wicked... . If you would Kindly let me see mother I should be so thankful to you.

Unfortunately, Alice continued to cause trouble at Clapham Park and the society returned her to the Westminster Guardians. She was not quite 13. The clerk to the guardians wrote to Rudolf: 'I cannot help thinking that it is wrong from every point of view that this little girl should be regarded as uncontrollable and irredeemable.' Rudolf agreed that Alice was not altogether irredeemable but explained she required special training and discipline, and it was the guardians' responsibility to decide her future. The guardians had no option but to accept Alice back, though the clerk responded, describing Alice as one of the brightest they had had in the union, adding, 'The action of your Committee in discharging her to the Workhouse is remarkable and certainly very disappointing.' It seems likely, however, that Alice only spent a few weeks in the workhouse before returning to the family home. She married in 1915 and had six children, so perhaps put her difficult childhood behind her.

Sometimes a family might request, even demand, the return of a child from care in a voluntary home, either because circumstances had changed, perhaps a lone parent had remarried, or the father was in a better paid job, or, more materialistically, because the child had reached an age when he or she could go out to work and contribute to the family income. The voluntary organisations could be quite obstructive, even devious, in their dealings with parents in such cases, often concerned about the welfare of the child or aggrieved that after they had trained and cared for the child, the parents could just resurface and claim the child when it suited them. Legally, in most cases, the parents retained parental rights over their children after they had been admitted to care.

Gladys Baldry was admitted to Rose Cottage in Dickleburgh in June 1909, on the referral of Miss Ledward, a voluntary worker for the Waifs and Strays Society, who advised that she had been told Gladys's widowed mother 'drinks rather badly & neglects her children but she seems fond of them & they of her.' Within months of Gladys's admission, Mrs Baldry applied to the society for her return, though she later withdrew the application, saying that she was thankful to Mr Rudolf for his kindness and delighted to have such cheerful letters from Gladys. A year later, the mother, now Mrs Cracknell, having remarried, was again agitating for the return of her daughter. Rudolf was determined not to let her go home, suggesting to the Dickleburgh rector that it would be advisable 'to stop any unsettling letters from the mother to the girl.' Miss Ledward visited Mr and Mrs Cracknell and advised Rudolf that she thought 'it would be the greatest pity for [Gladys] to return to such an untidy & unsatisfactory home, as she would probably only be running about the streets.' Rudolf advised that he had no legal power to 'withhold the child against the parents' wishes' and that Gladys's mother might get an order for her return through the magistrates, if there were no evidence against the characters of Mr and Mrs Cracknell.

Frederick Cracknell, Gladys's stepfather, now got involved and wrote to Rudolf asking for her return and querying why he had had no reply to an earlier letter: 'Parent can always claim their own children. It was an understood thing that before the child went. That Miss Ledwood know.' Rudolf continued to stall with a note on the reverse of the letter: 'Ignore for present. If writes back refer to letter of 11 June.' A month later Mrs Cracknell wrote to Rudolf demanding to know 'the reason of your Silence', adding 'I am her Mother & can claim My child.' Rudolf would still not agree to Gladys's return, writing:

May I again point out that the girl is very happy in our Home at Dickleburgh, and is making excellent progress, and having, as you have, your daughter's true welfare at heart, I feel sure you will agree with me that it is in her best interests for her to remain under the Society's care.

The matter went quiet for a while but resurfaced about a year later by which time both sides had calmed down and, perhaps significantly, Rose Cottage was scheduled to close within a few months, so Gladys returned to her mother, with Miss Ledward offering to keep an eye on the girl and encourage her to attend Bible classes and join the Girls Friendly Society.

Some children used their experience of being in care to help others. Emma Kennet emigrated to Canada when she was just 6, and her daughter recalled that some of the Home Children passed their door on the way to school or church, not always dressed appropriately for the Ontario winters. She said, 'Not once, but many times I have seen mother watch for these children and take them out her handknit mitts, and put them on cold little hands, or a new little cotton dress or shirt in summer.'[18] On Sundays her mother would treat the children returning from Sunday School to slices of watermelon or some home-baked treat. John Churcher, recalling his lack of proper schooling when he came to Canada, vowed to help others to get an education. Working with local officials and politicians, he established the North Hastings High School in Bancroft, Ontario, just a few miles from where he started his life in Canada at the age of 10. He was appointed the first chairman of the board.[19]

Others rose above their humble origins and their time in care to make their mark as adults, in politics, trade unions, teaching, entertainment, journalism and so forth. Will Crooks went into the Poplar workhouse with his father and four siblings after his father lost an arm in an accident. The children were then transferred to the district school at Sutton, but his mother got the family back together and in later life, Will, one of the leaders of the 1889 London Dock strike, was elected as a Progressive Party candidate at the first London County Council elections in 1892. He was elected to the Poplar Board of Guardians, eventually becoming chairman, and campaigned for improvements to the workhouse, some of which were adopted nationally. He became Mayor of Poplar, campaigned for the introduction of old age pensions and in 1903 became the MP for Woolwich.

In many ways, the adult lives of those who experienced life in care during the period of the new poor law probably differed little from those of their contemporaries who remained with their families during their childhood. They took up occupations mostly in keeping with their class in society; young men joined the armed forces, served and in some cases died in the First World War, many married and had children. In some respects, they may even have had advantages over their peers in the community. They may have been healthier, with access to medical care, better-nourished and better-clothed than other children who were still living in poverty. They almost certainly had better educational opportunities, especially before 1870. Even some with mental health issues may have been better cared for, at least during their childhood, than those who were not in care.

However, the emotional impact of a childhood spent in care, particularly in the large poor law institutions, and of the circumstances that brought them to that point, such as the death of their parents, desertion, abuse or homelessness, cannot be calculated. The need for these children, as they became adults, to find affection and a sense of belonging is evidenced by the many examples of young adults maintaining links with those who supported them during their childhood in care. They visited their old foster homes, industrial schools and children's homes, often calling themselves 'old boys' or 'old girls'. They asked for pictures of their benefactors, such as Edward Rudolf or the matron of the home in which they spent their childhood; they wrote letters with news of their lives or asking for help; they supported their foster parents in old age, made them beneficiaries in their wills and retained contact with subsequent generations, sometimes even marrying into their foster family.

Alice Louisa Hall, the child who had been sent away from Rose Cottage because she wrote 'improperly' on her slate at Dickleburgh School, emigrated to Canada when she was about 16. Following her emigration, it seems life improved for Alice. Mrs Bond Cabell, who had sponsored and supported her when she was fostered in Cromer as a child, contacted Rudolf in 1905, saying that Alice, who wrote frequently to her, was happily married and settled in Canada. The Alice Louisa Betz, née Hall, who died in the United States at the age of 80 in 1961, may be the same person of that name who spent some months in Dickleburgh during her childhood. [20] If so, she certainly seems to have turned her life around. Her obituary shows that she had four children and acquired nine stepchildren when she remarried after she was widowed. She was also very active in church and community organisations in Lockport in New York State where she had moved to from Canada with her husband and young family some fifty years before her death.

However, many who spent their childhood in care never found any love or ties of affection that would continue into their adult life, especially children in workhouses and district schools in England and those whose 'foster parents' on the Canadian farms treated them as child labour. For many former children in care, their fulfilment came from marrying and raising families of their own, giving and receiving unconditional love. Winnifred Jordan, who emigrated to Canada in 1920 aged 8, summed up the difference between care and love:

> I remember saying to the first lady in Nova Scotia 'How I wish I had someone to love me.'
> She said 'Well we love you.'
> 'I never get any hugs and kisses.'
> 'Well we feed and clothe you. What more do you want?'
> I saw to it that my own children and grandchildren got and still get lots of hugs and kisses. [21]

Conclusion

This world of mistakes, experiments, and stumbling advance.[1]

Florence Davenport-Hill, 1889

In 1834, the old parish-based system of poor relief, which provided in-relief through the parish poorhouse or out-relief to those living in their own homes, was replaced by the new poor law, which focused provision on the union workhouse. Children admitted to the workhouse were either permanent inmates, usually deserted and orphaned children with no family to support them, or 'ins and outs', who entered the workhouse for temporary respite, often with one or both parents, and were sometimes discharged and readmitted several times within a few months.

There were also thousands of children, both with and without parents, who never entered the workhouse, but lived in poverty within their communities – in desperate conditions in the family home, in lodgings, or on the streets. The sight of destitute children on the streets of London and elsewhere shocked many into action, including Thomas Barnardo, Annie Macpherson, John Pounds, and Edward Rudolf. They actively sought out destitute children in the poorer parts of towns and cities, they opened refuges, ragged schools, orphan asylums, training establishments and children's homes, and they formed charities, many of which still exist today.

Some poor law unions established separate or district schools for their pauper children, usually with enhanced training facilities, away from the workhouse and the possibility of corruption by adult paupers, to try to break the cycle of poverty. However, the size of many of these institutions created other problems, including loss of individuality and the rapid spread of disease. Many children remained in the workhouse, especially in rural areas where there were too few permanent child inmates to justify expenditure on a separate building for them. A few unions (and charities) provided grouped home complexes during the latter half of the nineteenth century, so the children lived in smaller groups, but still within a large institution. It was not until the very end of the nineteenth century that unions started to move away from large institutions, opening scattered or isolated homes within communities.

The voluntary sector was usually one step ahead of the poor law authorities in the way it provided for pauper children during much of the nineteenth century. Many children's charities provided more family-oriented care through small cottage homes and boarding-out schemes, so that the children lived in smaller groups or even proper families, with a parental substitute, and were part of the wider community, often attending the local school and supervised by the clergy or voluntary workers within the parish. However, rehabilitation within the birth family was not usually considered an option.

Until the 1860s, the poor law authorities and voluntary sector tended to operate in parallel; children who were taken into care were either admitted to a poor law institution, such as the workhouse, or taken in by a charity. However, as the century progressed, there were increasing concerns expressed by Jane Nassau Senior, Hannah Archer, Florence Davenport-Hill and others, that children housed in large institutions received no affection or 'mothering', or anything approaching family life, and were isolated from the outside community. They were becoming what we would now call 'institutionalised'. These concerns were answered, at least for some children, by legislation passed in the second half of the century that enabled unions to send their pauper children out of the union to certified homes and boarding-out schemes run by voluntary societies. This partnership between the state and the voluntary sector over the care of deprived children continues today. During the latter half of the nineteenth century and the early twentieth century, there was also a growing understanding of the meaning of childhood and the needs of children, not just destitute children, resulting in significant legislation relating to child labour, child protection and welfare, and education. Much of this formed the foundation of legislation in these areas that exists today.

From about 1870, poor law unions and charities enthusiastically embraced child migration, notably to Canada, as a solution to the problem of destitute children in Britain, although the schemes seemed out of kilter with more progressive thinking on child welfare in Britain at the time. Unions and charities were overwhelmed with children needing care, so emigration seemed to offer the ideal solution. Not only did it create room in the poor law institutions and children's homes in Britain, it also provided the children with an opportunity for a new life and answered the call for labour from the Canadian farmers. Many British Home Children were physically or emotionally ill-treated in Canada. They were often inadequately supervised and their employers or foster parents insufficiently vetted, but for some, emigration did change their lives for the better.

The 1834 Poor Law Amendment Act made little specific provision for pauper children, other than the requirement for three hours' teaching in the workhouse each day, so it is not surprising that progress towards finding appropriate means of looking after children in care was slow and sometimes faltered. By the second half of the nineteenth century, the entry of numerous charities not only expanded provision, but also provided new ideas on childcare and welfare, which eventually were taken up by the state. Although some developments were far from ideal, it is testament to the nineteenth century pioneers within both the voluntary and state sectors that small children's homes and fostering, two of the key forms of provision for looked-after children today, have been around for over 150 years. Adoption, the third main element of the children in care system in the twenty-first century, has also existed informally for a similar length of time and was legally regulated nearly a century ago.

Notes

Abbreviations

Ancestry – Ancestry website, www.ancestry.co.uk

TCSA – The Children's Society Archive

DCEPA – Dickleburgh Church of England Primary Academy

LGB – Local Government Board

LMA – London Metropolitan Archives

NALSL – Newham Archives and Local Studies Library

NRO – Norfolk Record Office

SAIB – Suffolk Archives, Ipswich Branch

SSTAS – Staffordshire and Stoke-on-Trent Archive Service

TNA – The National Archives

Introduction

1. John Stroud, *13 Penny Stamps* (1971), p. 109. The quotation is anonymous, but research has shown that she was Winifred Price, who came into care in Dickleburgh in 1908.

Chapter 1: Mrs Brandreth's Charity for Workhouse, Destitute and Orphaned Children

1. *Our Waifs and Strays*, Waifs and Strays Society Magazine, March 1895.
2. *Home Words*, Dickleburgh Parish Magazine, March 1886.
3. Waifs and Strays Society Children's Case Files, TCSA. Case file numbers are only cited if the quotation is taken from a case file other than that of the named child.
4. John Chapple & Alan Shelston (eds), *Further Letters of Mrs Gaskell*, Manchester University Press, Manchester, 2003, p. 156.
5. J. A. Venn (comp), *Alumni Cantabrigienses*, London, 1922–1954.
6. Green-Jamison letters, JN1 G/16/1871, quoted in Jenny Keaveney, 'Who was Louy Jackson?', *Gaskell Society Newsletter*, No. 57, Spring 2014, p. 29.
7. *Home Words*, June 1877.
8. The Children's Society Archive website, www.hiddenlivesrevealed.org.uk, accessed 9 May 2020.
9. Dickleburgh Baptism Register, 1844–1911, NRO PD 704/10.
10. Case File 5580.
11. Case File 3801.

12. Scarlatina is synonymous with scarlet fever, a highly contagious disease that occurs mainly in childhood and early youth. It is now usually successfully treated with antibiotics, but in the past the illness could prove fatal, especially in a severe epidemic or if there were complications, such as uremia (where the kidneys do not filter waste products from the blood) or septicaemia. See, Finley Ellingwood, *The Eclectic Practice of Medicine,* 1910, online www.henriettes-herb.com/eclectic/thomas/scarlatina.html, accessed 9 May 2020.

13. Stroud, pp. 109–110; Winifred Price was admitted to Rose Cottage in Dickleburgh in 1908, and her younger brother, Leonard, was sent to a Waifs and Strays home in Chislehurst, Kent about the same time.

14. Case File 3733; Dickleburgh School Log Book.

15. *Our Waifs and Strays,* March 1895. Until the early twentieth century, most girls of the labouring classes went into domestic service on leaving school, as housemaids, kitchen maids or cooks. Boys might go into service as grooms or gardeners.

16. Case File 6888.

17. Case File 6888.

18. *Our Waifs and Strays,* December 1897.

19. Case File 6888.

20. Case File 5580.

21. Case File 5580.

22. West Ham Union, Guardians' Minutes, 13 April 1911–4 April 1912, NALSL.

Chapter 2: Attitudes and Legislation Relating to the Poor

1. George Hadley, *A New and Complete History … of the Town of Kingston upon Hull,* 1788, quoted in Victor E. Neuburg, *Popular Education in Eighteenth Century England,* The Woburn Press, London, 1971, p. 4.

2. Churchwardens' Accounts, 1686–1950, Starston, Norfolk, NRO PD 119/97.

3. 1801 Census, Starston, NRO PD119/124.

4. Overseers of the Poor Account Book, 1774–1806, Starston, NRO PD 119/110.

5. Peter Higginbotham provides an excellent overview of poor law legislation over the centuries at www.workhouses.org.uk.

6. Stepney Poor Law Union, Ratcliffe Children's Receiving Home, Creed Register, 1906, LMA STBG/L/128/005/001,002.

7. West Ham Union, Guardians' Minutes, 1905–1906.

8. The terms 'house of industry' and 'workhouse' are synonymous; the former was generally used by the incorporations and the latter by the post-1834 unions.

9. Charles Chaplin, *My Early Years,* 1964, p. 19.

10. Charles Shaw, *When I was a Child,* 1903, p. 107.

11. Chaplin, p. 20.
12. Chaplin, pp. 21–22.
13. Quoted in Jean S. Heywood, *Children in Care: The Development of the Service for the Deprived Child*, 1965, p. 68.
14. Jack London, *People of the Abyss*, 1903, p. 35.
15. London, p. 40.
16. London, p. 43.
17. Aylsham Poor Law Union Out-Relief Book, 1836, NRO C/GP 1/293.
18. Hadley, quoted in Neuburg. *Popular Education*, p. 4.
19. *Hansard*, 10 April 1856, 141.804.
20. Quoted in Mary Sturt, *The Education of the People*, 1967, p. 4.
21. *Hansard*, 13 June 1807, 9.798.
22. James Kay, 1838, quoted in Sturt, p. 86.
23. Rev Thomas Spencer, *The Outcry Against the New Poor Law or Who is the Poor Man's Friend?*, 1841, p. 3.
24. Harriet Ward, 'The Charitable Relationship – Parents, Children and the Waifs and Strays Society', unpublished thesis, University of Bristol, 1990, p. 321.
25. Parr, *Labouring Children*, London, 1980, p. 78. 'Viciousness' is used here to indicate immorality.
26. Heywood, p. 65.
27. Harry Hendrick, *Child Welfare: England 1872–1989*, 1994, p. 51.
28. M. A. Crowther, 'From Workhouse to NHS Hospital in Britain, 1929–1948', in Hillam, C. and Bon, J. M. (eds.), *The Poor Law and After: Workhouse Hospitals and Public Welfare*, Liverpool Medical History Society, Liverpool, 1999, pp. 38-49.
29. Heywood, p. 108.
30. Heywood, pp. 110–113.

Chapter 3: The World of the Deprived Child

1. Henry Mayhew and John Binny, *The Criminal Prisons of London and Scenes of London Life*, (1862), p. 29.
2. Dickens in 'Household Words', Vol 1, No.23, pp. 549–552.
3. The quotations from Mayhew's *London Labour and the London Poor* used in this book were taken from the selections edited by Victor Neuburg, London, 1985; Rosemary O'Day and David Englander, Ware, 2008; and Robert Douglas-Fairhurst, Oxford, 2010.
4. The daguerreotype process was the first commercially successful method of producing permanent images from a camera, using silvered copper plate and mercury vapour.
5. London, pp. 149–150.
6. Charles Booth's introduction to the third series of volumes of *Life and Labour of the People in London*, 1902.

7. The quotations from Booth's book are taken from Albert Fried & Richard Elman (eds), *Charles Booth's London*, 1969.
8. Andrew Mearns, *The Bitter Cry of Outcast London: An Inquiry into the Condition of the Abject Poor*, 1883.
9. Barbara Leckie, 'The Bitter Cry of Outcast London, 1883: Print Expose and Print Reprise', online at: www.branchcollective.org/?ps_articles=barbara-leckie-the-bitter-cry-of-outcast-london-1883-print-expose-and-print-reprise, accessed 9 May 2020.
10. B. Seebohm Rowntree, *Poverty, A Study of Town Life*, 1901, 1922.
11. Rowntree, pp. 350–354.
12. Committee of Investigators on the Administration of Out-Relief in Norwich, *The Destitute of Norwich and How They Live*, 1913.
13. Mayhew, Letter to *the Morning Chronicle, The Morning Chronicle Survey of Labour and the Poor: The Metropolitan Districts*, vol. 1 p. 231, quoted in Helen Amy, *The Street Children of Dickens's London*, 2012, p. 66.
14. Children's Employment Commission, 1862, pp. 78–79.
15. The tips of lucifer matches were dipped in a highly toxic composition of white phosphorus, which enabled the match to ignite when struck against anything. Factory workers exposed to the vapours, especially the dippers and those who stirred the solution, were susceptible to phosphorus necrosis of the jaw, commonly called 'phossy jaw', which would start with severe toothache before the bones of the jaw started to rot. If the infected bones were not removed, the condition would often prove fatal.
16. Commission, 1862, p. 258.
17. *Norfolk News*, 30 June 1849.
18. Commission on the Employment of Children, Young Persons, and Women in Agriculture, 1867, p. 198.
19. Commission 1867, p. 197.
20. Commission 1867, p. 202.
21. *The Daily News*, 4 February 1846.

Chapter 4: Tipping Points – Reasons Children Came into Care

1. Waifs and Strays Annual Report 1892, p. 31.
2. Ward, pp. 70, 72.
3. Case File No. 2390.
4. *South Wales Daily News*, 9 November 1898; *Eastern Evening News*, 10 December 1898; *Essex County Standard*, 11 February 1899.
5. Suffolk Quarter Sessions, Convictions, 1874, SAIB, B105/5B/278.
6. Richard Deeks, *Transportees from Suffolk to Australia,1787–1867*, 2000, p. 150; England and Wales, Criminal Registers, Suffolk, 1791–1892, Ancestry.
7. Prison Hulk Registers and Letter Books, 1802–1849, Ancestry.
8. Deeks, p. 150.
9. Waifs and Strays Society Annual Report, 1897, Case File No. 5876.

Chapter 5: Workhouses and Other State Provision

1. Florence Davenport-Hill, *Children of the State*, 1889, p. 14.
2. E. C. Tufnell, 'Training of Pauper Children in the Workhouses of Kent, etc' Reports from Commissioners, 1841, pp. 401–402.
3. Peter Higginbotham, *Voices from the Workhouse*, 2012, pp. 43, 48.
4. Quoted in a letter from John R. Collins to *The Times*, Saturday, 4 June 1870.
5. Davenport-Hill, pp. 14–15.
6. Tufnell, 'Education of Pauper Children', Reports from Commissioners, 1841, p. 344.
7. LGB Annual Report 1873–74, p. 257.
8. Davenport-Hill, p. 36.
9. Tufnell, 'Education of Pauper Children', p. 349–350.
10. Frank Crompton, *Workhouse Children*, 1997, pp. 155–159.
11. Poor Law Commissioners' Correspondence 19 January 1846, TNA, MH12/14081, quoted in Crompton, p. 155.
12. *The Lancet*, 5 October 1867, quoted in Higginbotham, www.workhouses.org.uk.
13. *British Medical Journal*, 24 August 1895, p. 496 and 13 March 1897, p. 696.
14. *The Building News and Engineering Journal*, 23 January 1880.
15. Higginbotham, www.workhouses.org.uk, accessed 9 May 2020.
16. Davenport-Hill, p. 48.
17. *The Examiner*, 20 January 1849.
18. Education and Maintenance of Pauper Children in the Metropolis, 1896 (Mundella Report), p. 5.
19. Davenport-Hill, pp. 47–48.
20. Davenport-Hill, p. 58.
21. Mundella Report: Davenport-Hill, pp. 55–56.
22. Case File No. 2674.
23. Chaplin, p. 22
24. Davenport-Hill, pp. 76–83.
25. Chaplin, p. 26.
26. LGB Annual Report, 1885–86.
27. LGB Annual Report, 1873–74.
28. Reported in the *Sheffield Daily Telegraph*, Thursday, 28 February 1878.
29. F. J. Mouat and Captain J. D. Bowley, *Report on the Home and Cottage System of Training and Education the Children of the Poor*, LGB, 1878.
30. Higginbotham, *Children's Homes: A History of Institutional Care for Britain's Young*, 2017, p. 203.
31. Davenport-Hill, p. 90.
32. Quoted in Higginbotham, www.workhouses.org.uk, accessed 9 May 2020. The Band of Hope, which started in 1847 in Leeds, aimed to teach children about the dangers of alcoholic drink and was linked to the Christian temperance movement of the period. The national Band of Hope union

was formed in 1855 to support the growing number of groups around the country. The charity still exists today as Hope UK.

33. Higginbotham, Children's Homes website, www.childrenshomes.org.uk, accessed 9 May 2020; Phil Carradice, *Nautical Training Ships: An Illustrated History*, 2009, p. 43.

34. TS *Exmouth*, Training Records 1876–1918, accessed 9 May 2020, Ancestry; Chaplin, pp. 60–61.

35. Suffolk Reformatory, Admission and Licence Book, 1879–1882, SAIB, GB13/13/7.

36. Buxton Industrial School, Log Book, 1907–1911, NRO C/SS8/20.

37. Buxton Industrial School, Admission and Progress Register, NRO C/SS8/33.

38. LGB Annual Report, 1873–74.

Chapter 6: The Charitable Response

1. Quoted in Gillian Wagner, *Barnardo*, London, 1979, p. 32.

2. Quoted in *The Foundling Museum*, Museum Catalogue, 2009.

3. Accepted Petition of Maria Colby and other papers, Foundling Hospital, 1868, LMA. A/FH/A/08/001/002/077, No. 21284.

4. General Register, Foundling Hospital, LMA, A/FH/A/9/2/5, No. 21284.

5. The Surrey History Centre provides an excellent summary of the history of the institution in the introduction to its online catalogue of the records of the Orphan Working School, https://www.surreyarchives.org.uk/collections/getrecord/SHCOL_6129, accessed 9 May 2020.

6. Quoted in the Exploring Surrey's Past website, www.exploringsurreyspast.org.uk/themes/subjects/schools/london_orphan_asylum/, accessed 9 May 2020.

7. Surrey History Centre website, www.surreycc.gov.uk/culture-and-leisure/history-centre/researchers/guides/reports-of-reeds-school, accessed 9 May 2020.

8. Royal Hospital Chelsea Pensioner Soldier Service Records, TNA, WO 97, Find My Past, https://www.findmypast.co.uk/, accessed 9 May 2020.

9. Dickens, 'Brother Müller & his Orphan Work' in *Household Words*, 7 November 1857, p. 437.

10. Davenport-Hill, p. 101.

11. Davenport-Hill, p. 108.

12. Quoted in Wagner, *Barnardo*, p. 28.

13. Quoted in Wagner, *Barnardo*, p. 32.

14. Stroud, p. 10.

15. Stroud, p. 13.

16. Admission Register, Bethlem Hospital, April 1869–1 July 1871, Bethlem Museum of the Mind, https://museumofthemind.org.uk/collections/archives, accessed 9 May 2020.

17. Stroud, p. 29.

18. Children's Society website, www.hiddenlives.org.uk/, accessed 9 May 2020.
19. Stroud, pp. 111.
20. Stroud, p. 113.
21. Stroud, p. 114.
22. Stroud, p. 120.
23. Stroud, pp. 102–103.
24. Derek Fraser, *The Evolution of the British Welfare State*, 2003, p. 142.
25. Ward, pp. 160-183.
26. Ward, p. 172.

Chapter 7: Family Life in Care – Boarding Out and Adoption

1. Mundella Report.
2. Helen J. Macdonald, 'Boarding-Out and the Scottish Poor Law, 1845–1914', *The Scottish Historical Review*, Vol. LXXV, No 2, No. 200, 1996, pp. 197–220.
3. T. Ferguson, *The Dawn of Scottish Social Welfare*, 1948, quoted in Macdonald, p. 199.
4. Report from the Select Committee on the Poor Law (Scotland), 1868–9, p. 308.
5. *Seventh Annual Report of the Board of Supervision for the Relief of the Poor in Scotland*, 1852, p. vii.
6. 'Boarding-Out and The Wordsworths' based on Dorothy Wordsworth, *Narrative Concerning George and Sarah Green of the Parish of Grasmere.* Heywood, pp. 222–234.
7. 'The Wordsworths'.
8. 'Notes on the *Memoir of Kitty Wilkinson of Liverpool, 1786–1860*, 1835, Heywood, pp. 205–211.
9. Dickens, 'The Girl from the Workhouse', *All the Year Round*, Vol. VIII, p. 136, 18 October 1862.
10. Janet Horowitz Murray and Myra Stark (advisory eds), *The Englishwoman's Review of Social and Industrial Questions: 1866–1867*, October 1866, Routledge Library Editions, 2016.
11. J. J. Henley, *Report to the Poor Law Board on the Boarding-out of Pauper Children in Scotland*, 1870, p. 36.
12. Heywood, pp. 82–85, 214–219.
13. *Devon and Exeter Daily Gazette*, 26 June 1891.
14. Burton-upon-Trent Poor Law Union, Boarding-out Committee, Minutes, 1897–1905, SSTAS D25/2/5/1.
15. Depwade Poor Law Union, Boarding-out Committee, Correspondence Files, 1906–1915, NRO C/GP3/189,190.
16. Stroud, p. 74.
17. Stroud, p. 75.
18. Stroud, p. 74.

19. Stroud, p. 74

20. Depwade Poor Law Union, Boarding-out Committee, Correspondence Files.

21. A pelisse was a short military style jacket, particularly fashionable in Regency times, although in this case, it may have referred to a simple outer coat.

22. *Hull Daily Mail*, 12 June 1928.

23. Gill Rossini, *A History of Adoption in England & Wales, 1850–1961*, Barnsley, 2014, pp. 62–65.

24. Deborah Cohen, *Family Secrets: Living with Shame from the Victorians to the Present Day*, 2013, pp. 115–116.

Chapter 8: New Lives, a World Away – Child Migration

1. Phyllis Harrison (ed), *The Home Children: Their Personal Stories*, Winnipeg 1979, p. 51.

2. For an excellent summary of the earlier periods of child migration, see Gillian Wagner, *Children of the Empire*, London, 1982, pp. 1–18.

3. E. P. Brenton, *Observations on the Training and Education of the Children of Great Britain*, 1824, quoted in Wagner, *Children of the Empire*, p. 12.

4. Brenton, *The Bible and the Spade*, 1837, quoted in Wagner, *Children of the Empire*, p. 12.

5. Parr, p. 11.

6. Clara M. S. Lowe, *God's Answer*, London, 1882, quoted in Marjorie Kohli, *The Golden Bridge*, Toronto, 2003, pp. 90–91.

7. Lillian M. Birt, *The Children's Home-Finder*, 1913, quoted in Kohli, p. 93.

8. *Charges Made Against Miss M. Rye, Before the Poor Law Board at Islington, and Her Reply Thereto*, 1874, quoted in Kohli, pp. 76–78.

9. Quoted in Wagner, *Children of the Empire*, p. 52.

10. Andrew Doyle, *The Emigration of Pauper Children*, Report to the LGB, 1875.

11. *First Report of the Select Committee of the Parliament of the Dominion of Canada on Immigration and Colonization*, 1875.

12. *The Globe*, c.1875, quoted in Roger Kershaw and Janet Sacks, *New Lives for Old: The Story of Britain's Child Migrants*, Kew, 2008, p. 43.

13. Letter from Maria Rye to the President of the LGB, December 1876, published 1877; *The Times*, 23 April 1875.

14. Harrison, p. 18.

15. Gail H. Corbett, *Nation Builders: Barnardo Children in Canada*, Toronto, 1997, p. 88.

16. Harrison, p. 75; Steerage was the cheapest accommodation available for passengers, usually located in the bowels of the ship above the steering mechanism.

17. Stroud, p. 90.

18. Harrison, p. 87.
19. Stroud, p. 91.
20. Harrison, p. 82.
21. Harrison, p. 71.
22. Corbett, p. 83.
23. Corbett, p. 88.
24. Corbett, p. 87.
25. Corbett, pp. 91–92.
26. Harrison, pp. 82–83.
27. Corbett, pp. 108–109.
28. Harrison, pp. 78–79.
29. Harrison, p. 85.
30. Harrison, p. 19.
31. Harrison, p. 71.
32. Harrison, p. 81.
33. Phillip Bean and Joy Melville, *Lost Children of the Empire, The Untold Story of Britain's Child Migrants*, 1989, p. 144.
34. Bean and Melville, p. 143.
35. Bean and Melville, p. 148.
36. Harrison, p. 74.
37. Harrison, p. 85
38. Bean and Melville, p. 111.
39. Bean and Melville, p. 111.

Chapter 9: Life After Care

1. Harrison, p. 67.
2. Reported in *Home Words*, July 1877.
3. Quoted in Higginbotham, Children's Homes website, www.childrenshomes. org.uk/TrewintIH/, accessed 9 May 2020.
4. West Ham Guardians of the Poor, minute book, 18 April 1910–13 April 1911, NALSL.
5. Burton-upon-Trent Boarding-out Committee, SSTAS, D25/2/5/1.
6. Harrison, p. 37.
7. Harrison, p. 78.
8. Personnel Records of the First World War, Library and Archives Canada, www.bac-lac.gc.ca/eng/discover/military-heritage/first-world-war/ personnel-records/, accessed 9 May 2020.
9. Canadian Passenger Lists 1865–1935, Ancestry, accessed 9 May 2020.
10. Burton-upon-Trent Boarding-out Committee.
11. Soldiers' Effects Records, National Army Museum, Ancestry, accessed 9 May 2020.
12. Buxton Industrial School, Norfolk, Admission and Progress Register, 1894–1908, Norfolk Record Office, C/SS 8/33.

13. British Army WW1 Service Records, 1914–1920, Matthew Andrews, Ancestry, accessed 9 May 2020; soldiers had to be 19 years old to serve overseas, so it was quite common for underage recruits to lie about their age, sometimes with the active encouragement of the recruiting staff.
14. British Army WW1 Service Records, James Maynard.
15. Commonwealth War Graves Commission, Casualty Database, www.cwgc. org/, accessed 9 May 2020.
16. *Our Waifs and Strays*, September 1894, p. 327.
17. Although the police were called, the Rev John Forbes, Rector of Dickleburgh, decided not to press charges against Ada.
18. Harrison, p. 13.
19. Harrison, p. 19.
20. *The Union Sun and Journal*, Lockport, New York, 27 February 1961, Ancestry, Meister/Marcy/Hartline Family Tree, accessed 9 May 2020.
21. Harrison, p. 126.

Conclusion
1. Davenport-Hill, p. 99.

Select Bibliography and Further Reading

Birth, marriage and death records, census returns, the 1939 register, newspapers, poor law union records, passenger lists, parish registers, First World War casualty and service records, criminal registers and other genealogical sources have been consulted, mostly through online websites, as well as the specific sources listed below.

Primary Sources

Children's Society Records and Archive Centre, London: Waifs and Strays Society, Accepted Case Registers, 1882–1912, TCS/F/05; Children's Case Files, 1888–1912; Central Homes Register, 1897–1911, RCS/F/04/01.

Dickleburgh Church of England Primary Academy, Norfolk: Dickleburgh School, Admission Register 1911–1939 (some entries from 1900), Log Book 1900–1980.

London Metropolitan Archives: Stepney Poor Law Union, Ratcliffe Children's Receiving Home, Creed Register, 1906, STBG/L/128/005/001,002; Foundling Hospital, Accepted Petitions 1868, A/FH/A/08/001/002/077, General Register, A/FH/A/9/2/5, No. 21284.

Newham Archives and Local Studies Library: West Ham Poor Law Union, Minute Books, 1885–1914.

Norfolk Record Office: Depwade Poor Law Union, Minute Books, 1895–1897, C/GP 3/27-28; Children's Boarding-out Committee Correspondence Files, 1906–1915, C/GP 3/189-190; Dickleburgh Parish Registers, PD 704/9-11, 20; Red House (Farm) School, Buxton, Admissions and Progress Register 1894–1908, C/SS 8/33; Log Books, 1907–1915, C/SS 8/20;21; Starston Parish Records, PD 119.

Staffordshire and Stoke-on-Trent Archive Service: Burton-upon-Trent Poor Law Union, Admission and Discharge Register, 1880–1900, D25/4/2; Boarding-out Committee Minute Book, 1897–1905, D25/2/5/1; Year Books, 1890–1913 (with gaps), B/25/7/5/1-7.

Suffolk Archives, Ipswich: Quarter Sessions, Convictions, 1874, B105/ 5B/278; Suffolk Reformatory, Admission and Licence Book, 1879–1882, GB13/13/7.

Parliamentary Papers

The Training and Education of Pauper Children, Poor Law Commissioners, E. Chadwick; J. P. Kay; E. C. Tufnell etc, Report, 1841.

Children's Employment Commission, Report, 1863.

Commission on the Employment of Children, Young Persons, and Women in Agriculture, Report,1868.

The Boarding Out of Pauper Children, J. J. Henley, Report, 1870.

Annual Reports of the LGB, 1873–1892.

The Emigration of Pauper Children, Andrew Doyle, Report, 1875.

Immigration and Colonization, Select Committee of the Parliament of the Dominion of Canada, Report, 1875.

The Home and Cottage System of Training and Education of the Children of the Poor, F. J. Mouat and J. D. Bowley, Report, 1878.

Education and Maintenance of Pauper Children in the Metropolis, Mundella Report, 1896.

Books

Amy, Helen, *The Street Children of Dickens's London* (Amberley, Stroud, 2012).

Anonymous [Rudolf, Edward], *The First Forty Years: A Chronicle of the Church of England Waifs & Strays Society 1881-1920* (Waifs and Strays Society/ Society for Promoting Christian Knowledge, London, 1922).

Bean, Philip and Melville, Joy, *Lost Children of the Empire* (Unwin Hyman, London, 1989).

Booth, Charles, *Booth's Maps of London Poverty, East and West* (first published 1889, reprinted Old House Books, London, 2013).

Carradice, Phil, *Nautical Training Ships: An Illustrated History* (Amberley, Stroud, 2009).

Chaplin, Charles, *My Early Years* (The Bodley Head, London, 1964/1979).

Cohen, Deborah, *Family Secrets: Living with Shame from the Victorians to the Present Day* (Viking, London, 2013).

Corbett, Gail H., *Nation Builders: Barnardo Children in Canada* (Dundurn Press Ltd, Toronto, 1997/2002).

Crompton, Frank, *Workhouse Children* (Sutton Publishing, Stroud, 1997).

Crowther, M. A., *The Workhouse System: The History of an English Social Institution* (B. T. Batsford Limited, London, 1981).

Davenport-Hill, Florence, *Children of the State* (second edition, 1889).

Deeks, Richard, *Transportees from Suffolk to Australia, 1787–1867* (Seven Sparrows, Fressingfield, Suffolk, 2000).

Digby, Anne, *Pauper Palaces* (Routledge & Kegan Paul, London, 1978).

Fowler, Simon, *Workhouse: The People, The Places, The Life Behind Doors* (The National Archives, Kew, 2007).

Fraser, Derek, *The Evolution of the British Welfare State* (Palgrave Macmillan, Basingstoke, 1973/2009).

Fried, Alfred and Elman Richard M. (eds), *Charles Booth's London: A Portrait of the Poor at the Turn of the Century Drawn from his 'Life and Labour of the People in London'* (Hutchinson, London, 1969).

Harrison, Phyllis (ed), *The Home Children: Their Personal Stories* (J. Gordon Shillingford, Winnipeg, 1979).

Hendrick, Harry, *Child Welfare: England 1872–1989* (Routledge, London, 1994).

Heywood, Jean S., *Children in Care: The Development of the Service for the Deprived Child* (Routledge & Kegan Paul, London 1959/1978).

Higginbotham, Peter, *Voices from the Workhouse* (The History Press, Stroud, 2012).

Higginbotham, Peter, *Children's Homes: A History of Institutional Care for Britain's Young* (Pen and Sword, Barnsley, 2017).

Hillam, C. and Bon, J. M. (eds), *The Poor Law and After: Workhouse Hospitals and Public Welfare* (Liverpool Medical History Society, Liverpool, 1999).

Horn, Pamela, *Young Offenders: Juvenile Delinquency 1700–2000* (Amberley, Stroud, 2010).

Hulonce, Lesley, *Pauper Children and Poor Law Childhoods* (Kindle, 2016).

Humphreys, Margaret, *Empty Cradles,* (Doubleday, London, 1994).

Kershaw, Roger and Sacks, Janet, *New Lives for Old: The Story of Britain's Child Migrants* (The National Archives, Kew, 2000).

Kohli, Marjorie, *The Golden Bridge – Young Immigrants to Canada, 1833–1939* (Natural Heritage Books, Toronto, 2003).

London, Jack, *People of the Abyss* (1903, republished Workhouse Press, 2013).

Mayhew, Henry, *London Labour and the London Poor* (Charles Griffin, London, 1865, republished as selections: Neuburg, Victor (ed), Penguin Books, London, 1985; O'Day, Rosemary and Englander, David (eds), Wordsworth Editions, Ware, 2008; Douglas-Fairhurst, Robert (ed), Oxford University Press, Oxford, 2010).

Mayhew, Henry and Binny, John, *The Criminal Prisons of London and Scenes of London Life* (Griffin, Bohn & Co, London, 1862).

Middleton, Nigel, *When Family Failed: The Treatment of the Child in the Care of the Community in the First Half of the Twentieth Century* (Gollancz, London, 1971).

Parker, Roy, *Uprooted: The Shipment of Poor Children to Canada, 1867–1917* (The Policy Press, Bristol, 2010).

Parr, Joy, *Labouring Children: British Immigrant Apprentices to Canada, 1869–1924* (Croom Helm, London, 1980).

Pugh, Gillian, *London's Forgotten Children: Thomas Coram and the Foundling Hospital* (The History Press, Stroud, 2007).

Rossini, Gill, *A History of Adoption in England and Wales, 1850–1961* (Pen and Sword, Barnsley, 2014).

Rowntree, B. Seebohm, *Poverty, a Study of Town Life* (London, 1901/1922).

Shaw, Charles, *When I Was A Child* (1903, facsimile edition Caliban Books, Firle, 1977).

Stroud, John, *13 Penny Stamps: The Story of the Church of England Children's Society (Waifs and Strays) from 1881 to the 1970s* (Hodder and Stoughton, London, 1971).

Sturt, Mary, *The Education of the People* (Routledge & Kegan Paul, London, 1967).

Wagner, Gillian, *Barnardo* (Weidenfeld and Nicolson, London, 1979).

Wagner, Gillian, *Children of the Empire* (Weidenfeld and Nicolson, London, 1982).

Williams, A. E., *Barnardo of Stepney: Father of Nobody's Children* (G. Allen and Unwin Ltd, London, 1943).

Journals/Articles/Pamphlets

Archer, Hannah, *A Scheme for Befriending Orphan Pauper Girls*, 1861.

Brandreth, Henry (ed), *Home Words*, Dickleburgh Parish Magazine,1875–1899.

Committee of Investigators on the Administration of Out-Relief in Norwich, *The Destitute of Norwich and How They Live*, Jarrold & Sons, London, 1913.

Keaveney, Jenny, 'Who was Louy Jackson?', *Gaskell Society Newsletter*, No. 57, Spring 2014.

Macdonald, Helen J., 'Boarding-out and the Scottish Poor Law 1845–1914', in *Scottish Historical Review*, Vol. 75, 2, No. 200, October 1996.

Mearns, Andrew, *The Bitter Cry of Outcast London: An Inquiry into the Condition of the Abject Poor*, James Clarke & Co, London, 1883.

Spencer, Rev Thomas, *The Outcry Against the New Poor Law or Who is the Poor Man's Friend?*, 1841.

Waifs and Strays Society, *Our Waifs and Strays*, 1884–1900.

Unpublished Theses

Daniels, Barbara, 'Street Children and Philanthropy in the second half of the Nineteenth Century' (Ph.D. thesis, Open University, 2007).

Ross, Alexander, 'The Care and Education of Pauper Children in England and Wales, 1834–1896' (Ph.D. thesis, University of London, 1955).

Ward, Harriet, 'The Charitable Relationship: Parents, Children and the Waifs and Strays Society' (Ph.D. thesis, University of Bristol, 1990).

Websites

British Newspaper Archive (subscription site), www.britishnewspaperarchive. co.uk/

The Children's Society, 'Hidden Lives Revealed', www.hiddenlives.org.uk/

Commonwealth War Graves Commission, www.cwgc.org/

Higginbotham, Peter, 'Children's Homes', www.childrenshomes.org.uk/

Higginbotham, Peter, 'The History of the Workhouse', www.workhouses.org.uk/

Libraries and Archives, Canada, 'British Home Children' & '1st World War Soldiers', www.collectionscanada.gc.ca/

Index